Witness

Voices from the Holocaust

Edited by Joshua M. Greene and Shiva Kumar
in consultation with Joanne Weiner Rudof

Foreword by Lawrence L. Langer

A TOUCHSTONE BOOK
PUBLISHED BY SIMON & SCHUSTER
New York London Toronto Sydney Singapore

TOUCHSTONE
Rockefeller Center
1230 Avenue of the Americas
New York, NY 10020
Copyright © 2000 by Joshua M. Greene Productions, Inc.
All rights reserved, including the right of reproduction
in whole or in part in any form.
First Touchstone Edition 2001
TOUCHSTONE and colophon are registered trademarks of Simon & Schuster, Inc.
STORIES TO REMEMBER is a registered trademark of
Joshua M. Greene Productions, Inc.
Designed by Kim Llewellyn
Manufactured in the United States of America

9 10 8

The Library of Congress has cataloged the Free Press edition as follows:
Witness : voices from the Holocaust / edited by Joshua M. Greene and Shiva Kumar
in consultation with Joanne Weiner Rudof ; foreword by Lawrence L. Langer ;
in association with the Fortunoff Video Archive for Holocaust Testimonies,
Yale University.
p.   cm.
Includes bibliographical references and index.
1. Holocaust, Jewish (1939–1945)—Personal narratives. I. Greene, Joshua, 1950– .
II. Kumar, Shiva. III. Rudof, Joanne Weiner. IV. Fortunoff Video Archive
for Holocaust Testimonies.
D804.195.W58   2000
940.53'18—dc21   99-058401

ISBN-13: 978-0-684-86525-6
ISBN-10:   0-684-86525-4
ISBN-13: 978-0-684-86526-3 (Pbk)
ISBN-10:   0-684-86526-2 (Pbk)

To Adele, who knows the blessings of a full life,
Cara and Katu, who will soon know,
and Esther, who is my constant reminder.

—JMG

To my father,
who brought me so far,
and to my children,
who take it from here.

—SK

Sometimes at night I lay
and I can't believe what my eyes have seen.
I really cannot believe it.

—HELEN K.

CONTENTS

FOREWORD

Some students of the Holocaust pay so much attention to the crucial inquiry into how the murder of European Jewry could have happened that they often neglect the equally vital question of what in fact occurred. The Germans left archives of material that help us to understand how a bureaucracy of death was organized and transformed into a killing process, but they kept few records to verify how the ensuing ordeal was experienced by their victims. Without survivor testimony, the human dimension of the catastrophe would remain a subject of speculation. The voices of the victimized provide us with an intimate glimpse of daily existence in the ghettos and camps, of life before, during, and after the disaster. They tell of the anguish and humiliation of thousands of individuals who, by chronicling their own story and the fate of family members who did not return, furnish a version of the atrocity that the killers chose not to preserve. For example, published statistics may confirm the numerical truth that many Jews were forced to subsist on two or three hundred calories per day, a diet that, unless supplemented, led to death from malnutrition within about three months. But as witnesses in these testimonies grope for words to describe what "real" hunger was like, they animate the distress of starvation as mere statistics cannot. And when we hear someone confess abashedly, "I'll tell you what *real* hunger is; *real* hunger is when you look at another human being as something to eat," we know we have retrieved a phase of the agenda for destruction that no official document could reveal.

If, as one German sociologist has argued, collective crimes like the Holocaust are individual crimes in a collective, then from the point of view of the victimized the destruction of European Jewry might be described as the mass murder of individual men, women, and children. Inmates of Auschwitz and other camps may have been mere numbers to the Germans, but to themselves they were separate identities and their voices in these testimonies allow them to emerge from the anonymity in which their persecutors wished to see them perish. Contrary to our expectations and perhaps also to our desires, witnesses do not appear here as heroes or martyrs, labels they firmly reject, but as chroniclers of a melancholy and dreadful tale. For most of them gestures of defiance were beyond the realm of daily possibility. Their accounts help us to imagine their reality in unromantic terms, even when they speak, as several of them do, of uprisings, escapes, and other acts of resistance.

One of the problems with listening to or watching survivor testimonies is that we bring to the confrontation a mindset that has been nurtured by premises irrelevant to the stories we are about to hear. Living in a privileged world of moral choice where options for mutual support abound, we are ethically defenseless against the account of the Auschwitz witness who one night stole a piece of bread from the woman sleeping in the bunk above her. She is ashamed as she recalls the moment, but she also knows that at the time she was so driven by hunger that the moral principles she lives by today simply vanished from consciousness. Lamenting the absence of acceptable alternatives, she ends her memory of the episode, "So this wasn't good and that wasn't good, so what choice did we have?" The discomfort we feel after hearing about hundreds of such transgressions of what we deem decent behavior leaves us with two options: either we censure the victims for lapses of the moral will, or we revise our belief that in spite of assaults on the physical self it was still possible in places like Auschwitz to maintain an inviolable inward purity. If we embrace the latter option, we are forced to concede the inconsequence of familiar moral precepts under such unprecedented conditions.

For most of the victimized it was not possible, not because they suddenly abandoned their sense of civilized values but because the conditions imposed on them by the Germans left little room for the civilized values we are accustomed to cherish. When one witness shamefacedly confesses to the camera that in the ghetto he sneaked into the kitchen in the middle of the night to steal his sister's morning portion of bread, he is aghast at his remembered behavior. All his instincts today condemn what he did then, and we are inclined to agree with him. But as the evidence of what it was like to be living under impossible conditions mounts, we are drawn slowly into that milieu itself, and we are challenged to abandon the safeguards that protect us from the implications of a random universe where there is no connection between what one wishes and what one must do to remain alive.

When staying alive a little longer is the immediate, and for some the daily or even hourly, goal of existence, certain rules of conduct begin to disintegrate. Although few forgot the value of sharing and mutual concern, the struggle to stay alive eroded the durability of such universal ideals. Renowned Auschwitz survivors like Primo Levi and Charlotte Delbo admit that when they found additional sources of water in the camp, their extreme thirst forced them to conceal their discovery from others. Our familiar moral vocabulary might label this selfishness. But such language and the actions it supports were designed for a world that had never experienced the conditions the Germans imposed on their victims. Of course, some inmates proved utterly unable to adjust to their deprived milieu, and these soon died or were selected early for death. Most of those who outlasted the initial months learned to adjust to the new rules of survival not because they embraced them with enthusiasm but because pressing physical needs temporarily displaced other ethical considerations.

No one who listens carefully to Holocaust testimonies can avoid the disturbing implications embedded in these narratives. They mirror images of the distressed self that invite us to revise our romantic idea of the power of the individual will to resist and overcome adversity. The reasons leading to this summons are so unflattering to human nature that we are left wondering about the stamina and the very meaning of so-called civilized values. Long before deportation and the threats of death, we learn from these testimonies, Jews were forced to muse about the abrupt shift in attitude that suddenly left them isolated in a once familiar milieu. They give evidence about how Nazi ideology so infected formerly healthy social instincts that Christian neighbors and friends began to cross the street to avoid them. The perplexity that overwhelmed these witnesses then is still evident in their voices today, as they recount their long journey from bigotry through corridors of indifference and hostility to the destination where beating, torture, and starvation became one's normal fate, ending for those who were still alive in the doom of execution by bullet or gas.

Another kind of perplexity troubles audiences of these witnesses. Testimonies present survival as an unheroic experience. This contradicts the natural but misguided impulse to romanticize staying alive and to interpret painful endurance as a form of defiance or resistance. Such a response represents one style of revisionism that crept into the writing of Holocaust history after the liberation of the camps, when the world and survivors themselves had to face the memory of an ordeal that stunned the imagination into an equivalent of mute incomprehension. German atrocities were so unprecedented, the cruelty so extreme, the anguish of their victims so unfathomable that some balancing idea had to be found to offer relief from the frightful stories that accrued in survivor testimonies. One of the complicating factors in addressing the issue of the Holocaust, indeed, one of the reasons why the topic is still so fresh more than fifty years after the event, is the intensity of our psychological mutiny against the facts and details of mass murder as the Germans enacted it. The notion of a meaningless, uncompensated, and unredeemable suffering, the poverty of the very word *suffering* to capture the reality of the experience, breaches our response and creates an urgent need to bridge the ensuing gulf between unpalatable truths and our eager but beleaguered desire to understand.

Holocaust testimonies provoke us to build and cross that bridge but do not offer us a paradise of comprehension on the other side. If witnesses themselves are still disturbed by the chasm between their knowledge of events then and the difficulty they have in believing them today, we should not be surprised by our own distressed reactions to their stories. Although these stories do not fit into the familiar rhythms of existence with their alternating setbacks and triumphs, our instinct often drives us to adapt them to these rhythms as the easiest way of pretending that one "gets over" such experiences and reenters the normal flow of time. Our inclination leads us to equate staying alive with victory over oppression, an act of will worthy of celebration. Unhappily, the evidence in these narratives does not support that equation.

Quite the contrary. One of the clearest messages in the testimonies is the compartmentalized lives that survivors insist they lead, divided between their present reality and the moments of arrested memory they cannot (and often do not wish to) escape. This results in a recurrent crisis of moral identity and reflects one of their most consuming dilemmas. For example, one witness tells of a death march near the end of the war when he was walking alongside his exhausted brother, who finally pleaded with him to help him, since he had reached his physical limits. With a desolate look on his face the witness tells of his weakened condition and of his utter inability to find the strength to support his brother. He then explains that the Germans took his brother out of line and shot him. The instant seems fixed in his memory like a fossil encrusted in stone, and there is no evidence that it will ever decay.

It is clear from his words that he has a dual attitude toward what happened between him and his brother: he knows that his own frailty prevented him from offering aid, but he also believes today that he *should* have been able to make a fraternal gesture. He both justifies and censures himself for his failure to live up to his moral standards, caught in a riptide of contradiction that forces him to condemn himself because he can find no satisfactory end to his story. He leaves us mired in a similar conundrum as we try to accept a period of history that will never attain closure because there is no vision of human experience sufficient to contain it.

In the absence of such a vision, we may be tempted to substitute hackneyed images of passive Jews and Nazi monsters, or of a world where the "triumph of the spirit" dismisses in a verbal gesture the whole tale of physical agony and loss that surfaces repeatedly in survivor testimonies. These approaches, however, have more to do with the quest for comfort than the search for truth. They fail to face the disheartening fact that during the Holocaust, for the Jews and a multitude of other victims, the Germans and their collaborators calculatedly created situations where the only choices were between bad and worse. According to their system, as many survivors testify, even escape could not be viewed as a courageous deed because invariably others left behind were executed as warning and punishment. That explains what one witness means by his astonishing comment that in many instances resistance could be a form of murder. If passivity prevailed among prisoners it was not internally bred but induced by external threats that paralyzed the will to action. The German principle of collective responsibility was a macabre inversion of the Dostoevskian idea that all men were responsible to all men for all things. Everyone was hostage to the behavior of everyone else, so that the threat of reprisal hung over the heads of all with a menace that few could escape. It was a diabolical plan that snared an entire community in a web of death.

As viewers or readers of Holocaust testimonies, we have the benefit of being able to piece together the structure of this universe of death in a way that was not available to its inhabitants at the time. One of the most discouraging features of these narratives is the frequency with which witnesses blame themselves for consequences of which, as it seems to us, they are perfectly innocent. Repeatedly we hear survivors declare their guilt, for not having done enough, for having made mistaken choices, too soon or too late, as if the tidal wave of German hatred that was sweeping over them were *their* fault. This is perhaps the bitterest and most ironic legacy of the Holocaust: the spectacle of innocent victims assuming the guilt that their persecutors disowned both during and after the war.

The most striking omission we encounter in these testimonies is the virtual absence of individual criminals. If the Germans saw the Jews as anonymous masses, the Jews saw the Germans as anonymous killers. They describe expulsion from their homes, forced detention in ghettos, deportation to labor and death camps as if their persecutors were faceless and nameless. With the exception of Dr. Josef Mengele, who seems from these testimonies to have single-handedly selected a million Jews for the gas chambers, it is a rare moment when one of the criminals is identified by name. This is one reason why survivor testimonies are insufficient to reconstruct the history of mass murder. To gain insight into how the victimized were trapped in the infamous scheme to destroy all of European Jewry, it is indispensable to consult historians who identify the criminals and elaborate the context of their deeds.

Few viewers of Claude Lanzmann's classic film, *Shoah*, will forget the dramatic moment when renowned Holocaust historian Raul Hilberg declares that he's a "document man" and proceeds to "read" a wartime German railroad timetable listing way stations on the Jewish journey toward death as if he were a critic interpreting a text by Dostoevsky or Proust. Hilberg argues that no written record, however obscure, can be ignored in our pursuit of insight into the German plan for mass murder. And he is correct. Yet he and his fellow historians have shown less enthusiasm for another source of Holocaust information, survivor testimonies, partly because they are not written and partly because they usually are offered many years after the event and thus are based on the faculty of memory, which many consider untrustworthy. Recent neurological research, however, has suggested that some traumatic episodes are imprinted deeply on areas of the brain identified with long-term memory and do not fade with time. Certain details of oral Holocaust narratives are so vivid and precise that there is little practical reason for rejecting their authenticity, in spite of the theoretical objections to their value. To gain insight into the experience of entrapment it is indispensable to listen to the voices of those who were trapped, and the burden they still bear in spite of their survival.

The saddest legacy of all for those still alive is an inability to escape from the tainted memory that still hovers over their daily existence. When one witness exclaims that the Passover she celebrates with family and friends is "not the same," that "something is missing," that she wants to share it with "someone who knows me really," she evokes a severed intimacy whose absence still fills her with yearning. The violence of the rupture that separated her from her family without leaving, as she puts it, "even a grave to go and mourn to" reminds us that the Holocaust deprived its victims not only of their lives but of their deaths. Nothing is plainer from these testimonies than the lasting painful imprint of this unreconciled heritage, and it helps us to understand why, half a century later, the Holocaust continues to seem a fresh event to so many students of the subject.

It will also help us to understand why survivors are less than enthusiastic about fashionable requests for pardon and calls for reconciliation that have been issued by governments and church institutions on behalf of their guilty but silent predecessors. One wonders whether such spokespersons are familiar with the grim details of the barbarity for which they ask forgiveness in someone else's name. After World War II the criminals themselves, both the Germans and their collaborators, chose to remain mute and unrepentant or to deny personal responsibility for their collaboration or their crimes. Anyone hearing the tales of survival and loss in these testimonies will sympathize with witnesses' refusal to accept an armistice of memory and to embrace a future cleansed of resentment. As one witness declares with anguish, "It's not easy to live this way." If we can absorb into our consciousness the unspoken corollary to this complaint, "It's not easy to *die* this way," we will have validated the dual epitaph that governs her memory of her murdered family, from which she alone remains. We will also have embraced the deepest meaning of Holocaust testimonies, which joins in an indissoluble seal the will to live with the remembrance of mass murder. The radiance of the one seems shadowed by the gloom of the other, though distant centuries may reach different conclusions. Meanwhile, these narratives invite us to enter the overcast landscape of atrocity and to share with the voices of its former inhabitants their accounts of the lives and the deaths that transpired there.

LAWRENCE L. LANGER
Professor of English Emeritus
Simmons College

EDITOR'S INTRODUCTION

"I went to the movies by myself. Jews weren't allowed to go any-more, but on Sunday afternoons when they opened for children, I would leave my coat with my father, and he would wait outside while I went in to see the movie. We only had to wear the Jewish star on our outer garment, and I had curly blond hair and didn't really look Jewish." Renée H. paused in her tale. We had met for lunch in a restaurant.

"My curls were in an Afro direction—you know, up, not down?" she continued. "All the little girls in my neighborhood had their hair curled down in the Shirley Temple way. I wanted it like that, too, so I got my mother to curl my hair down. It was excruci-ating!" By 1942, Shirley Temple had topped all other Hollywood stars as the number one box office attraction worldwide. Sixteen movies featured the beautiful little girl whom so many other little girls wanted to be. While only a few of the films had been shown in Bratislava, where nine-year-old Renée H. lived with her sister and parents, Shirley Temple was still her idol. As a gift, Renée's parents bought her a tiny sepia-tint photo of her dimpled heroine.

"I kept the photo in a handkerchief," she said—the handker-chief her mom had given to her. I listened and tried to imagine what it had been like for her, surrounded by starvation and nightmares of every description, to pull the photo from its hiding place in her bunk at Bergen-Belsen and gaze on the image of a childhood she would never know. At liberation, she said, she was eleven years old but weighed no more than a three-year-old. Had the Allied forces taken so much as one day longer to arrive, she would not have survived. In the cheery restaurant, lunch piled high before us, it was almost impossible to connect my mental image of that emaciated child with the attractive white-haired woman sitting at the table.

The lunch was our first meeting, but it felt like a reunion. My colleague Shiva Kumar and I knew Renée H.'s stories almost by heart. We had screened her videotaped testimony dozens of times. We could recite her words, imitate the phrasing of her sentences. We knew that she had been the ears for her deaf parents and sister when the soldiers marched down the streets of Bratislava, rounding up Jews for deportation. We knew about the diary she wrote on toilet paper in Bergen-Belsen, about how it was discovered by German soldiers, and how they laughed and said, "She has a good sense of humor!" We could describe the pile of corpses across from her barrack. Our meeting in the restaurant felt incidental: we had known her for months.

Renée H. is one of more than four thousand witnesses to the Holocaust who have been interviewed for the Fortunoff Video Archive for Holocaust Testimonies at Yale University, the oldest such archive in the world. For almost twenty years, scholars at Yale's Video Archive have been painstakingly gathering thousands of hours of testimony from people in a dozen countries, cataloging the videotapes in databases available on the Internet, and producing educational programs available on a loan basis to schools and community groups worldwide.

When I first learned of the archive, the staff was concerned that the earliest tapes in the collection, dating back more than twenty years, were beginning to deteriorate from age and needed attention. Many of the people who had recorded their memories had since died; the videos were a precious legacy in danger of being lost. Along with others who had volunteered to raise restoration funds, I watched a number of the tapes. Person after person, many of them my current age, in their forties, spoke of things I had heard about but never understood: ghettos, cattle cars, concentration camps, death marches, liberation. Some of the witnesses had not spoken of their experiences for decades, if at all, and their words were spontaneous and powerful. Like others who received superficial exposure to the Holocaust in high-school classes, I thought I knew as much as necessary about this traumatic period in human history. The video testimonies made clear that an academic examination of prewar politics and social conditions conveys nothing of the experience itself. They showed not only how little I had understood but how impersonal my understanding had been.

Previously, my partner and I had worked with the Video Archive staff on half-hour programs for cable television. From that experience came the idea for a ninety-minute program that would bring further attention to the work of the archive.

What we had seen was revelatory. Play any of the ten thousand hours of video housed at the archive: all you see is a person sitting in one place, talking to a camera. The first lesson in film school is "Talking heads won't hold viewers' attention," but these "talking heads" are riveting. To make the film *Witness: Voices from the Holocaust*, Shiva and I screened more than six hundred hours of raw, relentless testimony. It was exhausting. What kept us going was a growing awareness that we were gaining insight into the seminal event of the twentieth century. Something incomprehensible was being clarified for us by hearing about it from the people to whom it had happened—and that generated the energy we needed to keep going for almost two years.

The book *Witness: Voices from the Holocaust* weaves together excerpts from twenty-seven of the one hundred witnesses whose testimonies we screened. Many of them had been inmates of concentration camps. Some recall surviving death marches and starvation as children. Others describe their experiences as resistance fighters or escaping by passing as non-Jews or hiding in bunkers for months, or even years. Most of the witnesses are Jewish. Among those who are not are a former Hitler Youth, an American prisoner of war, a U.S. army colonel who liberated the Austrian concentration camp, Mauthausen, a Jesuit priest, and a German woman who as a child saw columns of concentration camp prisoners—skeletons—stagger through her town. Our job has been not to comment on the testimonies but to carefully sequence them into a narrative that roughly traces life before, during, and after the Nazi era—to edit without editorializing.

The power of testimony is that it requires little commentary, for witnesses are the experts and they tell their own stories in their own words. The perpetrators worked diligently to silence their victims by taking away their names, homes, families, friends, possessions, and lives. The intent was to deny their victims any sense of humanness, to erase their individuality and rob them of all personal voice. Testimony reestablishes the individuality of the victims who survived—and in some instances of those who were killed—and demonstrates the power of their voices.

The format of *Witness* is consequently different from single-person narratives. *Witness* weaves together testimony from differing and often contradictory angles of vision. The result is a complicating of our thinking about the events being described. A memoir provides us with the continuity of one individual's personal odyssey. In a multivoice narrative such as *Witness*, we discover that such continuity can be misleading. Complexity and contradiction can often be greater tools for approaching an understanding of what happened. We may resist accepting the extremes of the Nazi regime's cruelty: a single witness's story might be exaggerated. Indeed, witnesses themselves often doubt what they went through, so unimaginable were the horrors. Helen K. tells us, "Sometimes at night I lay and I can't believe what my eyes have seen. I really cannot believe it." When we hear ten, a hundred, a thousand people describing extreme cruelty, however, each from his or her individual perspective, our resistance to the enormity of the crimes weakens.

Juxtaposing testimony reveals that each person reacted to events from a unique perspective. On arriving at Auschwitz, twenty-two-year-old Golly D. focused on the way women were separated by the SS into young and old, while eleven-year-old Arnold C. remembers the overwhelming size of the camp and the sense of having entered "a place out of the unreal." Edith P. recalls in Auschwitz: "When the sun came up, it was not like the sun—I swear to you! It was not bright." Clara L. remembers sounds: "Crying and whining and pleading with God and cursing God." And she remembers smells, like "fry[ing] liver . . . the blood as it dripped down had a very peculiar smell."

The multivoice approach reveals, too, that there is no single authoritative point of view, no one answer to the questions raised by the Holocaust. Rabbi Baruch G. tells us that in his circles there was faith that God would help. Did such faith help him to survive? "Possibly. I don't know. We knew some who didn't have that kind of faith and still survived. Many had more faith than I did, I'm sure, and did not survive. There's no rhyme or reason, no explanation of why one survived and the other did not." Clara L., on the other hand, did not come from a religious background, but she traded four days worth of bread for a book of psalms, memorized seven chapters, and tells us, "For months and months this Book of Psalms was my life." The diversity of reactions alerts us to the risk of oversimplifying the issues.

Not one of the hundred victims whose testimony we screened ever celebrated the act of survival. Hanna F., at the end of her interview, tells us it was "stupidity" that allowed her to live. Martin S. says he thinks he managed to survive by becoming "too inhuman." Rabbi Baruch G. tells us that the years immediately following liberation brought greater psychological pain than his time in the camps. No one speaks of having survived through bravery or courage. These are hard assessments for us to accept. We want to believe in a universe that rewards good character and exemplary behavior. We want to believe in the power of the human spirit to overcome adversity. It is difficult to live with the thought that human nature may not be noble or heroic and that under extreme conditions we, too, might turn brutal, selfish, "too inhuman." It is even more difficult to accept that a cultured, educated nation, not an uncivilized band of fanatics, almost destroyed an entire people.

Yet this is the reality that witnesses knew, and their descriptions do not include redemptive messages or happy endings. These are concepts we who were not there create for ourselves, perhaps because confronting the reality is more than we can bear. We showed our film to the person in charge of Holocaust studies for a prestigious Jewish organization, and she commented, "Your film has a very unhappy ending. Can't you change that?" The challenge we faced in editing the testimonies was to guard against our own tendency to emphasize isolated acts of bravery, to gloss over the harsh reality in favor of a more romantic, fictionalized vision of resistance and survival.

When the British liberated Bergen-Belsen concentration camp in April 1945, eleven-year-old Renée was so delirious from typhus that she has no recollection of what happened. From Bergen-Belsen she was shipped to Sweden to recuperate, and from there flown to America, where she lived with a great-aunt in Brooklyn. The Shirley Temple photo went with her all the way to Brooklyn in a suitcase, along with souvenirs of Sweden: a collection of colorful bird feathers, flat rocks for skimming, and a collection of Hebrew-language magazine inserts called *Kochavim Yehudim Be Olam* (*Jewish Stars of the World*) that featured photos of Hedy Lamarr, Lauren Bacall, Kirk Douglas, Burgess Meredith, and other famous actors and actresses.

"I was star-struck," Renée conceded. "One of the most delicious moments for me was when Shirley Temple became ambassador to Czechoslovakia. I never met her, never knew anything about her, but I was so delighted that the little child who only sang and danced and showed her dimples turned into such a remarkable woman—that she had made something of herself!"

We have met some of the other men and women whose words appear in this book. Joseph K., who went from ghetto to concentration camp to death march, attended a screening of *Witness* in New Haven, as energized as when interviewed twenty years ago. "Still here!" he announced, and reported his frequent talks to high-school students. Werner F. visited us in my home on Long Island. In Auschwitz, he bunked with a famous magician. Now he has a magic act of his own that he performs at public gatherings. Sadly, we will not get to meet many of the others. Father John S., who observed the brutality of deportations through the knothole of a train yard fence, died in 1992. Hanna F. died in 1994, Walter S. in 1995, and Celia K. in 1994.

Their stories are still here, compelling us to rethink the way we perceive history. Just after World War II, many who were not a part of it could not bear to hear the truth of what had happened, and many witnesses gave up trying to explain. Martin S., who was only a child when he returned from the camps, talked to his schoolmates about his experiences, until one day another student prodded him, "Why don't you tell one of your bullshit stories?" He did not say another word about his experiences for thirty years.

In the 1960s, witness testimony resurfaced, particularly during the Eichmann trial. Previously, documentaries focused more on footage of the camps than on the words of the witnesses. Since the Fortunoff Video Archive began its work in the late 1970s, witnesses themselves have become the focus of attention. Many of the people in this book were among the first to speak and allow their words to be videotaped for the archive. They had no guarantees that anyone would listen. Nor did they even believe that speaking up would necessarily make a difference to anyone, but some did hope their testimony might help avoid such catastrophes in the future. Others looked to Cambodia, shrugged, and like Martin S., said, "What's new?" Helen K. ends her testimony by asking, "But did we learn anything? I don't know."

If testimony offers no assurance of averting catastrophe in the future, it at least assures that what occurred in the past will not be forgotten. That alone would be a remarkable accomplishment. And if there is any credit to be given for the work in hand, it is to be offered first to the witnesses for their willingness to share with us their anguished memories. Credit must next be offered to the dedicated people of the Fortunoff Video Archive for Holocaust Testimonies, who for two decades have made testimony available, without romanticizing, without fanfare, in a manner that reflects meticulous research and inquiry, and with profound respect for the words of the witnesses. We are grateful for having the chance to assist them through this publication.

JOSHUA M. GREENE
New York, July 1999

ACKNOWLEDGMENTS

It is awkward to acknowledge others for their help when the work in question is truly their own. As editors, we feel we have merely provided a vehicle for the years of recording, research, and insight generated by the Fortunoff Video Archive.

Archivist Joanne Weiner Rudof deserves recognition for vetting every line, word, fact, and figure in this book. Her attention to detail reminded us that when we editorialize human experience, in the name of theory or creativity, we blur the line between what truth is and what we wish it to be. As impressive as her meticulous review of the work was her sensitivity and loyalty to the witnesses. She gently but firmly refused to allow anything to impinge on their privacy, and that, too, was a reminder: human experience is not a commodity to be traded in a marketplace of goods and services.

The book owes its genesis to editor Linda Kahn, who brought a newspaper article about the film to the attention of literary agent Linda Chester. Ms. Kahn's expert editorial input complemented Ms. Chester's firm conviction that *Witness* would be an important literary work. We hope that the results have met their expectations. Our representative at the Linda Chester Agency, Joanna Pulcini, provided constant encouragement during the months it took to transcribe and edit hundreds of hours of testimony. She was the able messenger who brought the book to the attention of its publisher, and for her expertise and guidance we are immensely grateful.

Lawrence Langer and Geoffrey Hartman, who also supervised the manuscript in its various stages, offered reassurances and assuaged our discomfort at navigating unfamiliar terrain. Their groundbreaking work in the field of witness testimony sets a standard for academic and intellectual integrity, and we are honored to be in such company.

The staff of Yale's Fortunoff Video Archive and Manuscripts and Archives deserves much recognition for their many hours of research and videotape identification for this book. Debra Bush; L. Christopher Burns; and Richard Szary, Head, and Nancy F. Lyon, Archivist, Manuscripts and Archives, at the Yale University Library all have our heartfelt thanks, as do the good people at Yale's Audio Visual Center, where the book's photographic needs were always given prompt attention.

Paul Golob, our editor at The Free Press, carries on a tradition that has begun to fade into memory: the editor as co-creator. His contributions were substantive, informed by a deep personal sensitivity to the subject and a craftsman's expertise. Sometimes you pick the right horse.

Alan Fortunoff provided support, wisdom, and the strength to keep going when frustration threatened to overwhelm the work at hand. It was Alan's inspiration that first pointed us in the direction of the Video Archive. Both for their help and their exemplary life, he and his wife, Helene, have earned our respect, admiration, and love.

The witnesses probably would prefer not to be acknowledged. They are, nonetheless, the subject of this book—men and women who lived through extraordinary events. For having given permission to use their words and images, we offer our sincere thanks.

EDITOR'S NOTE

We have not altered the words of the witnesses; however, for the sake of readability, we have omitted many hesitations and duplications that normally occur in speech but not in writing. These are not indicated in the text. We have not corrected any of the grammar, in English or other languages. Some of these errors occur simply because spoken language is more informal than written, or the hesitations which have been omitted led to changes in mid-speech. Other grammatical errors occur because the witnesses are using a foreign language which they have never formally studied or are repeating informal or vernacular speech that they heard.

I would like to thank Professor Edward Stankiewicz for assisting me in transcribing all the foreign language phrases. I am in awe of his knowledge of every language that appears in this text, and then some. Any errors, however, are mine, not his.

JOANNE WEINER RUDOF

"A Way of Life"

EUROPE, 1930s

European Jewish cultures were as diverse as the larger European communities around them. Some extended back many generations and were an integral part of the surrounding populations. Others were more isolated. The response by these varied Jewish communities to the Nazi threat was mixed. Even in Germany, some witnesses say that Hitler's rise to power increased hostility among their Christian neighbors, while others recall Jews and non-Jews continuing to live together comfortably.

Many people found it difficult to believe the rumors about Nazi plans for the Jews. There had been thousands of years of waxing and waning European antisemitism, including the Spanish Inquisition, the Crusades, and the Dreyfus affair. Hitler's racial ideology at first did not appear any more dangerous than what had come before, and many Jews continued to feel a part of the society around them.

That delusion was shattered for German Jews on Kristallnacht *(Night of Broken Glass), November 9, 1938, when Nazis smashed Jewish stores, homes, and offices; destroyed synagogues and prayer rooms; and deported thirty thousand Jews to concentration camps. By the time the Nazis' true intentions were clear, it was too late for almost any Jew to escape.*

WITNESS

Joseph W.
Born Przemyśl, Poland, 1922
Raised in Krzywcza, Poland

The small town of Krzywcza was, as is known in the Yiddish vernacular as a *shtetl*—a hundred Jewish families out of a population of two or three thousand. And they all clustered around a central square. We lived with my grandparents, who had a house, a large house.

My mother was the oldest daughter. She was the first one married. My father had just come back from the [first world] war. He was a soldier in the Austrian army. I guess it was a *shiddukh*, [which] means an arranged marriage, but they knew each other. . . . I do remember going to *cheder*, which was a Jewish school. And boys, particularly, started at the age of three Jewish instruction, especially reading, learning the alphabet, and learning the prayers, which was the most important. The morning prayers, the *Modeh Ani*, which means, "I thank you, God, for waking up and being alive." Then the prayers before, making the *Motzi* [prayer over bread] before you ate anything.

My father had two sisters living there. Their children, we were very close. We knew each other—houses all around. And what I remember distinctly was a certain spirit there, a spirit very Jewish, deeply Jewish, religious, but custom, traditional. The Sabbath was the centerpiece of the week. Starting Thursday, people starting preparing for the Sabbath. The women would prepare starting with the flour and the baking. I remember my grandmother's house. My mother was not [baking] because she was in business. But my grandmother used to send everything over. By my grandmother everything was turned upside down. The stove was going. I used to go Friday, and she had a little *pletzl* there, a little piece of dough was left with some onions, delicious. And the smells of the baking! Thursday was the preparation, Friday afternoon nobody did any more. The men went to the *mikvah* [ritual baths] to get themselves purified. The women started preparing the children. So, it was a certain, it was a way of life that is—I don't know if it's

2

Joseph W. (second from left) in *cheder* class with other children of Krzywcza, a *shtetl* near Przemyśl, Poland (1929). "It was a way of life . . . that was the culmination of hundreds of years of Jewish life in Eastern Europe."

duplicated any place unless in the Hasidic communities. But that was a way of life that was the culmination of hundreds of years of Jewish life in Eastern Europe. That was the spirit in this little town.

The Sabbath was an expression, it was a deep expression, made a deep, deep impression on children. But the outside world beckoned. We loved it, and we wanted to break free. It was like a tug-of-war. Then after the Sabbath, the evening at the end of the Sabbath, was also a feeling that you're losing something, something very precious is passed. And you prepared yourself for the week. So people had to work. People had to make a living. You had to go out to the villages. Either they bought up produce or cattle or chicken, whatever, or selling them in your stores. We had hardware stores, textile stores. There were no ready-made goods yet. Manufacturing was not very well developed.

Ninety-nine percent of our clientele was non-Jewish. People from the surrounding villages used to come in and buy. Of course it was tough. There was competition. And they didn't have money, so they paid in kind. They paid in eggs and butter and potatoes, whatever. But somehow this worked. This was right after the prayers that separate, *Havdalah* service, which is a separation between the holy and the profane. The weekday was profane, the Sabbath was the holy. So right after that, people went out, opened their stores because the peasants were coming in, because Sunday was a big day.

This is how life went. We were enveloped in this. The outside world was only through the books, through contact. But the contact with the peasantry was not much. It was just the day-to-day. The Jewish life was the essential.

Golly D.
Born Bremen, Germany, 1922

I had one brother who was five years my senior. We were both products of a mixed marriage. My father had come from an Orthodox family, which was one of the reason[s], therefore, my mother converted to Judaism prior to her marriage. And my brother and I were raised in the Jewish faith, in fact in a kosher and Orthodox home. My early childhood passed by rather uneventfully, even though in the early twenties the Brown Shirts started marching through the streets singing antisemitic songs, which somehow didn't faze us all that much because we lived in our own little world. I never felt at that point in time that I was discriminated against. And so it went until Hitler came to power in January 1933.

I was well accepted and also liked by most of my classmates. Fortunately, I very much exceeded in art as well as in sports. I just loved sports. In fact, they had considered even that I should participate in the Olympic Games in 1936—which, of course, was impossible because of my—my being Jewish.

"We lived in our own little world."

Golly D.
Born Bremen, Germany, 1922
Recorded 1992, age 70

The child of a Jewish father and a Christian mother who had converted to Judaism, Golly was raised in an Orthodox family surrounded by an antisemitic environment. She was an Olympic-level athlete, but was unable to compete in the 1936 games because she was Jewish. Later she would attribute her survival partly to her physical strength and endurance.

Mrs. D.'s brother and father were arrested on *Kristallnacht*, and she was expelled from school. After an unsuccessful attempt to emigrate, she began nursing studies in Berlin in 1940. Mrs. D. worked in the Jewish Hospital, where she met her future husband, a physician. When he was deported to Theresienstadt in 1943, she volunteered to join him. They were married in Theresienstadt by Dr. Leo Baeck, a leading German rabbi who after the war became chair of the World Union for Progressive Judaism. Theresienstadt was used by the Nazis as a "model ghetto" for propaganda purposes. Life was harsh, and sham improvements were implemented for a Red Cross visit. After her husband was deported to Auschwitz/Birkenau, in 1944, she again decided to follow him. However, she never saw him again. Mrs. D. was transferred to Gross-Rosen concentration camp and from there sent on a death march through Bohemia and Moravia. Those who could not keep up were shot. Starved and near death, she and a friend escaped from the column and then hid with the help of a local woman until they were discovered by United States soldiers. After recuperating in a hospital, she met her second husband, a Polish survivor, and together they emigrated to the United States in 1946. Mrs. D. travels frequently to Israel to visit her daughter and grandchildren.

Frank S.
Born Breslau, Germany, 1921

The *Reichswehr* [German army], which was only allowed one hundred thousand men at that time by the Treaty of Versailles, they all marched in front of my window. You know, this was the parade street. And I, we watched the *Reichswehr*, and we were very proud because after all we felt very German. Germany was a very militaristic country and everybody wore uniforms. Even we [Jews] wore uniforms. As soon as you had a club or an organization, you had to have a uniform. So there were a variety of uniforms and the whole country marched—it was a militaristic kind of a thing. In school, when we went out anywhere, we had to march. That was the most important thing: left, right, left, right, and so we went. Even the school children. Everybody. The whole country marched. I can remember even when my mother and father went for a walk with us, my father used to remind us, "Fall into step."

Walter S.
Born Steinbach, Germany, 1924

In 1933, everything seemed to be cozy for us because we, as Jewish people in Germany, were first Germans and then Jewish—like you would be an American, and then your religion is the secondary. Because we had all the privileges [of] any other citizen of the German government. In 1936, when the Olympic Games were staged in Berlin, I was rooting for the German people, the German athletes to win as many medals as they could.

Chaim E.
Born Brudzew, Poland, 1916

My father had a textile store, and he always was called "the millionaire." Not that he was a millionaire, but maybe was a little better situated than others. And he felt a certain antisemitism, so he left it. So when I was five we moved to Łódź. And, well, [we] had better times and worse times. It was not so easy, but he had to leave it because he

Frank S.

We didn't know much about antisemitis[m]
years, when I went to elementary sch[ool]
famously with everybody. There w[...]
together.

I remember the day whe[n...]
believed him! Everyone [...]
was *Abwirtschaften*. If y[ou...]
selves to ruin" with [...]
they put forwar[d...]
lous and is a[...]
wildest dr[...]
whole [...]

Frank S. (right) with father and brother. "Even we [Jews] ...
ber even when my mother and father went for a walk with us, my father used to remind us,
'Fall into step.' "

felt the antisemitism is very strong there. We always felt some hate to
Jews, but we lived with [it] because we didn't know differently.

We grew up mostly with Jewish kids. Where we lived in Łódź,
there were sections where not Jews lived there. I wouldn't dare to
go at night there because the antisemitism was big. So we felt it,
but because we lived with the Jews alone, we didn't see it every
day, but we knew it is present there or here. So we kept, in a way,
separate. When I went in the army, the antisemitism was very,
very strong. A matter of fact, when it came already to go in the
war, when the war broke out I was afraid, just the same from the
Polish soldiers because I'm a Jew, the same way as the not-known
enemy what was the Germans. Whether you felt it every day or
not, but it was present there. A Jew was something different.

...n because in the early
...ool, we got along very
...ere Jews and non-Jews all

...n Hitler came to power, nobody
...aughed. The platform against the Nazis
...ou can translate that, "They will work them-
...the silly and ridiculous kind of ideology that
...d. What they want to do with Germany is ridicu-
...bsolutely stupid. Nobody could even dream, in their
...eams, that some day Hitler would come to power. The
country sort of laughed about him.

In 1933, we were sitting at the supper table. We read in the paper, I believe, that Hitler had won the election. And I remember like today my mother said, "Oh my God, this is terrible. That means war."

Renée G.
Born Łosice, Poland, 1932

I was born in Poland in a small town the name of which is Łosice, in eastern Poland near the Bug River. The majority of the people were shopkeepers, merchants. I lived in an extended family situation in a big house that my grandfather built that consisted of three floors. The bottom floor, the middle floor was my apartment, and the top floor was another uncle and aunt and family. Throughout my early childhood and throughout the German occupation I watched everything that was going on through this window.

Before the war, the only time I was at times unhappy was when we children tried to go outside of town a little bit and sometimes Polish children would run after us and would yell *"Żyd! Żyd! Żydowka!"* which meant little Jewish boy, little Jewish girl, and throw stones at us. Also at times the teacher would occasionally hit the Jewish kids, and I remember being hit over my face because I didn't speak loud enough. But for some reason all the Jewish children, we used to get hit more than the others.

My dad would buy the grains from the peasants all around and had lots of friends in the countryside. The town was a very happy Jewish community, even though there was quite a bit of poverty, and one Jewish family would always help out another one. Friday afternoons, for example, I remember lots and lots of beggars standing in front of the door, and I would run out and hand out bread and change—money. I remember my little cousin even, who was very good-hearted, helped out a blind Jewish beggar who couldn't walk by himself, and he would lead him around so he wouldn't go hungry on a Saturday. This was all very good until 1939, when we heard that war broke out.

Robert S.
Born Weissenstadt, Germany, 1927
Member of Hitler Youth

One of the members of the family, who lived on the same street as I did, was a Brown Shirt, an SA man [Storm Troopers, early paramilitary supporters of National Socialism]. And as far as I remember, apparently in a leading position because I remember very well, and I can't remember exactly what year it was, but it was in one of the years before the war the SA marching around in town. They were very prominent, and one night they marched by our window with torches and singing SA songs, and stopping at the house of this relative of mine, and bringing him some sort of a salute. I don't remember if it was his birthday or whether it was a party day of significance. I just remember the fact itself, and I also remember how impressed I was that somebody would get a whole torchlight parade. I also remember my grandmother putting torches or small, little lights, candle lights into the window for some kind of Nazi celebrations, much like people do here at Christmas.

In '37 I was ten [shows his Hitler Youth membership card].

Hitler Youth card of Robert S. "This is me as a ten-year-old—very proud, as a matter of fact, to have this uniform."

This is me as a ten-year-old—very proud, as a matter of fact, to have this uniform which was, you know as you see it, a regulation uniform. I believe, and it's possible that I'm wrong, I believe at that time in '37, everybody reaching a certain age had to join the Hitler Youth. I did have an uncle who was a Social Democrat, Willy Brandt–variety, a really strong believer in the Social Democrats. I visited him when I was fourteen years old, and I was wearing this uniform here when I visited him. I opened the door. I had traveled on the train all day, and I opened the door, and he looked at me and said, "Why did you have to come in this uniform?" And I—I didn't understand, really, what he was so unhappy about. In fact, I lectured him about whatever I knew, whatever I had learned, what was in my mind about the great— [*das*] *grosse deutsche Reich* and the whole propaganda spiel, and he just sort of sat down and let me talk, and then we went on being relatives. You can surmise from this that I—even though I wasn't thinking very much at that time or I don't recall having heavy thoughts about anything—I was accepting what was given to me, what was told me, was accepting the regime, really, without any second thoughts. And even to people who were telling me, "This is madness!" I, I as a fourteen-year-old, felt I had to put them straight.

Christa M.
Born Saarbrücken, Germany, 1930

Home life was very comfortable—summer vacations, winter skiing, in the summer we went to the sea, and everything was very comfortable. The first very subtle [change] is that I was exposed to a lot of the Brown Shirts. To this day I can't stand even the sound of a motorcycle—they were always tearing around on motorcycles and screaming.

It had to be around when I was five, [my nanny] had taken me into town to go shopping. There was what I had thought was a church across the street, and it was all in flames. And I thought, "Oh, my God! The church is burning!" because there was a lot of commotion on the street. And then I saw a whole bunch of Brown Shirts, with their boots and caps and armbands—they always wore the swastika armband. In the center there was a man in a long black robe and a long beard. They had put a big drum around his neck. They were pushing him and shoving him. And he had to beat the drum, and he had to say to the drum, "I'm a filthy Jew. I'm a filthy Jew." And they shoved him and tried to even trip him. Every time he staggered or fell, they kicked him again. It was just horrible, horrible, horrible, horrible. And I was very scared, and I didn't know what was going on. Somewhere, there was my father's car and they scooped us up and drove us home. I remember my father saying, "From now on nobody in this house goes into town without my permission."

Frank S.

The small Nazis, the young people, called *Jungvolk*—the young folk, the young people—they had little black short-shorts and brown shirts and black ties. They were the young ones. These were the ones I went to school with. They came to school in uniform after 1933. In high school, I was still a very popular man and I walked together with a couple of my friends from high school who were not Jewish. As a matter of fact, they were members of the young peoples, the *Jungvolk*, the Young Nazis. I said, "Well, what do you have against the Jews?" or something to the effect. And they said, "Well, we have nothing against you. If they were all like you it would be all right. But it's the other Jews that we don't like." This kind of talk I got from my friends.

At that time, they were reading the newspaper *Der Stürmer*, which was a racist paper with caricatures of Jews with long noses and black hair and whatever—ugly-looking people. This was the propaganda paper. . . . Anyway, they read this, and their picture of a Jew was an ugly, miserable person. And this is what happened when my mother came to pick me up from school. I came to school the next day, and they told me, "Who was that dirty Jew woman that picked you up from school?" I said, "That was my mother." "Oh, my God," they said. "You should be ashamed of yourself to have a mother like this." I had a fight, I think, because my mother was insulted. I came home and I cried and I said [to] my mother, "Please don't pick me up anymore because the boys are bothering me," and I told her what they said. She was very offended and cried bitterly.

Christa M.

You couldn't go anywhere unless you raised your arm and said, "*Heil Hitler*," and that gets to be really, I mean—even to your friends! I mean when you used just [to] shake hands and whatnot. Not anymore. You had to go and say, "*Heil Hitler*." And, of

"We have nothing
against you . . .
it's the other Jews
that we don't like."

Frank S.
Born Breslau, Germany, 1921
Recorded 1980, age 59

As a child in Breslau, Frank S. remembers his mother gently kneading his younger brother's large nose to make it straight and thus protect him from attacks by Nazis. Her advice to young Frank was to try not to be noticeable, "to shrink into oblivion." Mr. S. discusses the introduction of "raceology" in the school curriculum, which emphasized the superiority of the "Aryan" race and the inferiority of Jews.

At age fifteen he left school to apprentice with a Nazi electrician who treated him "just a little better than an animal," abusing him physically and mentally and making him pull huge cartloads of materials. During *Kristallnacht* Frank S. was protected by his family's Gentile cleaning lady, who warned him in time for Frank to run and hide.

In 1938, he emigrated to England. After the outbreak of war in 1939, Mr. S. was confined as an "enemy alien," as were many other Germans, both Jews and non-Jews.

course, we were silly kids. I remember sometimes I used to go around and I'd [do] like this [*raises and lowers her arm very fast*] "*heilhitlerheilhitler*" and laugh and think I get away with it. [*Shakes her head no.*] You were reported. By the time you get back home, your whole family knew about it. How quickly you were reported.

Frank S.

Then all of a sudden, the teachers came in, and in uniform. Every teacher had to have a uniform. So my biology teacher had an SS uniform, a Gestapo uniform with a skull and, you know, the bones, the crossbones and the skull. My other teacher, the Latin teacher, who always said "*Salvete, discipuli,*" he came in a storm trooper uniform, the brown uniform. And the greetings were changed from "*Salvete, discipuli*" and "*Salve Magister . . .*" to "*Heil Hitler.*" He came in and he said, "*Heil Hitler,* students," and we had to stand up and say, "*Heil Hitler,* teacher." Then we had a different curriculum because we had this *Rassenkunde,* which was race-ology. That was a regular subject we had. And we were supposed to learn what an Aryan is, the Aryan race. Opposed to the Aryan race, we were the Jews. And the students were to learn what makes the difference between a blond, blue-eyed pure Aryan to a Jew. And I hated this biology teacher with a passion. He always pulled me up on my sideburns and he put me in front of the class and you see how, "Here's a Jew," and he started to describe my nose and my cheekbones, and my hair and my features, and how to recognize a Jew. And I was very humiliated. And I hated it, and I felt terrible about the whole thing.

Golly D.

We were not permitted to have any social contact with non-Jews. . . . One day I remember, a young German, a childhood friend, a youth friend, came to pick me up from school after school was out. We had about a one-hour walk from school to home and we were about halfway home and were suddenly stopped by a Gestapo agent who had obviously followed us all along. He approached this young boy. We were about sixteen years old. I didn't hear exactly what he said, but I could see that he argued with him severely. He made his father appear at Gestapo headquarters and threatened the father that if his son would ever be seen again with a Jew or Jewess, he and the son would end up in concentration camp.

"Raceology" chart comparing physical traits of German and Jewish youth. Such classes in *Rassenkunde* were a part of school curricula for Frank S., who grew up in Breslau, Germany. "[The biology teacher] always pulled me up on my sideburns and he put me in front of the class and [said], 'Here's a Jew.' " *Archive Photo*

Christa M.

Well, I was really proud of myself—really. I don't know where I got it, but for some reason it was one of my favorites. Maybe because of the mysticism, the siren who was on the rock calling, combing her golden locks, the romanticism and all this. And I loved it. And of course, the way the music was set to Schumann. I memorized the whole thing. In my class, we had to do some recital of some nature. Here comes my big, big performance. And I got up on the stage and started to sing "The Lorelei." And I got two lines, that I remember. The first two lines, and these two very bullish women, big bullish—they just marched up and literally just ripped me off the stage. And I know I got slapped across the face and I was scared. I still didn't know what I'd done. And they just, you know, said, "Get your stuff together!" They took me home and investigated, and all kinds of sessions with my father and whatnot. And then I found out my big crime, that "The Lorelei" was written by Heinrich Heine, who happened to be a Jew.

Frank S.

On the street they were all Nazis. You didn't dare to ask anybody, "Are you [a] Nazi or aren't you a Nazi?" You know, everybody was a Nazi because God forbid you're not. Somebody might walk next to you and hear the remark, and immediately you get arrested because they were training people to listen in. The Hitler Youth was trained to give their parents away. They were trained to listen at home. There were quite a few families where the parents—fathers or mothers—were arrested for something they have said against Hitler because their own son, their own child had given them away.

Robert S.
Member of Hitler Youth

As far as I remember, it was mostly teaching about the *Fuehrer*. That was topic number one. It was always the *Fuehrer*. Okay, what the *Fuehrer* did here and there, and so on. And what the *Fuehrer* will do, what Hitler's plans were, for, you know, the greatness of our country. It was really more either biographical things about Hitler or it was singing a lot of Nazi songs. We would then march around singing them. There were references to Roosevelt as "the sick man in the White House," surrounded by Jewish advisers.

Werner R.
Born Berlin, Germany, 1927

My father was an engineer. My mother was a housewife from a prominent, old Sephardic family. We lived on the outskirts of Berlin. In 1933, my father lost his job. He was asked to resign because he was Jewish.

During World War I my father was in the Austro-Hungarian army. He was a captain, and he spent considerable time in what afterwards became Yugoslavia. So in 1933, when he lost his job and people were already ending up in camps and getting beaten up, he decided he wanted to leave Germany. So we went to Zagreb in December 1933.

Croatia, where we lived, was a predominantly Catholic area. [In high school] there would be Greek Orthodox students, Russian Orthodox, Lutherans, Muslims. As a result of this I had friends of every religion and I got a very, very good understanding of their religions. And I celebrated with them their holidays. People are sometimes amazed how much I know about Moslem holidays and Greek Orthodox holidays. And this has remained with me, and this is probably one of the reasons why I never use the term *goi*, for instance. I never use it. I never have any anti-Christian feelings and so on. It's just I was brought up in this particular environment. There never was a question of—I never experienced any antisemitism while I went to school. The only antisemitism which I ever experienced was on the part of a couple of teachers, just before the Nazis marched in.

Werner R., age 11 (1938).

Rabbi Baruch G.
Born Mława, Poland, 1923

[I had] one brother, one sister, I would say a lower-middle-class family in terms of financial status, as I can think back. But nothing was lacking in the house in terms of what we needed and wanted. Childhood normal, uneventful, but rather surrounded by warm family. He [my father] owned a dry goods store. It was bad times and good times, you know, businesswise. I remember those days in the 1930s, years of tension, a bit of tension, socially speaking.

There was an isolation between Jews and Christians in my hometown, you know. I try to compare it with what we have here [in the United States]: Jewish boys and girls mixing in open society with non-Jewish kids. That was not my experience, growing up. We went to Jewish schools, we had our Jewish areas, we had our Jewish synagogues, and frequently, or occasionally at least, being beaten up by a bunch of Christian kids who called me a Christ killer or something of that nature. We grew up in a kind of isolation as far as the Jewish community was concerned. Obviously it wasn't the open society, the democracy that we have here. And so we learned to accept the reality of what it is and to making no waves about it.

Bessie K.
Born Vilna, Poland, 1924

We had Christian friends, we had Jewish friends, and I think we were always protected. As I look back, the bad things were never told, they were never mentioned in the house. Because I went to a private school, only Jewish children went there. We heard that something is going on with Jewish people, but it was not there. So in other words, if it's not your home, it's okay.

Abraham P.
Born Beclean, Romania, 1924

I am from Transylvania, Romania. I come from a small town. The name of the town was Beclean. My family was father, mother, six brothers. My older brother, his name was Isaac. After him I had a brother Menachem. He died in Auschwitz, and I am next. And then, I have a brother Yossi [who] is after me. He lives now in New York. He used to live in South America. After that is Schloima, who lives in Israel. And then I had a little kid brother. His name was Metzalah. He died in Auschwitz. My parents died in Auschwitz. Most of my aunts and uncles died—all of them died in Auschwitz. It was a large family, forty, fifty. Maybe twelve of us, fourteen of us have survived.

The community had about five thousand people living there. There were two hundred fifty Jewish families. There were Hungarians living there, Romanians, Germans, Gypsies, and Jews. After the war, there were about six or seven families who came home.

Friday we used to get ready for the *Shabes*. . . . We used [to] clean up the house, scrub the floor, clean the windows. My mother, may she rest in peace, was cooking and baking. We shined our shoes, we brushed our clothes. It was a busy day. It was delightful. Oh God! We used to press our own shirts, then after that we went to the bathhouse because they didn't have showers or bathtubs like we have over here. As children we were forced to sleep in the afternoon on Friday so we should be able to stay up for the Friday night meal and to be able to go to the synagogue. It was happiness!

Except once in a while, some of the Gentiles used to scream and yell from the other side, "You dirty Jew!" or something like that. There was always antisemitism. There hasn't been a week that went by when I wasn't told, "You dirty Jew, go back to Palestine!" Our household was very religious; we all wore the side curls, *peyes*, and we wore the dark clothes, the traditional clothes. It started to change around the late '30s. We were forced to go and do all the menial labor, work for the officials, clean the toilets, sweep the streets, and to top it all off, they blamed you for the war. They blamed you for all the troubles that had been going on. One day we were walking down the street, and a priest, a Catholic priest, stopped and he said, "Do you know these people are responsible for the war?" I'm fourteen, fifteen years old. I'm responsible for a war that's been going on over there in Europe? We were always hoping it's not going to last very long.

In late 1943, one Friday afternoon, one soldier wanted to show off to his girlfriend, and the girl happens to be the daughter of the people who used to buy our milk. They used to come into our store to buy on credit, and we always trusted them. He says to me, "Let me look at you." He looked at me and he saw that I have *peies*. So I remember he cut off this one over here, the left *peie*. He cut it up and showed it off to his girlfriend, the very same girl, and she didn't say a word.

We just lived and we tried to stay away from the streets. On

German soldiers cutting off side locks (*peyes*) and beard of an Orthodox Jewish man. Abraham P. describes how in 1943 a Nazi soldier cut off one of his *peyes* to impress a girl-friend, and how Mr. P.'s mother broke down seeing his father forcibly shaved and without a beard for the first time in their marriage. *Courtesy U.S. Holocaust Memorial Museum*

May the third in 1944, they put out an order that everybody has to shave off their beards, their hair, everything. My mother asked me, "Did you see your father?" He was with his back to her. I said, "He's right here!" And he turned around, and she saw him. She's never seen my father without a beard. She broke down and she cried. I'll never forget it. She just—she looked so stunned—she couldn't believe it.

Abraham P.
Born Beclean, Romania, 1922
Recorded 1984, age 62

Abraham P. fondly recalls his large, close-knit family and the small Jewish community in which he was raised. For eighteen months he attended a yeshiva in the nearby town of Sighet. He describes increased antisemitism after the Hungarian occupation of western Romania, when his two older brothers were conscripted into a Hungarian slave labor battalion. After the German occupation in 1944, Mr. P. and his family were transported to Dej, where they were forced to work for three weeks in open fields before being deported to Auschwitz/Birkenau.

Mr. P. vividly describes concentration camp life: the days punctuated by wrenching hunger, hours of roll calls, and the incessant screaming of the guards, *"'Los! Los! Mach los!'* Every minute they were driving you out of your mind!" He was transferred to Buchenwald, Zeitz, back to Buchenwald, Schlieben, where he was a slave laborer in a munitions factory, then to Flossenbürg. He was transferred one final time to Theresienstadt, where he was liberated by Soviet troops. Mr. P. was hospitalized after the war and eventually reunited with two of his brothers. After a brief return to Beclean, Mr. P. moved to Hungary and then to a displaced persons camp in Ulm, Germany. He emigrated to the United States, where he was drafted and served as a chaplain in the United States army. Mr. P. frequently visits junior and senior high schools to speak about his experiences.

Joseph K.
Born Gorlice, Poland, 1926

When we lived amongst these people before 1939, we knew that they hated us, because in Poland, there was nothing hidden. Ever since I could remember as a child going to school, I would see on the street—be it on a fence or on a building of a Jewish home or in front on a Jewish store or on the sidewalk—there were signs, we call it graffiti here today, signs all over the place: "Jew Go to Palestine. You Filthy Jew, We Don't Want You in Poland."

Jacob K.
Born Zwoleń, Poland, 1923

In school all my friends, that I was good friends, that I never would think that they would do it, they were singing antisemitic songs. And they made up songs and I recall one, one song that they were singing it. It says:

> *Remember Jew you are on Polish soil.*
> *Your bones we will pile on a heap.*
> *Hitler's calamity you will not avoid,*
> *And we will beat your crippled destiny with a whip.*

Joseph W.
Attended gymnasium (high school) in Przemyśl, Poland

We had a Latin teacher—I forgot his name. Orloffsky? He was a humanist—a real *mensch*, a real human being. When he died suddenly of a heart attack, we went to this [student government] committee and asked what should we do. Should we buy flowers? He [student committee member] says, "We don't want any Jews to participate in Professor Orloffsky's funeral. Get out of here! We will make it. He was a Catholic. You Jews have nothing to do." Just like that.

I had a professor [for] math. He was very antisemitic. He would denigrate you. He would imitate a Yiddish accent, which I didn't have, but he would do it just to *grizhen* [aggravate] you. I'll never forget we had a Jewish boy in class. His name was Pulver. He came from a Jewish family from an old Jewish section of Prze-myśl. The Jewish boys there spoke Yiddish. [A] professor taught history and he used to make fun of this Pulver because of his accent. It was so—I wanted to sink in the ground. He used to call him up and say, "Elu Pulver. Why do you want to come here? Why can't you become a tailor, a shoemaker, a *shoḥet* [kosher slaughterer]? What do you want to go to a gymnasium? What do you? Go home. Tell your parents." It was, for a child, young person to hear such blatant—nobody could censor them. They were free to do whatever they wanted.

Christa M.
Describes German elementary school curriculum

[We were taught that] Jews are dirty. They are root of all evil. Whatever is going to happen to us that's bad, whatever that did happen that's bad, it's all the fault of the Jews. The Jews own all the money. The Jews are all crooks and all Jews are going to cheat you. Never to trust them. And then, of course, never to have a Jewish friend. We were taken to some propaganda films, one that I remember distinctly because I was an enormous animal lover and I am an animal lover. And they would show, you know, Jews bleed animals to death and they slit their throats, and there were some horrible pictures in there. Then they say, "See? You know Jews mistreat everybody and therefore we must get rid of them. Look what they did to the animals." I would, at that point, I said, "That's awful! Anybody who did that to animals. . . ."

Joseph W.

Of course, the antisemitism in Poland was becoming more open because Hitler was in Germany and the Nazi party had a great influence on the Polish Nationalist Party. They had a priest, he published a newspaper. His name was Ksiądz Trzeciak, Father

Trzeciak. He published the most antisemitic newspaper. There's a joke—is it okay if I tell a joke? There's a Jewish man sitting in Warsaw on a bench and he has this antisemitic paper and he's reading it. And so another friend, a Jew, passes by and he says, *"Rab Chaim, vus laynst di didozike tsaytung?"* What are you reading this paper? He says, *"Rab Schloime,* if a *Yid* read the Jewish papers, all I read is about *tsores* [troubles]: 'The Jews are pogrommed. They're this, they're that. Look what they are doing in Germany'—and I'm depressed. So if I want to feel good, I take the antisemitic paper, and it says, 'The Jews own all the apartment houses in Poland! The Jews own all the factories! The Jews are the richest! They control the world! They control America, and Roosevelt is a Jew!'—It makes me feel good!" That's the kind of a life that was going on. And this was the '30s. It was getting—the clouds were getting darker, darker.

Father John S.
Born Košice, Czechoslovakia, 1922
Jesuit Seminarian

For me, the first indication, but again, not thinking in terms of what might happen to Jewish people, but in terms of what might happen to all of us or Czechoslovakia—was the *Anschluss*. Until then we didn't really notice Hitler so much, but with the *Anschluss*, with Austria being taken by Germany [March 1938], the whole of Czechoslovakia became depressed and restless, to some degree. There was fear around and I was young, but I sensed that. And I had a foreboding of tragedy. I felt that a vise was closing in on Czechoslovakia. I might add right now that I lived six years in the People's Republic of China, Communist China, so I went through many stressful and fearful situations. But I never in any situation experienced the kind of terrible fear that [the] Nazi regime and ideology, the presence of Nazis could inculcate, could create in people. I like to stress that because it is a fear for which I find no parallel.

Edith P.
Born Michalovce, Czechoslovakia, 1920

I come from the eastern part of Czechoslovakia, from a middle-class Jewish family. My father was a high official, very religious man. We were six children. Four boys. My sister was the oldest. I was the youngest. Czechoslovakia being a very democratic country, we had a very good life there. As far as antisemitism, actually I never felt it really. I knew there was antisemitism in Czechoslovakia, but it never hit us. And if it did, we were always able to defend ourselves. Just like here. When I came to this country democracy was nothing new to me because I was used to it. I come from a family where there were two emphases: education and love for the family. And I suppose these were the two principles that have guided me.

Times became hard because Hitler became more powerful, and it disturbed our beautiful life. We didn't know from one day to the other what's going to happen. The family was very strong and it was just unthinkable, absolutely unthinkable, that somebody or some power would be able to uproot us.

Walter S.
15 years old in Mannheim, Germany,
during *Kristallnacht*

1938, Crystal Night. I remember vividly. I wanted to go to school. We went all together, and we saw all along the streets every Jewish store had broken windows. And we didn't know what was going on. We come to the school. The gates were closed. The principal of the school told us, "Kids, please go home. Something is happening. Please go home and hide." We went back and I remember exactly. We looked [from] behind the curtains to see what was going on in the street. We saw the Nazis smashing windows, and about a block, a block and a half away was a dentist's office, a Jewish dentist. We could see how they broke into the doors and smashing everything. We were young and were scared.

Edith P. (child at center of table) surrounded by her family in Michalovce, Czechoslovakia, early 1920s. "The family was very strong and it was just unthinkable, absolutely unthinkable, that somebody or some power would be able to uproot us."

Golly D.
16 years old in Bremen, Germany,
during *Kristallnacht*

We were fast asleep. I and my family, the four of us fast asleep when we heard pounding on the front door. Heavy pounding. My father quickly went down the steps, opened the door, and there were two Brown [Shirt] Nazi troopers standing there. "Tell your family get dressed quickly and come with us. Come along!" We had no choice. We quickly got dressed and the two troopers delivered us to a mess hall which was in the center of town. And as we entered, we realized that all the other Jews from the city had also been rounded up and also been brought to this mess hall. Nobody knew why. Nobody knew what was going to happen. They let us sit there for hours on end, hour after hour after hour, until finally they separated the women from the men and the men were taken away. We didn't know where to, and so was my father and my brother.

In the morning, my mother and I and all women were allowed
to return home. And that's when we found out what had been
happening during the night while we were gathered together there
in the mess hall. That the Brown Shirts were busy smashing the
Jewish store windows, entering the Jewish homes and apartments,
smashing everything that they could. My father's business was
destroyed that night. And of course we had one synagogue in Bremen, which was burned down.

The next day, not suspecting anything, I returned to school,
the day after the *Kristallnacht*. [I] walked up the steps trying to get
to my classroom, and my homeroom teacher, Mr. Koch, came
down the steps, by coincidence, and approached me and said to
me really with sad eyes, "Miss Golly, I'm awfully sorry, but Jews
are no longer to attend school." So, I had no choice but to turn
back. And I walked home with my head down, and I realized that
my plans for the future had been shattered.

The next day the doorbell rings again and one of my classmates
stands by the door. Now after I told you that social contact with
Jews was taboo—more than taboo. Now this pure Aryan classmate
of mine, coming from a very prominent family—her father was the
most prominent lawyer in Bremen—came to our house, came
upstairs, and she said she only came with one message. In the name
of her family, she wanted to express how terribly embarrassed and
ashamed they were about what had happened the previous night,
the *Kristallnacht*, night before. And I could never forget this gesture
and I'm still in contact. I'm still corresponding with her. And whenever I do go home to Bremen, we do get together.

Frank S.

The only one purpose that we all had in common was to get out.
The only Jewish organizations that were allowed were the emigra-
tion organizations. They were allowed to exist for the single purpose of expediting Jews out of the country.

28

Walter S.
Age 16, Germany

At that time, it was a funny deal. In Germany they still let you emigrate to Palestine. So I went near Berlin on a farm to prepare myself to emigrate to Israel. I didn't know that was the beginning of hard labor and hardship in my life because soon afterwards those farm camps were taken over by the Gestapo. We were restricted of movement, we could not go anywhere else, the band around our arms.

We were harvesting everything, potatoes and so on, but we were starving from hunger more or less, because we were not allowed to eat what we harvested. That was for the "German people." We knew already we couldn't go to Palestine anymore. We prepared ourselves for the worst, like army soldiers preparing for survival. We packed our things. We had backpacks. We put in medication and things like this, just in case we would be deported, because we knew already at that time that people were taken away. But where, we did not know.

"I Grew Up Overnight"

THE OUTBREAK OF WAR

On September 1, 1939, World War II began in Europe with Germany's invasion of Poland. In German-occupied territories, Jews were forbidden to congregate, pray, or own books, bicycles, radios, and many other items. Even then, few could predict where German policies would lead. Information was scarce: the press was censored and radios were forbidden.

In June 1941, Germany invaded the Soviet Union, including those parts of Eastern Europe occupied by the Red Army. Following behind the German invasion forces were Einsatzgruppen (special squads). These mobile killing units murdered as many as 1.5 million Jews as German forces advanced.

Forced labor became a fact of life in occupied territories. German soldiers seized Jews from streets and homes and put them to work. Many were sent to slave labor camps where the work was excruciating, the conditions unbearable.

The toll on young Jews was severe. They were no longer allowed to attend school, former non-Jewish friends shunned them, family members disappeared, and corpses littered their towns.

Robert S.
Member of Hitler Youth

I remember the beginning of the war. I remember the speech of
Hitler. I remember the whole frenzy that all of a sudden rose up.
And where I was, in the environment that I was, the people I
knew, including my teachers, [were] all for the war. And I think in
conjunction with that, for whatever stood in its way to be
destroyed. And tanks were rolling by day and night. We were sitting in the windows, we were so caught up by this display of might
that I thought, "My God, I'm so glad I'm here!" It may reflect on
the limits of my mind. I wasn't even unhappy about that. I
thought, "War! I'm going to be a hero!"

Helen K.
Born Warsaw, Poland, 1924
Age 15, Germany invades Poland

First of all, we felt that if there's going to be a war, it is going to
be like a *Blitzkreig*. It's going to last a month or so, and then it
will be over. So we felt, well, if it is only going to last a little
while, the Jews will survive. They always somehow do. We
didn't think it was going to last long, first of all. Number two,
we didn't believe what [Hitler] said or what he was going to do,
it's going to really happen. We didn't believe it. My parents
lived in Warsaw all their life. They had four children, and I
guess by the time we really realized what's going to happen, it
was too late. We couldn't leave. So we were caught like millions
of others.

I was a very, very immature, very sheltered little girl. And
when the world war broke out, I grew up overnight. I became
really so strong. I didn't know that I was able to do all the things I
did. My mother had a diamond ring, and I wanted to get papers
for my mother and my brother. I remember I went over to a German and I said to him, "I'll give a diamond ring. Give me papers

Helen K. (second from left) with her three brothers in Warsaw, Poland, early 1930s. "I was a very, very immature, very sheltered little girl. And when the world war broke out, I grew up overnight."

for my brother, my mother." A girl of fifteen. Who would dare do that? I did. He did give me the papers, and it did buy a little time for them. You know, without papers you just didn't have a chance.

Abraham P.
Beclean, Romania

There was no place to go. You know, we were not prepared for this. I didn't know anything about the concentration camps. We'd heard that the Germans are persecuting Jews, so we thought maybe they put them in jail. They leave them in jail for a month and then let them go. The newspapers we used to get in the community were strictly censored. The only thing you saw over there was the glorious German army, the way they were advancing and how they are capturing one country after the other. We never knew. There were a couple of radios, but you had to be careful. If they catch you listening to it, they kill you without any hesitation. It means you are a traitor.

Edith P.
In Hungarian-occupied Czechoslovakia

We did not hear much, because by this time the Hungarian press most likely was censored. We listened to the BBC and we knew that there were concentration camps, but in some miraculous way we thought we are never going to go there. It's impossible. We had refugees from Poland, Polish Jews who told us, "Do something! Go! Go to America! Go to Israel! Go to Palestine! Do something! Escape, because that's what is going to happen to you." And we thought, "That's impossible. I mean, my father was born here, his father was born here, and my grand-grandfather was born here. It's impossible." But we didn't know enough. Had we known enough, I think we would have done more.

Joseph K.
Age 13, Germany invades Poland

In 1939, September 1, when the Germans occupied our town within a few days after the war broke out, we immediately began to feel the pressure of the occupation forces on the Jewish population. Shortly after the occupation by the Germans, the Jewish High Holidays came about and we were not allowed to go to the synagogue. [We] were not allowed to pray. We were not allowed to gather more than three people at first. The synagogues were destroyed, Torahs were burned, prayer books were burned. We immediately began to feel the oppressor's boot.

Martin S.
Born Tarnobrzeg, Poland, 1933
Age 6, Germany invades Poland

I remember the war coming to our town with a very severe air raid. I remember the whole city was just an inferno, and we all ran for our lives. We crossed a river called the Visla [Vistula], and certain things you can remember. And one of the things I remember as we were crossing in a little boat, we just looked at a wall of fire in back of us.

Renée G.
Age 7, Germany invades Poland

We as little children didn't quite understand the whole impact of it. All of a sudden in this little dead town which the big adventure was usually to go to Warsaw for excitement, and all of a sudden we heard war [and we said,] "Oh, good!" The kids were terribly excited to see new people, tanks. Until one day, we saw three planes overhead. And all of a sudden this excitement started dying down. Fear took over. We heard screaming and screeching and explosions and fire and smoke. My dad was still in the town, and we were terribly afraid that he might have been hit. But he came in the afternoon and related that, yes, the town was bombed and lots of people were killed. But saddest thing of all was that the beautiful synagogue that was built before the war was completely leveled. I remember at the time thinking, "Why the Jewish synagogue? Why not the church? Why not anything else in town?" And right away, my parents explained to me this is a war, perhaps, against the Jews.

Celia K.
Born Szarkowszczyzna, Poland, 1923
Attending boarding school as Germany attacks
Soviet Union, June 1941

They said war broke out, and it was bombing, constant bombing. And everyone was going towards east. The roads were littered with trucks and bodies, bodies and bodies everywhere. And I was swept with this tide of people going east. I had no idea how to get home. I had no idea how my family fared. And everyone was trying to evacuate, but there was no way. No way! After some time I realized I want to go home. So instead of going east, I started heading west. There was a Polish girl in my dormitory who was very good to me, who helped me out a lot. And I figured out, "Gee, she's only a couple of miles away from here. I'll stop there and I'll get something to wear, to cover myself." I had a flimsy nightgown on. As soon as I came down to her gate, she said, "Get away from here, you dirty Jew!" And this is the first time it hit me, that I really understood what it's all about. It really didn't hit me until then.

Arnold C.
Born Kovno, Lithuania, 1933
Age 8 as Germany invades Kovno, June 1941

I was part of a family of four. There was my sister, six-years-older Sarah, and my mother, Tanya, and my father, Lazar. In June— 23rd, 1941—at five o'clock in the morning we encountered the first waves of German bombers over Kovno. And this is when we realized that war has broken out. We went down in the basement, sat out the rest of the day there, and at night my parents decided that the safest thing for us would be to move out of Kovno. We had decided to move towards the Russian border. This was the safest place to go, to the interior of the Soviet Union. This was on Sunday. On Monday morning we packed a few belongings, we

Arnold C. (middle) with his father and sister in Kovno, Lithuania, approximately 1934.

took a bicycle and started walking out of the city of Kovno. As we left the outskirts of Kovno and entered the highway, the highway was mobbed with people. Everyone had the same idea. German planes were overhead. They strafed us. We had to duck and run. There were dead bodies all over the place. We just kept on going. By midday, there was a heavy bombardment and we got separated. My mother, my sister and I lost our father. We decided to continue on. [After two days] we decided at that time to then return back to Kovno. We were afraid to use the highway because the highway was loaded with German military troops. So we rented a little boat with another Jewish family. And as we rode the boat towards Kovno, the first shock of war came to me because I saw bodies floating in the river.

Renée H.
Born Bratislava, Czechoslovakia, 1933

I was born in Bratislava in Czechoslovakia, which was a community, very old Jewish community established there. I felt very much a part of that community. I was a child during the war. When the Germans came into Czechoslovakia I was not yet six years old. I have one recollection of the German presence of that time, which was when Hitler supposedly went through the town. And I do remember my father saying that I was not to go in the streets. I couldn't understand why it was. He didn't explain anything to me, but I remember him saying, "We are not going to show any support." I saw everybody else in the neighborhood going out in the street and participating.

Slowly there was abuse, and the abuse came not so much from the Germans alone as it came from the native population, the Slovaks. There would be all sorts of nasty things being said as Jews passed in the street. One of the things I remember very strongly was that this kind of abuse escalated as soon as we were supposed to wear the Jewish star. And that was for me a very traumatic experience. I remember coming home one day and seeing my

Renée H. (child in the middle) with her sister and parents, who were deaf, in Bratislava, Czechoslovakia, approximately 1935. "When the Germans came into Czechoslovakia I was not yet six years old."

mother sewing on the star on my coat. And I was aware of the fact that this was a way of singling us out. I remember saying, "Let's not do this, because then we can't hide." And she said, "We have to. That is the decree." And what happened in the town itself was the closing in of the neighborhood.

Edith P.

I can't say that all Gentiles were against us. I won't say that. They didn't help us. They were passive. Maybe they were scared. Our best neighbors, the day that we had been deported, came in to our house. Our best neighbor. And I recall it's the first time in my life I got two pairs of new shoes, because in Europe you don't buy two pair of shoes, not in our family. You bought one pair of new shoes. I don't know why I bought two pair of new shoes. And she knew about it. Maybe I told her four weeks before. And just before, we were just looking around what to take with us—we were [being] deported—she came in. She said, "Where are your new shoes? You don't need it anyhow."

Abraham P.

We had some money, and my mother decided that she's going to go over to a friend of hers who happens to be a German. They went to school together, they grew up together. She went to her friend and said to her, "Look here, I don't know what is going to happen to us. I got here some money. Keep it for me. Keep it. I don't know whether I'm going to come back, but if the kids are going to come home, give it to them. If not, keep it." This very friend of hers went to the authorities and she turned in my mother. My mother came in, came back. She was pale and blue. They must have hurt her. They must have beaten her up.

Father John S.

The real fear was of denunciation. Suppose you would try to hide a Jewish person. In our city, it was not safe. Somebody would denounce you. So this I hold up as a crime, as a collective crime. Our people were still too antisemitic and even the best, even those who had close Jewish friendships and relationships, were not strong enough to buckle this. And they were not prepared to act. The nice, the good people on whom their Jewish friends could have counted, were the most scared, the most weak, the least prepared to take on this huge, brutal machinery which exploded all around them. We were just not ready to see, understand anything. And that was the fault of our upbringing, both familywise, church-wise, and educationwise.

Father John S.
Born Košice, Czechoslovakia, 1922
Recorded 1983, age 61. Died 1990

In his childhood, Father John S. enjoyed friendships with many Jewish neighbors in Košice. The Hungarian occupation of his region of Czechoslovakia resulted in increased and institutionalized antisemitism. After spending three years secluded in a monastery in Budapest, Father S. returned to Košice and was stunned by the shift in attitude toward Jews. When a group of non-Jewish partisans were slated for deportation, he helped hide them. He remembers that "even the good people, on whom their Jewish friends could have counted," were unprepared to deal with the evil of the Holocaust.

Father S. saw a group of Jews being deported in cattle cars and was particularly shaken when, through the knothole of a wooden fence surrounding a train yard, he witnessed the brutal beating of someone who dared to ask for water. He recalls awakening at night to the wailing of Jews in cattle cars when at the railroad station German guards took over from the Hungarians.

"I see it, personally, as the greatest tragedy of my life that Jewish people were deported all around me, I didn't do anything. I panicked—not even panic. . . . I just didn't know what to do."

After the war, Father S. served as a missionary in China for six years before emigrating to the United States. He frequently lectured about the Holocaust and taught communications at a Jesuit university until his death in 1990.

Golly D.

I was sent several times to work as a nurse in one of the collecting camps in Berlin, collecting halls. It was in Hamburgerstrasse, where they gathered the Jewish families together, and where they had to wait sometimes two weeks, sometimes three weeks, till a train was available to transfer them wherever—east. It was always called "east." When I worked there, it became clear to me what was really going on. The families would just get an order to report in this place on a certain day, in the certain time, and they packed their suitcases and they went and waited, not suspecting that anything so terrible could happen because it was just unimaginable. One day I see all these children we had been working with in the children's home with the head nurse. The home was vacated. The head nurse had to take all these children, dozens of them, dozens of little children, and I met them in the collection hall, and knew, of course, what their fate would be. They were all sent to be exterminated in Auschwitz.

I'm sorry to say that some of my friends who managed to go into hiding, their hiding places were given away by young Jewish people who, in order to save their own skin, cooperated with the Gestapo and gave the hiding places away. And that was the end of them. I suppose that in those years too good a character was not a great advantage; I don't condemn them. Everybody tries to save his own skin, but I also cannot respect them, to say the least. Especially because in the end they were also put into a transfer and sent away, so they were just used by the Gestapo.

As far as the staff of the hospital, the head of the hospital made the selections as to who was supposed to be deported and who was not. That was a supposedly reputable older man named Dr. Lustig. He was ordered by the Gestapo to make the selections inside the hospital. But he was a rather willing accomplice of the Gestapo. In fact he was so willing that when the Russians liberated Berlin in 1945, Dr. Lustig was hanged. Anyway, he had the power to select who was supposed to be deported and who was not. So naturally, he protected those whom he liked or were related to him or who slept with him, while the others got the order to go. He got the order, let's say, "We need today two hundred people." So he had to select two hundred people.

Joseph W.

They sent out propaganda, the Germans, that, Wow! Jews are being resettled in a certain area in the Lublin district and [it's a] wonderful life! A couple of weeks before, maybe three weeks before, we had a postcard from my mother's younger sister, my aunt—she had a husband, a child—that they are now traveling on a train, and they are going to the Jewish area where they are resettling Jews. She hopes everything will work out fine, and she hopes that everything is fine with us. It was a postcard stamped with the post office stamp. We thought that was the truth. And other people came, [saying,] "We got postcards! We got postcards!" Later we found out that people were made—and it was her signature!—that people were made to write those cards, and the Germans took those postcards and dropped them in the mail to assuage people's fears that they are only deporting people for work and for resettlement, not to be exterminated. But it didn't take us long to find out. There was a Pole who was the engineer who ran those trains to Chelmno, Belzec, and he confided in somebody. He says, "You know, Jews think they're going to work. They're all being gassed." This came back. "Can't be!" Nobody wanted to believe it. So you want to delude yourself. You don't want to believe that's what awaits you.

Joseph K.

We still couldn't believe what the Germans had in mind: total annihilation of our people. It was still beyond comprehension. As a matter of fact, for the bulk of the sixty-eight months under the German occupation, at no time did I realize or believe that the—this was a total annihilation process going on.

"We got
postcards!"

Joseph W.
Born Przemyśl, Poland, 1922
Recorded 1994, age 72

Joseph W. grew up in Krzywcza and attended gymnasium in Przemyśl. The atmosphere was antisemitic, fueled by Polish laws that restricted the rights of Jews. He and his father participated in Zionist activities.

The area was under Soviet occupation from September 13, 1939, until the German invasion of the Soviet Union in June 1941. Mr. W. recounts formation of the *Judenrat* (Jewish Council), forced labor, and deportations. When a friend escaped from a nearby camp and returned with news of a "camp of killing," Joseph W.'s family decided not to register and instead went into hiding.

Mr. W. was separated from his family during the last roundup in Przemyśl. He escaped and hid with a friend in a bunker in the woods, with the help of a Polish farmer, until they were liberated by Soviet troops. He describes constructing the underground bunker where they lived for months, near-discovery by a German hunting party, and the Polish farmer who brought them food and supplies. Mr. W. served in the Soviet military after liberation. He emigrated to the United States as a yeshiva student and later testified at two war crimes trials.

3

"A Whole Town Cried"

GHETTOS

As an interim step between persecution and extermination, the Germans and their collaborators gathered Jews in designated areas called ghettos: congested slums where food was scarce and disease and death were rampant. Ghetto residents were stripped of possessions and rights, abused, terrorized, and executed at random. The larger ghettos were built along railroad lines in anticipation of transporting Jews to concentration or extermination camps. The largest, in Warsaw, housed more than four hundred thousand people—30 percent of the city's population, compressed into 2.4 percent of the city's area. If the Germans determined that a ghetto's population had grown too large, random executions and deportations ensued.

In most ghettos, a Jewish Council (Judenrat) was appointed and made responsible for administration of ghetto life and for transmitting and implementing German orders. In the summer of 1942, with gas chambers and crematoria in full operation, the Germans began liquidating the ghettos of Eastern Europe. Within two years, more than two million Jews had been transported to concentration or death camps.

Helen K.
Warsaw, Poland

The beginning, they organized the ghetto. They pushed in all the people from the small little towns. They pushed us in about I don't know how many square blocks and they built walls around the Warsaw ghetto. You were trapped! I don't know if anybody can feel this feeling. You know, with all the freedom we have today, nobody can feel this feeling of being trapped.

Jay M.
Born Białystok, Poland, 1925
Germany invades Soviet-occupied territory, June 1941

The first day they got together [a] thousand or more Jewish men and collected them all in the big temple—the biggest temple in Białystok—and burned all of them alive. I was horrified to witness a portion of the burning, of the fire, from a three-story building where we lived. I walked up in the attic, removed some of the tiles, terra cotta tiles, put my head through it and was watching in horror as a whole big section of the city, which surrounded the big temple, the big *schul*, was all in flames.

Renée G.
Łosice, Poland

People were getting sick in the ghetto because of lack of food and lack of sanitation facilities and lack of water. The Germans were very, very clever because when they built the ghetto, they probably purposely avoided a well in the ghetto. The well, the water well, was outside of the ghetto, and in order to get water people had to go out. Well, some people had special passes, or there were special water carriers that would bring in the water. At times when somebody got out to get water and didn't have a pass, the Germans would just shoot them.

Celia K.
Szarkowszczyzna, Poland

They organized a ghetto. It wasn't enough that just our people, our town. They had to bring in all the Jews from the surrounding little towns, and our ghetto became the main ghetto for this region. People were pushed in like sardines. And they kept on bringing more and more and more people every single day, and there was no room anymore to put them in. The windows were boarded up. We were not allowed to look out the window, ever. Everything was boarded up. We were not allowed to go out and get water. Every day there were different decrees. "Jews turn in your bicycles. Jews turn in your valuables. Jews turn in your winter coats. [Jewish] children are not allowed to go to school. Jews, don't walk on sidewalks." Of course, we had to walk on the streets, and the Germans had the pleasure of riding over us with cars, with anything they wanted to hit us.

One day, they said they want twenty-five bookkeepers. So, of course, people who were bookkeepers volunteered. They were all shot on the spot. The second day, they would say they want other professionals. They kept on shooting off the intelligentsia every day. Someone that had a little intelligence, a little education, went first.

Renée G.

To my parents, education was very important, and this was a big tragedy. One of my old teachers that was very sympathetic and he was a friend of the family used to send in books so we children could study at home. And the Germans, not only didn't allow us to go to the public schools, but we weren't allowed to study, even at home. If they caught us, they would throw us into jail, or burn the books, or punish us in one way or another. I remember locking the doors when we studied at home. We studied everything from math to Hebrew, to history—even Polish history. We would lock the doors, and if we heard anybody coming we would throw the books under the bed and hide them. These were daily proclamations. One was Jews had to hand in all furs and coats and good clothes. Jews would just give it away willingly. After all, our lives were spared. The next day, they would collect pots. The next day, they would collect something else—our furniture. One specific moment that I remember [was] when the Germans came out to take our furniture away. My mother got hysterical and started crying. Little did she know how unimportant that was at the time. But my little brother, who was age five at the time, was so mad to see my mother so upset that he grabbed an axe and ran after the Germans and wanted to bang at the furniture and smash it up. And just as I ran after him, I saw the German grabbing his gun. I pulled him away. If I hadn't pulled him away, he probably would have been shot.

Joseph K.
Gorlice, Poland

Then there began a succession of edicts. Some of them were of the nature that every Jew over the age of twelve had to register for work. After that, the edict came out that every Jew had to wear the Star of David on a white band on the outside garment at all times. Failure to do so was punishable by death. Many of our people were executed for failure to wear the Star of David band. Then came about the edict of hostages. Ten Jewish men were named as hostages, and their names were posted on placards all over town. Should anything happen to a German, those ten men would be executed. That was, I think, one of the most difficult edicts to live with.

I recall distinctly the winter of 1941 to '42. That winter, they began to kill Jews at random in the street. In our town there were approximately a half a dozen Gestapo men. But these men had complete control over the entire Jewish population. They knew, because of the hostage system, nothing would happen to them. This perhaps is also one of the reasons why the majority of people in the free world cannot comprehend why six million people could

"It is very difficult to raise a finger against a machine gun."

Joseph K.
Born Gorlice, Poland, 1926
Recorded 1979, age 52

"These people . . . hated us . . . in Poland, there was nothing hidden," Joseph K. said of his childhood, remembering graffiti such as "Jew Go to Palestine" on walls and sidewalks. As a teenager, he witnessed the German invasion of Poland, the destruction of the synagogues, and the implementation of anti-Jewish laws.

Life in the ghetto, he commented, was worse than life in the camps, because in the camps he accepted that he was going to die, while in the ghetto he saw people he loved in agony and was unable to help them. In 1943, Mr. K. was deported to Mielec, where he worked in a Heinkel airplane factory. He was subsequently transferred to Wieliczka, Auschwitz, Flossenbürg, Leitmeritz, Hersbruck, and then back to Flossenbürg. He recalled "walking around naked day and night," being inspected by a German doctor, and then having a number painted on his forehead and back "like cattle." He saw bodies being dropped onto the grate of the crematorium all day long. In a selection, he was one of fifty not chosen out of a group of one thousand. Of those one thousand, he knows of only three who survived.

In 1945 he was sent on a death march. Several thousand set off; only a few hundred survived. Upon liberation, he was handed a gun by a G.I. who offered him the opportunity to shoot German prisoners. He refused, unable to believe that the Germans were actually defeated, or that there was a force more powerful than the Nazis.

OGŁOSZENIE.

Zarząd Miejski wyznacza na jedenasty
14-wy okres t. j. od 8 do 21 czerwca 1940 r.
włącznie na zakładników niżej wymienionych
Obywateli miasta Gorlic:

Bodzioch Kazimierz Józef
Dr. Borysiewicz Roman
Brożyna Bronisław
Burnatowski Michał
Dec Stanisław
Drabyna Mikołaj

Hersz Lazar Mozes
Herzberg Bernard
Johanes Dawid
Kornreich Zabel ← MY FATHER

Zarząd Miejski wzywa mieszkańców miasta Gorlic do
zachowania spokoju i ładu w mieście,
wyznaczeni bowiem zakładnicy odpowiadają wobec Władz
Niemieckich swoją wolnością.

GORLICE, dnia 8 czerwca 1940 r.

BURMISTRZ:
Andrzej Kwiatkowski

"*The City Council designates as hostages . . . from June 8th through June 21st, 1940, the following citizens of the city of Gorlice: [Joseph K.'s father is listed].* The City Council appeals to the residents to maintain peace and order which is insured to German authorities with the hostages' freedom."

allow themselves to be led to the slaughter—[*long silence*]—like sheep, without lifting a finger in their defense. It is very difficult to raise a finger against a machine gun. It was also difficult to live knowing that because of my foolish act ten men have been executed, and there are widows and orphans.

Renée G.

My little brother, the same one that was trying to smash up the furniture, he was a very adventurous little kid and he was running around all over town with some kids that were trying to pick out food out of garbage. He came home one day with a very high fever. He contracted typhus. My mother was sure that we were going to lose him. But one day, somehow miraculously, he got up and he says, "Mommy, I'm well." And he recovered without any medical care or anything. But typhus was a big killer in the ghetto. I remember again, with my big eyes, through the window, watching daily through the window, people being carried out into the cemetery, sometimes hundreds of people a day.

Joseph K.

The life in the ghetto, for me personally, was more difficult to endure than in the concentration camps or the slave labor camps, because in the ghetto I was with my family. And there was the constant fear of something happening to my family. You see people that you grew up with—neighbors, relatives—and you see them in a state of agony, screaming, crying, and you're helpless. You just stand and observe it. Of course, you sort of rationalize, most likely that they are taken away to the east for resettlement, as some of the rumors at the time persisted.

Renée H.
Bratislava, Slovakia

We did not have a ghetto, and yet there was a ghetto atmosphere. I do remember slowly the sense that even though there were no gates in the ghetto, there were no wires, that we were not welcome beyond certain streets. And I had always been a child that used to roam around—to my parents' despair—so I got to know the city terribly well. And what I would do, in order to be able to continue that sense of freedom that I had, would be constantly to try to wear a scarf to cover up the Jewish star. And I would pretend that, if anybody addressed me in some way, I wouldn't understand what they were saying. But I did feel that every exit into the town, outside of my immediate home, was into a very hostile and dangerous environment—that I always could be found out. And I would have fantasies about what would happen to me if they found me out. And it was always accompanied by my immediately running home, to touch base.

The Jewish Council (*Judenrat*) of Gorlice, Poland (1941), where Joseph K. lived until his deportation. "Life in the ghetto, for me personally, was more difficult to endure than in the concentration camps."

Rabbi Baruch G.
Mława, Poland

Every Jew must register. Every Jew must have a number. A Jew must have a white round sign that [says] is he a Jew, on front and on back. Later on, it was changed to yellow. A Jew must take off his hat if he sees a German. A German has the right to call on any Jew, any time, for work. Any kind of work he wants. My parents particularly were very much concerned about me, being the oldest, being at the age where I can be caught to work at any times. So they would send me off to the fields. I would take some books along and study for all day. Nights I would spend in the cellar. We organized a study group among students of my age group.

Rabbi Baruch G.
Born Mława, Poland, 1923
Recorded 1984, age 61

Rabbi Baruch G. is the sole survivor of an extended family that enjoyed a rich traditional life despite the antisemitism he remembers in prewar Poland. The Jews of Mława were ghettoized following the German invasion in 1939. When compelled to perform forced labor, Rabbi G. was beaten for the petty offense of not knowing how to properly stack bricks. He recalls that the humiliation was far more painful than the beating itself. After he and his family were transferred to the town of Lubartów, Rabbi G. managed to smuggle himself, his mother, and his brother back to Mława—only to be deported to Auschwitz/Birkenau when the Nazis liquidated the Mława ghetto in the summer of 1943. There, Rabbi G. was trained as a bricklayer.

Coming from a religious environment, he questions whether belief was a factor in having survived the camps of Auschwitz/Birkenau, Buchenwald, Ohrdruf, and Crawinkel. "Many who had more faith than I did, I'm sure, did not survive. . . . There is no rhyme or reason, no explanation why one survived and the other did not." Toward the close of the war, Rabbi G. was subjected to death marches and transports. After liberation, he awoke to find himself in a Russian hospital in Theresienstadt. Rabbi G. feels he suffered psychologically more after liberation than in the camps: the daily struggle for survival preoccupied him, while afterward awareness of his losses led to overwhelming loneliness and isolation. A practicing rabbi, Baruch G. regrets not having shared his experiences with his son while he was growing up, immersing himself in his work, and avoiding confronting his past until shortly before his testimony was recorded.

We met daily, we studied—secretly, of course. One time I remember on a Saturday a Polish policeman came in and he obviously knew that in the secret cellar of a mill we had a service going on. That was the first time, I remember how terrible I felt. This is the Sabbath day, and it's the first time I had to work on the Sabbath. And since, of course, they gave us some food, but since it wasn't kosher I wouldn't eat. Of course I got smarter later, unfortunately. But to me it was a trauma of the worst kind, being a sheltered young man.

Thinking back on what happened afterwards, things were not so bad. Okay, so I was beaten up. So what? Talking about beating up, I'll never forget the first time I was beaten up. And that really got to me, not so much the pain from the beating but the mental anguish. Instead of telling me how to put bricks together—they had to be placed in a certain way in order for them to be stacked up and—he simply went over and beat me for it, without knowing why. And I couldn't even cry. When I went home, this is when I burst out crying. I mean—animal! And I was conscientious. I had to go to work. I knew one thing, I had to do the best I can, it's forced labor. But why [the beatings]? What right? It was incomprehensible to me. I mean, these things are forgotten, you know, because there are so many other things that we are to deal with, so many things of horrifying results that are outstanding in our minds. So those little things are forgotten. But if you come to analyze them, they were terribly painful for me.

Jay M.
Białystok, Poland

Everybody would have to gather in one designated part of the city, and that portion would be called a ghetto. They allotted three square meters per person. And usually a house that two or three people lived [in] before, as many as ten or fifteen had to move in. In the ghetto, conditions were rough because of the crowded quarters, lack of food, irritation. Especially those that owned their homes and/or apartments, and here new people moved in on their privacy. And jobs were not available. The food rationing every other day, a very small slice of bread per person and perhaps some potatoes. People tried to smuggle in food into the ghetto for valuables that they still had.

Joseph W.
Przemyśl, Poland

During the night, they fanned out. I think they had a list this time. I don't know how they obtained that list. German police, auxiliary Polish police, Ukrainian police, and they grabbed one thousand men—men only, maybe from the ages of fifteen, sixteen up—and they loaded them on trucks and they took them away. We didn't know where, but then we found out the next day. They were taken to a camp outside Lwów called Janowska.

Entrance to the Janowska concentration camp. Joseph W. describes, "[A schoolmate who escaped from Janowska] came back [and told us it was] 'a camp of killing, a killing ground.'" *Courtesy U.S. Holocaust Memorial Museum*

We didn't know yet what it meant. What does Janowska [mean]? Is it a labor camp? Within two, three days, four days, escapees started trickling back to Przemyśl. One of my friends, his name is Rechev, a schoolmate, came back. In four days he was like a cadaver. He had lost all his weight 'cause he ate nothing. They gave him no food, no drink, and they made him work and endure beatings. And he saw that he isn't going to survive. So somehow he managed to hide in a pile of railroad ties, and at night he hopped on a train that was going west. And he came back to Przemyśl. He told us what happened. He says most of the people taken, nobody's going to live. Unless you escaped, Janowska is a camp of extermination. He didn't use that word. He said, "camp of killing, a killing ground." And he said also that a lot of people from the Lwów Jewish population were being killed right there. So, first found out there was such a thing as a killing machine in camps. This was the first realization that that is the destination, that this is the intent of the Germans. It was just horrendous.

Renée H.
Bratislava, Slovakia

The worst part for me was watching the transports. The transport would just suddenly appear. The transports used to terrify me, because the speed of them was so horrendous. Where they were trying to force, they would yell at the people and say, "Get out! Get out! Quickly! Get out! Gather together. You can't take this suitcase. No, you mustn't take this blanket." In the process also there would be a lot of hitting, especially of old people, and of sick people, and children. And shoving and pushing. And those gatherings of people just terrified me. It was a way of behaving which I could never experience, not even in nightmares. What was terrible was that it was the behavior toward the very people that the Jewish religion says you must have a great deal of kindness, which are the sick, the old, and the children. And I saw everything being

56

done which was opposed to what I believed in and what I had grown up in.

I remember that we would hear certain sounds of boots on the street. And usually whenever there was a transport, it was accompanied by ten or twelve soldiers coming marching together from house to house and gathering all the people, knocking on the doors and saying, "You have an hour." People had only an hour in which they could gather families together. And we used to live in terror of these boots. My parents were both deaf, and I had a deaf sister. So I became the ears. I would have to warn them that the transport was coming. What I would do, we would all rush into the back room and when they knocked on the door, we didn't answer. We were in the back room, just trying to be as quiet as possible. And what happened was that, as a result of this, the responsibility was on me to always hear what was going on. Every time I would hear ten boots marching around the corner, I'd run immediately home and tell everybody to go into the apartment. We used to pray that nobody would be coming up the stairs.

Renée G.
Łosice, Poland

One of my cousins, who lived upstairs in the house, built a hiding place in the house. He essentially built a wall in the room and covered it with wallpaper and made a little opening on the bottom of the wall, and put a cot against the opening, so that in order to get into the hiding place you had to crawl under the cot. It was very hard to tell that it was a different room because of the wallpaper. By that time, things started coming through from other towns—all kinds of stories that Jews were being killed, that Jews were being taken away in trucks and shot. But nobody really wanted to believe it. Except that this cousin that built this hiding place heard it from another cousin who ran away—who escaped from such a massacre, and he believed it. So by this time, he

House in Łosice, Poland, where Renée G. grew up. From the porthole in the front of the house, she witnessed the killing and deportation of townspeople, relatives, and friends in August 1942. "And a whole town cried."

declared that if anything happens, there is no point in going with the crowd. The best thing to try to do is to hide and at least we'd have a fighting chance for life, not just walk to your death.

That day came in August 1942. I remember waking up on a Saturday morning. I heard shots. Again I quickly ran to my window. That was my observation point. I looked around and I saw dead people, all around on the square. Nobody moved and I couldn't understand that. About an hour later, I heard German voices: "'*Raus!* '*Raus!* '*Raus!*'" That was one word that I learned very quickly. That meant "Out! Out! Out!" It was like dogs barking. And there were German voices telling everybody, "All Jews out! All Jews out on the square!" We heard people beginning to cry and chaos. Everybody was running up and down in my building. My cousin finally started yelling to my family. My cousin finally shut the door and said, "All right, now you're in. Nobody out." He closed the door, and he said, "Nobody's moving out of here. If you're going to die, you're going to die right here." I started crying, but then he made me shut up. The only opening for air was a porthole under the roof. And I looked out and I saw lots of Jews with little packages walking towards the square. And I also saw my grandfather and my grandma coming over, and they were looking up and deciding whether to come up, to come and hide with us or to go away. And finally I saw them walk again, walk away, and I never saw them again. I heard people yelling and screaming and crying and shooting. And a whole town cried.

Jacob K.
Zwoleń, Poland

One night we heard footstep[s]. So I quickly run into my room. And we were sleeping, the whole family, five of us, were sleeping in one bed. And I undressed myself quickly and jumped into the bed, make believe that I'm sleeping already. Finally, we all got frightened. We heard noise outside the house. They were yelling, the Germans. And they came to the door and they burst into the room. They kicked the door open, with bayonets, fixed bayonets, steel helmets strapped around their heads. All paraphernalia they wore, bullets and everything. And they started to yell we should undress. So we all undressed, mother, and women and men. And then one of them said that my father didn't undress quick enough. And he started to beat him on the face with a bayonet, poking, like this [gestures] and blood started to come out. My father became very frightened, became pale. We were all standing up, my mother naked, all of us, three brothers, my father, the other ladies, naked. It was a terrible sight for a young man to see. They took out matches, and I thought they're going to strike the matches. No. They took out and they struck our genitals—the women's and the men's. They were only a few minutes in the room, maybe ten minutes. It was so frightening.

Renée G.
Age 10

The houses in our town didn't have modern plumbing. There was an outhouse outside, but you had to go outside. There was no running water. There were twenty-seven of us in the August heat, in a small place, under the roof and it must have been about ninety degrees there. No water. No food. We all knew that it was no way we could survive for very long in that hiding place. So this one family tried to try their luck. So they walked downstairs and tried to get out. All of a sudden, we heard, "Halt!" And the Germans stopped them. We heard some scuffles and yelling and screaming. One of the sons started arguing with the soldier and said, "You can't do that to us! You're not going to get away with it!" And he says something to him like, "You're a dog!" or "You're a pig!" And we heard a shot, and he was killed on the spot. The rest of them were taken away. We also heard the mother pleading to be able to take the body with them. And we heard them all going away, and no more noise.

On the second day, people in the hiding place were getting desperate and were thirsty and were becoming wild because of no food and all and heat. Some of them started drinking urine and were getting sick and throwing up.

On the third day, when things were really bad, my parents decided that my brother and I, the older brother and I, had to try our luck. They talked to us very quietly. [My mother] said, "You've got to try and see if you can survive." They literally pushed us out, and my mother gave me instructions, told me where to go, to this village. She tried to convince me that she and dad had friends there and gave me specific names who to go to. They told us two things. They told us number one, to try and get shelter and two, to see if we can find people to come and help them to get them out from the hiding place and give them shelter. I started crying, but my mother literally pushed me out through the door and she said, "Go!" And my older brother, too. So I held his hand and we walked out, and was a bright, sunny day. We walked down on the street. It was like a ghost town. There was nobody there, except for the very end of the town there was a guard. And somehow he either disregarded us or thought we were Polish. When we were young, we were both very blond and probably taken as little Polish kids and were not touched.

We passed through the guard all right and went to the small village. I knew those people. I knocked on the door and they recognized us. The woman said, "No! You can't come in here. No! We don't want you here. Get away! Get away!" I pleaded with her. I said, "All right. Never mind," I said, "We'll lie down in the field and we'll just sleep over there until mommy and daddy come." She came running after us and chased us away. We tried in another place, [but] the people sent the dogs after us. So we had to start walking again. I started crying, and I told my brother I wanted to go back to the hiding place. My brother didn't think it was a good idea, but he finally relented.

It was already late at night, and we walked very close to one building to another and so nobody would see us. We heard voices, [a] little Polish kid running after us and yelling, "*Żyd! Żydowka! Żyd! Żydowka!*" which meant "Little Jewish boy! Little Jewish girl!" And then we heard, "Stop or I'll shoot!" in Polish. "Hands up!" And I remember, you know, putting my hands up, and my brother putting—that was an automatic reflex. We stood next to the wall, you know like this [*puts her hands up over her head*] and he came over and he started asking us, "Where are you from? Where are your parents?" And we said they went away, they went with everybody else. So he took us to the police post. I remember him calling the German office, asking them what to do with us, whether to shoot us on the spot or to throw us in jail. Then he said, "Let's go." At gunpoint he started marching us.

On the way, I talked to my brother. "Perhaps one of us could live by starting to run." I said. I told him, "You run right, and I'll run left and one of us, maybe, will have a chance to survive." He

"Stop or
I'll shoot!"

Renée G.
Born Łosice, Poland, 1932
Recorded 1980, age 48

The Germans occupied Renée G.'s town in 1939, and then created a ghetto. Renée G., her brothers, parents, relatives, and neighbors hid in a crawl space inside an attic during a roundup. Sent out by their parents to get help, eight-year-old Renée G. and her brother were arrested. They narrowly escaped execution before being transferred to the "small ghetto." A non-Jewish family friend helped them escape. Her father arranged for her to live in hiding with a Polish policeman. She later joined her parents, older brother, and other relatives, who were hidden by a Polish farmer in a five-foot by eight-foot pit under a manure pile.

In the pit, Mrs. G.'s cousin Oscar taught her languages and math. When asked what she would like for her birthday, she chose scrambled eggs, which her father obtained in trade for her gold earrings. Soviet troops arrived and, after living in the pit for eighteen months, Renée G. and her family were liberated.

She returned to school, but teachers and students alike called her a Christ killer and made her studies impossible. With her family, she eventually emigrated to the United States. Many years later she returned to Poland, and to the hiding place in the barn. She was reunited with the widow of the farmer who had hidden them. Then, visiting Treblinka, she found the tombstone of her town. "I had my last cry, and we left."

thought about it. He said, "No. It won't do any good. He'll probably shoot both of us." Before we knew it, we were in a jail cell on the third floor in the town jail. We just sat there and we just knew that at night somebody would take us out and shoot us. The only thing we were afraid of was getting a whipping, or the Germans trying to use torture to try and find out where our parents were. And we made up that no matter what, we would not squeal or tell. My brother also decided that he wanted, if there are any survivors left, [for them] to know what happened to us. So he cut his finger and got out some blood and wrote on the wall that he and I were in jail on such and such a date. He must have been about thirteen at the time.

That same night, we finally heard them coming. We heard the dogs barking and we heard them yelling and screaming, "Jews!" and "Jews!" and "Dirty Jews! *Schwein! Schwein!*" We were standing ready at the door. We waited there, and I held my brother's hand. We heard them come up—and then we heard voices on the second floor! Two Polish children yelling, "We are not Jews! We are not Jews! They're upstairs! They're upstairs!" A lot of children, a lot of Poles were jailed because they were looting the leftover goods from the Jewish homes. The Germans were probably drunk, and we heard the dogs barking and a lot of noise and they maybe didn't understand Polish. And they took those children out instead of us. About fifteen minutes later, we heard two shots. And that was it.

On this third day, I think there were nine or ten of us in the cell. They [other prisoners] mentioned something that created sort of a flicker of hope, of possible life. They said that they heard that the Germans no longer killed all the leftovers in the town. They were now gathering them to help clean out the town, to help put the leftover Jews to work. We didn't quite believe it until that morning, the doors opened and again. Polish policemen came and at gunpoint told us start walking. So [we] all lined up and my brother and I, being the youngest, were the first ones in a row. We walked through the town and the whole town stared and

watched, and I remember my teacher looking at me. As we passed
the street going to the cemetery, I was sure that they were going
to shoot us, so I made a left turn to go onto the cemetery. The
policeman started yelling, "No! No! Straight! Straight!" And I
looked at my brother, and I think that must have been the first
time I started to grin. Maybe the story is true. Maybe we're not
going to be shot. Then he [the policeman] said, "Walk into that
block on the right." When we got in there, there were more Jews.
It was a small ghetto left over, and there must have been about a
hundred people. They told me that my parents did get out from
the hiding place, and that was a great joy. They didn't know
where they were, but they knew that they did get out.

We were taken to work, my brother and I. I was so proud that
I was finally taken to work because I was one of the youngest. I
tried to do a very good job. I came back that day to the small
ghetto and talked to my brother and tried to plan some sort of
strategy how to find out where our parents were so we could join
them. The next morning came and he was taken away to work.
They didn't pick me that day, so I was standing around. A guy on
a bicycle came by and said, "Come on. I'm taking you to your
father." Well, I didn't quite know what he was talking about.
"Your father is alive. He wants to take you to his hiding place." I
said, "No, I won't go without my brother." He said, "But I'll come
for your brother the following day." Now that's the only way I
agreed to go with him. So I left a note for my brother that we're
going to come here for him the next day and I hopped on the
bike. This messenger took me, sure enough, to my father, who was
hiding out in a village in a stable. When he saw me, he just, you
know, started crying.

Rumors had it that in some other town there was still a func-
tioning ghetto and Jews. We went there. One evening in that
ghetto the word came that all Jews are going to be gathered.
There was again a proclamation: all Jews are going to be deported
again. Sometimes these proclamations said that you were being

deported to another town, sometimes to a beautiful "colony." At this point already we knew what those "colonies" meant. Some of the family from that town had a very good friend, a Polish farmer who risked his life and decided to take us out, back to the small ghetto where my brother was. [That farmer] was shot after the war by Polish underground because he was helping the Jews. He was a wonderful guy. All the way through, he helped us, for no money at all. [He took us] back to Łosice at night.

I remember walking and walking and walking. Finally, I remember my little brother just lay down on the ground. He said, "Mommy, I can't walk," he said. I remember he said, "You go. You save yourselves. You go, but leave me here." He—the Pole, this Polish farmer—picked him up on his back and carried him all the way so we would make it before dawn. We arrived to this small town, to the ghetto. By this time, rumors have come through about what was really happening to all the deportations. There was one who somehow miraculously escaped from Treblinka and told us exactly what the score was, that there [were] gas chambers there, that people were being burned and gassed.

Joseph W.

One day we're looking out the window, and a truck pulled up in the center of Przemyśl and soldiers fanned out through town, and they started taking young men. They knocked on the door and they motioned me to come. "*Komm!*" So my mother ran to them and says, "He's a child!" So he looked at me and he said [*gestures to go away*], "Okay, don't come." [Then he looked at] my father so [*gestures to come*]: "Come!" He told my father to come. My father went to him, and I see they are taking him to that truck. And my father had a picture of himself—a soldier. He was in the Austrian army. And he showed it to the officer that was standing by that truck. My mother was begging like this [*clasping his hands*] and my father was standing. He [the officer] turned around, he looked here, there, then gave my father a kick and he says, "*Verschwinde!* Disappear!" Somehow, maybe he was Austrian. So my father came running back in with my mother.

But then I see they're loading, they took ten men, just ten. [They] drove off. Nobody knew where they went. This was like one o'clock in the afternoon. By seven o'clock in the evening, a couple of peasants [from] two miles out of town came back and they said, "You know, we were taken to put earth on the grave where they shot these ten men." And they described the scene: "They made these men undress. They made them dig their own grave. Then, as they were standing in the open pit, they shot every one of them. Then they came to our houses in the village. They took a few of us and said, 'If you cover this up, we'll give you their clothing.' So they gave us their clothing."

Arnold C.

In 1943, we were selected to be taken out of the [Kovno] ghetto and to be sent to a working camp. That was the first selection where they took the children away. [It] was called the *kinder aktsye*. My father was selected to be the camp engineer, even though he wasn't an engineer by profession. He was able to arrange certain things in the camp, construction and so on. And one morning the German soldiers and Ukrainian helpers drove into the camp. My father immediately realized that something is going to happen here. He took me and six more children and hid us in the loft of one of the barracks. It was a very shallow area. We could just barely squeeze in. And what happened is that they proceeded to take away all the children from that camp. Now, all the adults were away working. When they came from work, none of the children were there. The crying and the yelling was unbelievable. There were six grateful parents. They kissed my father's hands for saving their children. After that, it was decided that I should go to work. It wasn't safe to stay in camp. So they got me a big pair of shoes, a long coat, and every morning when the groups went out to work they made sure I was always in the middle, flanked by adults, so the Germans would not notice there is a child standing there. I was about nine.

Jay M.
Białystok, Poland

The Germans at one time decided that the population was greater than what they planned to have it, and they had an *Aktion*, an action. What it simply meant, that they would come in and shoot and kill. And to the best estimates, there were about ten thousand people [deported to Treblinka]. Those that couldn't walk out were killed in their beds—I witnessed. After this ended, the job of collecting the dead began. The cemetery was created in a lot that was contained inside of the ghetto. It was winter, and the bodies collected from the streets were frozen in positions that they fell, many of them with their hands in front of the face, as if that would yield some protection from a bullet. But it didn't.

Joseph K.

I saw with my own eyes Germans tossing babies in the air and shooting them. I couldn't believe it, but I saw it. It did happen! And they were laughing as they were doing this. The Germans were the most enlightened and educated people in all of Europe at that time. Those were university-educated people, and yet they were killing infants. Unbelievable!

Bessie K.
Born Vilna, Poland, 1924. Age 19, deported from Kovno to concentration camp in Estonia

We always were ready. When they gave orders, all our possessions came with us—the coats, the shoes, and if you had dresses. And I took the baby with me. Nearby were trains, the cattle trains. And as I look back, I think that for a while I was in a daze. I didn't know what was happening, actually. I saw they taking away the men separate, the children separate, and the women separate. So I had the baby, and I took the coats and I wrapped around the baby and I put it on my left side, because I saw the Germans were saying, left and right. And I went through with the baby. But the baby was short of breath, started to choke, and it started to cry. So the German called me back. He says, "What do you have there?" in German. Now, I didn't know what to do because everything was so fast, everything happened so suddenly. I wasn't prepared for it. To look back, the experience was—I think I was numb or something happened to me. I don't know. But I wasn't— I wasn't there, even. He stretched his arms, I should hand him over the bundle. And I hand him over the bundle. And this was the last time I had the bundle.

Rabbi Baruch G.
Age 17, deported from Mława ghetto to Lubartów, 1940

It became more restrictive. The ghetto became more scarce in food, and so forth, till finally we heard rumors again about the liquidations of the ghetto. Some knowledge of concentration camps came in, but the word was very strange to us. We didn't know what it was. We interpreted a concentration camp meaning labor camp where people go to work. The ghetto received an order, the *Judenrat* received, [that] this ghetto must be liquidated and the people evacuated. And unless this is done in an orderly fashion followed by a certain order, everybody is going to be shot to death.

The leadership of the Jewish community did establish occasionally some good rapport with some of the leaders of the Gestapo in the hometown. That, too, was a ploy. It was a way of setting the community at ease. One [Jew] was extremely successful, I remember. And then all of a sudden one morning he was called to the Gestapo and he was shot there in the offices there.

By that time rumors went back and forth that they're going to evacuate all Jews from Mław. Then reassurance would come from the German authorities to the leaders of the *Judenrat*, "No, that's not going to happen." [These were] agonizing months. We would sleep dressed. Each one of us had a package prepared of whatever one could carry, so that if it does happen—The following morning, Friday, my mother used to get up very early on Fridays to prepare for the Sabbath. She would go to the bakery. She came back and she woke everybody up, [saying] "That's it." There were Germans all over town. It was impossible to go out without being stopped. We lived a little bit outside the town, and we were standing all depressed. There were eight of us, each one ready to go. We were hoping maybe they wouldn't see us. Then we saw a Polish kid was telling the Germans, "Here are Jews." So they came up with dogs and whips and whipped us out. My father was holding on to his mother. She couldn't run as fast as the rest of us. It was snowing. Here he was, holding on to his mother, and dogs attacked him, and with a German whipping him, and his mother on the floor, on the ground.

We were taken to a place like a high school sports place. There were thousands of us there. We looked for each other. We found my father there, crying, missing his mother, and the rest of us were waiting. After some time, they wheeled my grandmother to the group in a wagon. That group consisted [of] about seven thousand Jews, all the Jews from the town. Obviously they decided to create a ghetto there, and they decided the ghetto should be only about three thousand and the rest of us must be evacuated. So my family together was evacuated. We were put on trains. My group came to a town by the name of Lubartów, near Lublin. It was after two days travel. They assigned us to different homes. The following day we got together, and my grandmother had died at night, sitting on my mother's lap. You know, there was no room there, so they sat together and hugged each other. And she just expired.

Chaim E.
Age 26, deported to Sobibór death camp

At night, the Germans broke in and drove all the Jews out into the street. We were still hiding in an attic there somewhere. But the same story—you can hide one day, two days, but eventually you have to come out. And we came out from there, and there were already full with Germans all over. They were just waiting. They didn't even try to draw you out, because they know you will come out anyway. So then they took us in wagon, horses. Eventually they bring us to some train, a train with the cattle. They packed us full, standing full, to full capacity. They filled up this train and they drove us the whole night till we arrived in Sobibór.

Joseph W.
Przemyśl, Poland

They took everybody from the *Judenrat* during this first or the second action in July. They took Dr. Duldig [head of the *Judenrat*], his wife and children out there while people was waiting to be put on the trains. One of the Gestapo, by name Reisner, shot them right there in front. That was just to show that no matter how big you are, as a Jew there is no future.

Jacob K.
Zwoleń, Poland

Some of them refused to go, so the Germans killed them right there. So we piled up the dead people, and while we were digging at the cemetery, a mass grave, somebody brought a little girl to the grave. A Jewish girl. She was maybe four years old, a blond little girl. The parents gave her away to Polish people to hide, and the Germans gave an order: anybody who is [hiding a Jew] is going to be killed. So they brought a little girl. And the *gendarme* was standing there on top of a little hill, watching us work. We knew him because we used to work, and mainly the work was done to take care of the German police department—cleaning and washing and whatever, everything that they need. They brought the little girl. She was four years old, curly hair. So he went over to her, and he gave her an apple and he asked her, "What's this?" in Polish. So she named it, *jabłko*, which is in Polish "apple." He asked her name and he repeated it in broken Polish. He went back to his post and he started to lecture us about the Jewish mother. He says, "*Dies ist keine Mutter*—This is not a mother who leaves her child." And he said, "I assure you that she is not going to go far, that mother who run away and left this child. We're going to get her." And while the girl was eating the apple, he shoot her. He aimed at her. And the bullet went through her hair. And it screamed, the child screamed. Then he shoot her again and killed her. And the child fell dead to the ground, and the apple rolled away. And we buried her with the rest of the others.

Celia K.
Age 18, Szarkowszczyzna, Poland

My mother volunteered in the ghetto to bake bread, since our oven was equipped to handle this large amount of baking. We had had a restaurant. She really added more water and more water every single day. She diluted it [so much] that the bread finally wasn't a dough. It was like milk, it wasn't enough. They were dying like flies. She said to us, "Look, kids, we took care of you up until now. From now on, you are on your own. Run. Scatter. Look for a hiding place."

I worked in the *Kommandantur* [German command post]. I was picked from a lot of girls to be their waitress, to serve them meals three times a day. This helped me a lot because I could see and hear what was going on, and this is how we found out that the action will take place in the ghetto. We knew the date and the time. And this is one reason that our ghetto had the largest amount of survivors at that time. We knew the Lithuanians are coming in, in truckloads, every single day, more and more, and we knew it spelled trouble. The only way they come is for extermination of the ghetto. We saw them come in at night. We were on guard in our house, in the attic. We had guards watching the *Kommandantur*, which was across from the ghetto. We saw them jumping off the trucks.

Jay M.
Białystok, Poland

[On] August 16, 1943, it was announced that the whole population of the ghetto is going to be moved. Of course, everybody knew what it meant: it's going to be the end. Shooting started, and all the Germans that were then in the ghetto opened fire on everybody. The house was littered with bullets. It was a four-unit structure. We ran from one house to the next, and wherever we came in we were met by a hail of gunfire. Briefly looking out through one of the windows, in the backyard I saw a great number of people there [that ran] in and hiding in the bushes and trees. One German walked in with a submachine gun and just sprayed bullets, and everybody was falling like little wooden soldiers. We heard the steps of a German soldier walking in. In the split second, I told my sister to get under a bed and my mother into a closet, and I hid under the same bed. And again, a minute later, he walked in, with his boots perhaps inches away from my nose where I was under the bed. Fortunately, he did not see us, and we survived.

This [hiding place] was then to be our home for the next two-and-a-half months, from August the seventeen through November third, 1943. There was no food to be obtained except for some leftovers: dried-out bread, wilted. Maybe some grain. And whatever we found, we ate. Pretty soon they shut off the water in the whole area. We would then go to the toilets and empty out the toilet tanks until there was no more water in the tanks. One evening we found a bathtub full of water. Apparently someone had taken a bath when the deportation of the ghetto started. There was a thick film of soap and dirt and grime and perhaps algae from a couple of months. But it didn't bother us. We used all of that.

Arnold C.
Age 11, after nearly a year in labor camp with his family

[In] 1944, the Germans decided to move us again. They took us all out, marched us to trains, and we were shipped off to the interior of Germany. We arrived in Stutthof. They took us all out of the trains and separated the men from the women. They sent the women to Stutthof concentration camp. My mother and sister were taken there and I remained with my father. We continued on in the train to the interior of Germany and we came to Landsberg concentration camp, which was a satellite camp of Dachau. From the gate of the camp to the area of the huts, we had to walk the gauntlet. There were SS men standing on both sides and as we walked through. Each one of us was clobbered with sticks. And we ran as we tried to get away from the beating.

In Landsberg, I was with my father for about a week. Then they decided to take away the children, the youngsters, from Landsberg. They had the morning count, and they picked up all the little ones, the small ones. It was a hundred and thirty-one [of us]. They put us in a separate tent and we were told that we were being taken to a children's camp. My father knew this is another children's selection, but he was helpless. There was nothing he could do. His last words to me were, "Whoever survives, contact family in Evanston, Illinois." He gave me the address: 1819 Wesley Avenue in Evanston. I remember it. He said this is where our *mishpokhe* [family] went before the war. This is how we're going to meet—whoever survives. This was his last few words to me as they took me away. I saw him standing there, waving.

Renée H.
Age 9, Bratislava, Slovakia

By 1943, my parents realized it was just hopeless, that there was no point in trying to live in this fearful way. So they decided to send my sister and me to a farm family out in the country, for which they paid great sums. I had to hide the fact that I was Jewish, and I remember my mother taking all the stars off my clothes and sending me off. I was taken by a person, who was also deaf, to his mother's house in the countryside somewhere near the Tatra Mountains. I was introduced as a very distant relationship whose parents were in the hospital and sick, and I had to be taken care of for a certain amount of time until I got the message to come back. I was told never to tell anyone I was Jewish. I was told that, even though I didn't have to go to church, that I had to pretend that everything Christian was very familiar to me and very desired by me. So that, for example, if the priest went by I had to cross myself. It used to be terrible to do that for me, because I felt that I was going in some way have to pay for this. But I nevertheless knew that I had my sister as well to take care of, who was a year and a half younger than myself.

I never saw my parents again afterwards. I did hear from them occasionally, either through letters or through messages or to codes. For example, "We are all together, still," meaning my mother and my father, would be said, "We are visiting relatives in Vienna." And I knew that they were still all right.

But then, in the spring of 1944, the son came back to the farm and announced to me that my parents had failed to pay for the last five months of my stay there, and consequently somebody else was going to take care of us in Bratislava itself. He bundled us up and we went back to Bratislava with him. I had a great sense of relief because I really could not adjust to the wild ways of the children in the village where we lived. They never went to school, and they always wanted to take my shoes away, and they used to poke fun at my sister, who was deaf. I would be very protective of her, because I was really told to take care of her.

When we went back to Bratislava, there were various people we knew who had papers, forged papers, and they told us that it would be impossible for us to have the forged papers. When we said, "Well, where are our parents?" they said that they didn't know, that they were still in hiding. They never told us that they had already been taken by the last transport out of Bratislava. I remember one evening, hiding on the third floor of a building, which was really the place where a tailor kept his workshop. We had to stay out of the place all day long because he had workmen there, and he explained to us that many of the workmen were very antisemitic and if they knew we were there, spending the night in the dark, they would betray us without a doubt. So I remember spending three weeks on the streets, going into shops, going into the church, going all over the place.

I remember one episode, which was very harrowing. Somebody who knew my parents recognized me. It was rather easy to recognize me at that time because I had very blond, very tightly curled hair—sort of like an Afro in blond—and he immediately says, "Come here. I am going to take care of you." And I knew immediately that I just could not trust him. In fact, I had lost trust in everybody. I was very suspicious and very careful to watch and listen for any false or difficult notes. I said, "No," I wasn't going to come, and I started to run and he chased me. And it was very good thing that my knowledge of Bratislava came to my aid, because I was able to weave my way around streets and corners and little openings in buildings. Finally, I managed to lose him.

After three weeks of living on the streets, being terrified of the thought of meeting the man who had chased me again—being terrified of meeting anyone who knew me as a Jew—I had been away from the town for about nine months, so I had hoped that somehow in growing I had somehow become less noticeable—but after three weeks of living like that, [the tailor] said the people have gotten suspicious because they had found bread crumbs. So he finally told me he couldn't keep me. I had to find some other accommodation. And I took my suitcase and my sister, looking for a place to stay. I would go to places where I knew people who were Christians. I knocked on the door, and they slammed the door right in my face. Not saying a word, not explaining, just as if I were just a beggar at the door, they closed the door in my face.

Finally, I went to the home of these friends of my parents who were living on a forged passport—and they did the same thing. And I felt that I was the last Jew left.

There was nothing for me to do. For two days we were scrounging—we had no money—we were scrounging around trying to find food. Finally, I said to my sister, we can't live that way. We will die on the street. So we might as well go to the police. And I went to the police and I said my name, and I said my parents' name, and I said I'd like to join them. And the police were amused. They first laughed, and then they realized that I was perfectly serious. Suddenly I realized that I had presented them with a problem. They didn't know what to do with me. So they told me I could sit on the bench, and I spent the night in the police station on the bench while they were trying to find out what to do with me. They didn't explain anything to me. One of the policemen said, I remember, "Well, we're trying to find where your parents are." And they finally must have found out somehow, because we were immediately put on a truck and driven into Hungary, and that was in Sered´, which was a gathering point for the last remaining transports coming out of Bratislava, because nothing was going directly from Bratislava. I arrived there to discover that two weeks before my parents had been put on the train to Auschwitz. This was the first time I heard about Auschwitz. I didn't know anything about it.

There was this very nice woman who immediately took me under her care. For two weeks I was in Sered´, and she gathered food for me. She gave me two blankets, and she said, "Do not let anybody know you have that." And I was put on one train. It was a cattle car and I, in some ways, was terribly relieved to be there because here I was among Jews again. They were all strangers, but still the fact that they were Jews was very important to me. At that time I was nine years old, and I had my sister who was seven and a half, and to whom I had to explain everything because she only knew sign language. She didn't know how to communicate yet with the hearing people and so I was really constantly having to

"And I felt
that I was the
last Jew left."

Renée H.
Born Bratislava, Czechoslovakia, 1933
Recorded 1979, age 45

Renée H.'s parents and younger sister were deaf, so growing up in Bratislava she was the "ears" for them, gathering information and alerting them to roundups of Jews signaled by the sound of boots coming up the stairs. Realizing their danger, her parents paid a farm family to hide the two girls in the country-side. After many months, claiming her parents had failed to pay, the farmer's son returned the children to Bratislava. Going door to door, sister in hand, Mrs. H. attempted to find a place to stay. When all doors slammed in their faces, she walked into the police station, stated her name, and asked to join her parents, who, unbeknownst to her, had been deported to Auschwitz/Birkenau.

From a transit camp in Sered', she and her sister were placed on a deporta-tion train to Auschwitz/Birkenau. When the tracks were bombed, the train was diverted to Bergen-Belsen. As a child, she was surrounded by corpses, by peo-ple "going mad." She remained there one year, and at liberation weighed only "as much as a three-year-old." After recuperating in Sweden, she and her sister emigrated to "the bounty" of Brooklyn, where she lived with her relatives. Renée H. found the Orthodox Jews she encountered reluctant to hear her stories of what had happened. "It was a way in which they were telling me they could not bear to listen."

In her testimony, Renée H. describes feeling as if she is two people: one who lives today, the other who lived through the horror.

hold her by her hand because I couldn't call her. I couldn't ever lose sight of her, because in the milling of the people we could have been separated. We finally were put on the train and I was told I would be going Auschwitz. To me, of course, it was just an image of my rejoining my parents.

Golly D.
Age 21, working in Berlin Jewish hospital

In May 1943, my then fiancé was included in one of the transports which were supposed to go to Theresienstadt, and Theresienstadt, we knew, was the lesser of many evils. He went to one of the collection camps, and I was left behind. I didn't know what to do. I was safe. As a half-Jew, I was safe in Germany, especially in Berlin, while in some different cities the half-Jews were not safe. My heart said, "Yes, I better go with him. Maybe I can help him." And my common sense said, "Careful. Caution." I debated with myself. I debated with some of my colleagues. I remember my head nurse said to me, "Golly, for something like that, one does not volunteer." Maybe she knew more than I did, because she was Dr. Lustig's girlfriend. Finally, the heart won out over the common sense, and I did volunteer. I packed my things. I joined him at the collection camp, and on May 31, 1943, we arrived in Theresienstadt.

As we entered, we were immediately separated, my [future] husband and I. I was placed into women's barrack and I don't know what they did with him. I was lying on the bunk bed all night long [and] I said, "What did I do? What did I do? Now I volunteered for this! I don't know if I'll ever see him again. I'm trapped!" I cried like a baby all night long.

[In] Theresienstadt, people could move about freely. Next day I went out into the street, and lo and behold, I ran into him! We set the wedding. There weren't many weddings in Theresienstadt, so mine must be one of the few exceptions. We set the wedding for June 13, 1943, and the super rabbi, Dr. Leo Baeck, conducted the ceremony. We scraped a little food together and we made a so-called celebration. After that we were able to move into the room that was assigned to us but had to share that one room with another young couple—which was pretty peculiar, but it was better than being separated into different barracks.

Food was scarce. We were allowed to receive packages. We were allowed to send out letters and receive letters. All in all, I must say that life in Theresienstadt was bearable, even though someone who has been only in Theresienstadt may not feel that way, but everything in life is relative. If I compare it with what was to come after Theresienstadt, to me it was a paradise because there were no gas chambers. People died naturally. Food, as I say, was scarce, but we were allowed to keep our own clothes. We looked civilized. There were little shops and there were lots of cultural activities. But this was also an illusion. In fact, the whole camp was a facade.

Members of the Red Cross [came] to check out the camp. [It] received a face-lift, so to speak. Everything was scrubbed and cleaned, and we received extra rations of food, and we had to put on our Sunday clothes, so to speak, and we were walking—had to walk around on the streets. So I remember the people from the Red Cross were walking. Pictures were taken, movies were taken. I wouldn't be surprised if everybody thought, "Well, they don't really treat the Jews so badly." That's why I say it was merely a facade. Transports came and transports went.

In September 1944, my husband was again taken into a transport. That was the day, I remember, after Yom Kippur, because I remember he was praying all day long. But it didn't help very much. The next day he had to pack his duffel bag, and I remember on top of the duffel bag he packed his *tefillin* [phylacteries] so that he would be able to say the morning prayer in the cattle car. The last time I saw him, Zolly happened to get a standing place where the cattle car had a little opening with the bars. So he looked out. He smiled at me. I waved at him. And that was the last thing I ever saw of him.

A few days later an announcement was given out by the Gestapo that the relatives of those who were deported in this particular transport on this particular day may volunteer to join their relatives at this working camp. Again, I didn't know what to do. Again I volunteered. So did thousands of others. I packed my backpack. I went over to the train, just like everybody else, looking forward to be united with our loved ones. And after hours and hours—we had learned German geography in school—we saw the train pass towns such as Gliwice, Katowice, Hindenburg—all leading to Auschwitz. Then it became clear to us. It goes to Auschwitz! We were in shock. We were absolutely in shock.

Werner R.
Born Berlin, Germany, 1927
Moved to Zagreb, Yugoslavia, 1933

Then I was put with a whole bunch of other people into one of these cattle cars and shipped to Theresienstadt. At this point, it was slightly an adventure, and I felt that if I cooperate, I had a better chance of survival than if I tried to run away. I had this tremendous optimism that nothing is going to happen to me. I had this, I don't know what, maybe to the point of hubris, I would say, of nothing is going to happen to me. But I had one advantage. I had the advantage that I didn't know details about concentration camps. I didn't know of gas chambers. I didn't know of tortures and all these things. I had an advantage over adults. I was fifteen years old, I never had any possessions. I had a tremendous—how do you call it—feeling of survival. And to me, the most important thing was survival. The older people had this tremendous feeling of justice, of ethics, of righteousness, and so on. They had family, and they lost, you know, they left children and parents and so on behind. The only person I left behind was my mother, whom I didn't have to worry about because she was an American citizen [through her father's U.S. citizenship] with a German Iron Cross. So I had this tremendous advantage. I did not stand there like many people who were bemoaning fate and who were bemoaning the loss of businesses, and stuff like that, or families.

Theresienstadt was a completely different situation. Theresienstadt was called at that time *Stadt der jüdischen Selbstverwaltung*, which means "City of Jewish Self-Government." But they used to call it jokingly *Stadt der jüdischen Selbstvergewaltung*, which means "City of Jewish Self-Rape." Theresienstadt had a cabaret. They were performing opera. The food was relatively good. There was money, ghetto money. There was a sort of social life, if you will. Then in '44, I was packed into a railroad car, given a couple of cans of sardines, and we were shipped to Birkenau, which is Auschwitz, really. Now this was concentration camp, you know. This was already much, much more serious.

4

"A Ladder Made of Rope"

ESCAPE, HIDING, AND RESISTANCE

Resistance took many forms. Individuals with contacts, money, the "right" hair and eye color, and no accent could acquire false identity papers and pass as non-Jews. Others went into hiding, although this often required money for bribes and food. Both strategies were dangerous: living conditions could be unbearable and betrayal was a constant threat.

Those who planned uprisings and resistance did not delude themselves that they could defeat the Germans or liberate large numbers. Rather, uprisings usually occurred when all hope of survival was lost. Occasionally a small number escaped to the woods where partisan units operated.

The best-known act of resistance was the Warsaw ghetto uprising that began on April 19, 1943. Several hundred young Jews obtained a small number of weapons and for nearly a month withstood German efforts to liquidate the ghetto. A few of these fighters escaped to Warsaw proper through the sewers. Most were killed and the rest, together with the remaining ghetto population, were deported to concentration or death camps. Other uprisings occurred, some in ghettos and even in the Treblinka, Sobibór, and Birkenau death camps.

Hanna F.
Born Czemierniki, Poland, 1923
Deported to Parczew with her family, 1942

We knew that we are going for destruction, but we just didn't know when and how, until one afternoon we did receive a message that [there were] a lot of trains at the train depot, and we knew that something is going to happen. Everybody [who was] able to went into hiding. I really don't remember how long it lasted because days didn't mean anything to you. [When we] came out from the hiding from the bunker, [there] were hardly any people left. A bunker was built in the backyard, and you went through like in a tunnel from the house through the cellar and into the hiding.

My mother gave us permission. She said, "It's time for us to separate, because maybe somebody [will] remain alive." I got to my brother's house, and my brother said, "Listen, you are the only one have a chance to survive. I know somebody who will get you a birth certificate as a Polish woman. You are going to go to Germany. Maybe you'll survive there." The same night, I parted with my brother and sister. Far away, I could hear the screaming and crying, "Don't go, because they're going to kill you!" They didn't know what it was in store for them.

I went to that man and he gave me that birth certificate, and I went to Germany. A transport of Polish workers were leaving that particular day, and with a heavy heart I climbed on that truck. I know this is the end, and I had nothing to lose. If they catch me, they'll kill me, regardless if I am here or wherever I'm going to be. Standing on the bus, on the truck, going towards the gathering-point, to Lublin, they called my name. But I did not memorize my name—I couldn't remember my name! They hollered, "Urszula Jurkowska! Urszula Jurkowska!" I was facing the other way, and I didn't hear because I had a heavy scarf on my head. Somebody poked, "Are you Urszula Jurkowska?" and that crying saved me, because they figured that I'm really very sorry leaving, you know, going to Germany to work. They didn't know my feelings, my heart. I knew I'm leaving everything and everybody behind to die. And from there I went into Germany.

I was in Germany from 1942, from around October. Days, you know, didn't mean anything. It just more or less [marked] the months or the time of the season or whatever. A woman that suspected me worked in the same airport as I did. She worked there too, and she denounced us and the Gestapo came and they took us away. [She] denounced me being Jewish and she denounced three other women. The verdict came from the higher echelon to send us to Auschwitz. The following day they took us for interrogation and I never admitted that I'm a full-blooded Jew, but the three others did. I lost two teeth in the process, I got a terrible beating. Actually, I was the only one that got the beating because I never wanted to admit that I'm—the others admitted right away.

> ### Celia K.
> ### Szarkowszczyzna, Poland

The wires were cut beforehand. We all pushed towards the back of the ghetto, and we all ran in the woods. A lot of people escaped. I turned around and saw a classmate of mine who was a policeman, and his rifle jammed. He looked at me and I looked at him. And that's the only reason I am alive. His rifle jammed. He couldn't shoot me. So I escaped.

We were all little groups of Jews in the woods. I ran into a group of Jews, maybe twelve, fifteen. And there was a cousin of mine with her children, a little girl of four or five and a little boy of maybe eight, ten, eleven months. And he had a voice. It was such a raspy voice. It was impossible. And in the woods, when a child cries it really rings out, and the Germans would really come very fast. So the group of Jews said to her, "Look, Teitle. You can't be in the woods with this child. Either get away or kill him." She became wild. Anyway, she had to do it. There was no choice. She had the little girl and herself to think of. I saw her put the child in the swamp. With her foot on his neck, she drowned him. I

"I saw her put
the child in
the swamp."

Celia K.
Born Szarkowszczyzna, Poland, 1923
Recorded 1980, age 57. Died 1994

In the small town near Vilna where Celia K. grew up a ghetto was established after the German occupation. Celia K.'s good looks earned her a job as waitress in the German officers' dining hall. She and her family escaped to the woods but had to surrender or they could not survive. They were taken to the ghetto in Glubokoye. She again escaped and spent eighteen months hidden by a Polish farmer under the floor of a barn fighting off the rats and overhearing the peasants discussing how many Jews they had captured and turned in for rewards. The farmer finally insisted she leave, fearing discovery.

Celia K. joined her two brothers in a partisan camp in the woods. There she learned to ride and shoot, raid villages for food, and blow up German installations. "We killed mercilessly . . . indiscriminately. . . . I stayed in the partisans until the Russians liberated us in 1944. Then my soldier's life finished. I began a civilian life—of insanity, I would say. I was pretty insane."

She speaks of not knowing how to reconstruct a life without money, without skills. So she went out "to look for a man" and married "the first man that wanted me." They emigrated to the United States when her son was three years old, where she had two daughters. Celia K. sought counseling when her children were young, recognizing that her problems were having an impact on her family. Her children and their families attended a ceremony in 1999 in which Yad Vashem, the Israeli national institution dedicated to Holocaust education and memorialization, recognized the family that hid their mother.

saw it with my own eyes. And that wasn't the only isolated incident. There were a lot of incidents like this. One man was running
from the ghetto with a bundle and a child. And in the shooting,
he got so confused he dropped the child and he saved the bundle.
When he came to a safe place, he realized the child was gone.
And he had the bundle.

Joseph W.
Przemyśl, Poland

One day I saw two Gestapo men walking with three girls, banter-
ing, joking. Three pretty girls, maybe eighteen, nineteen, and they
walk with them, and I say "Phee! What's two Gestapo doing with
three Jewish girls?" They're walking to an area where the building
was bombed, and they walked into the courtyard. I looked, and I
see [them] draw pistols and *boom, boom, boom!* All three, dead. I ran
away. [I] found out later that they were three girls who got themselves false Aryan papers. They were caught on the railroad station
in Przemyśl, pretending to go to Germany for work in Germany
as non-Jews. But somebody identified them, pointed them out.
They were arrested. The perfidy! The way they were joking with
them as if they were friends! They didn't tell them anything. They
just walked and shot them right there.

Celia K.

When they exterminated our ghetto and the surrounding little ghettos, the Germans were afraid of Jews congregating in the woods. So
they sent out *shelihim* [messengers] to the woods with loudspeakers:
"You'll be safe if you all come to Glubokoye," which is a big
ghetto. "You'll be given work. You'll be given housing. Please come
to the ghetto, to Glubokoye." Well, of course, we knew that
eventually Glubokoye would be exterminated, too. But we had no
choice. You couldn't live in the woods anymore because you were
hunted down like animals. So a lot of people started going towards
Glubokoye, including myself and my little sister.

When I came to Glubokoye, all of a sudden, my mother comes up. I didn't know she was alive! She said to me, "What business did you have to come here? I fed you and clothed you for so many years, and now you're a parasite. Out you go! You were in hiding. Why did you come here?" My mother was really vicious, but she had a purpose. She wanted me to live. And then she broke down. She started crying, and she said, "Look, darling, I do love you. You know I do. The reason I want you to go is because at least one person should remain alive of the family." She said, "You know we are all going to be killed in here. Please go."

Chaim E.
Serving in the Polish military

I went in the army. The duty was one and a half year. September the fifteenth [1939] was really the day what [I] would have gone home—and the war broke out September the first. So I was caught in the war, and we were soldiers in the front. The war was over by about two, three weeks, and we were caught on the front as prisoners of war. The Germans took us. The first experience I had with a German when he took me prisoner, he said, "*Bist du Jude?*" "Are you a Jew?" I said yes really, but somehow nothing happened, and he pushed me aside. They kept us outside for about two, three days. We didn't really have to eat anything. They took us to some camp. All the prisoners of war they sent to Gemany to work there. But when we arrived in Germany, they separated the Jews from the not-Jews.

We didn't get hardly anything to eat. We worked in the street for clean the street in Leipzig. I have to admit there was a German guard what was an old soldier. He stole sometimes bread for us in the kitchen. But that is the very, very big exception. They kept us for about a half year, and then all the Jewish prisoners of war they sent back to Poland. When I came back, so I decided, let me go work at a farm. On a farm is always food and shelter and maybe make a few dollars, you can help your family. And what I did and I worked there, started to work there and later for my brother I found a spot for him too.

Working on a farm was really one of the few things a Jew was allowed to do. Then came the rule: Jews are not allowed to be in no place, no working, nothing. They have to concentrate in the nearest, biggest city. And from there they took them to the concentration camps. A friend of mine had [been] working also on a farm there. So we decided, "Let's see what happen [if we do] not go to this nearest city. Let's go in the woods, maybe find partisans or whatever, and we can somehow get away." We heard a lot of sayings that they take the Jews to concentration camps and gas them and do that kind of things. But with a straight human mind, you couldn't believe that things like that happened. You figured maybe they take him and they send him some hard work or whatever. But to the extreme like they said, you really, normally you couldn't imagine that something like that really goes to happen. Not believing the stories, we still tried to get away.

We went to the woods, but with an empty stomach for two, three days. And don't forget, even you ran away, you're not in freedom because the population was not cooperating with you. You were in just [as much] in big danger outside than inside. After three, four days we were in the woods and we couldn't have food and things, so we said, that doesn't make any sense, and we walked another little city and we heard there are still—we noticed there are Jews there. We came then during the day, and one Jew immediately helps the other one. They took us in somewhere, and we slept in some house.

Renée G.
Hiding with her family

My dad came and told me not to worry, that he found a place in a stable underground, a pit about five-by-eight, dug underneath the stable underneath the manure. I thought it was just the greatest thing to be together. Boards [were] propping up the ceiling and some of the side walls. There were two long benches on the

side and one bench in the middle. The bench in the middle served
as a table in the daytime. At night, that middle bench was leveled
with the other two benches so we were able to sleep sideways,
eight of us. We stayed there for about—well, for them it was
almost two years. For me it was about fifteen months. The food
consisted of morning coffee made from burned grain and a loaf of
bread for eight people every other day. Lunch consisted of soup
and occasionally some potatoes in it. Supper was again coffee.
They used burned wheat to make the coffee. If we wanted to take
a bath or wash our hair, we had to use our share of coffee.

We only could go out one at a time, because in case of danger
we had to get in very quickly and close the opening. We were
sealed in, almost without air. A couple of times people were passing out. This farmer was a very poor farmer, and when the idea
came about of possibly hiding out eight Jews, this good farmer
[the one who had previously helped them] negotiated with him for
money, that we would pay him so much a month. The manure
was laid on top, so that it was the same level as the whole stable.
The ground with the animals [was] right over us, so nobody could
tell there was anything going on underneath. And the farmer usually brought in food for the animals anyway, so the neighbors
thought that the food was for animals.

The two female cousins bribed my [cousin] Oscar, the one
who kept the diary of the war in hiding to teaching us language
and math. He bargained for paper. He said, "If you can get me
paper, I will give you lessons in those things." He himself and his
father were going crazy for lack of activities. [He] one night risked
his life and went to one of the ghettos that was still existing. It was
a good forty kilometers away, and [he] went to go to that town to
get books and came back with a sack full of books. So naturally,
we read these books over and over and over again. I learned plain
arithmetic, I believe, and perhaps we got into algebra. He taught
us the Polish language and a little bit of English. . . . The books
we read were mostly in Yiddish.

The biggest treat was when a newspaper came in. Every time that the farmer went to market, we put in our order. We would give him something extra to bring the paper for us. We would follow the war, and I remember the big heading of Stalingrad. And also we had to feed him information to encourage him that there was an end to all this, because several times he came in and he said, "No more! You are getting out tonight! I'm chasing you out! I'm not risking my life anymore." Besides, we ran out of money. I think the last three months or so, we didn't have any more money to give him and he wanted to chase us out. We kept on encouraging him that there will be money after we get out and we'll pay him back, and that [the] war was almost over. We would show him the headlines in German, which he couldn't read anyway. Finally one day, he was in a good mood—I think maybe some good news came through or some other farmer told him that the Russians were coming close. He came in and he said, "Well, maybe we're actually making it after all." He says, "I'm not chasing you out anymore." He said, "I now like you." He says, "You are almost as good as my cow and my sheep and my pigs. I've gotten used to you," he said.

When my birthday came around, my dad wanted me to have something special for dinner. He asked me what I want and I said, "I would love to have some scrambled eggs." So he traded. He gave the farmer a pair of golden earrings to get me scrambled eggs. And I'll never forget, those were the best-tasting scrambled eggs I have ever had in my life.

Jay M.
November 1943, Białystok, Poland

We started planning an escape. We did not know where to go, except the other fellow had heard about the partisans in the woods and he thought that he had directions how to get there. We prepared a ladder made out of rope and the following night we made the escape. November third, we escaped from the ghetto, had to cut all the barbed wire, climb out the fence, and we knew we had to walk north to get to a highway, and then walk east on the highway to get to the woods.

We walked for four nights. During the days, we rested. Until the fourth night we met some partisans. They then invited us to come along with them, and we joined with that group of five people. After a period of time, one of the groups in that same area was discovered by the Germans. A few of them were killed and the rest of them ran away and came to us. The rule in the partisans is that whatever is available in food it is shared by everybody and shared alike. Within a week, another group was knocked out from their place, and they came to us. Pretty soon, our supply of food that we thought would last for a few months was all gone. Of course, it didn't feel good, but if it were the other way around, we would expect them to treat us the same way. So, being realistic, this was the only rational way, the only decent way to handle the situation. There were many days that we had no food at all, stretches of two, three, and once five days.

Two people went and brought back a horse with them the following morning. We killed it, and it was a feast the first day. The whole liver was divided and we broiled it on charcoal, and I think it was the best delicacy that I've had in years. Again, things looked up that time until the meat started running out. And again period of reduced rations, and then no food at all. We reminded ourselves that some weeks ago we had buried the intestines, head, tail, and whole skin of the horse. Someone suggested to open up the hole and start using it. Well, we did. First we cleaned the intestines. They were already decomposing. I remember washing it and the meat part of it was coming apart. But we washed it, cooked it, and ate it. The last thing was the skin, and this was the toughest. And it was tough! We tried to boil it in hot water to remove the hair, but it did not budge. So we had to burn it off in the flame and scrape it. We finally managed to clean a good portion of it, and we cut it up in small pieces, put it in a big pot of

"Two people went
and brought back a
horse with them the
following morning."

Jay M.
Born Białystok, Poland, 1925
Recorded 1983, age 58

Jay M. grew up in a Jewish neighborhood and witnessed the brief German occupation of his town followed by Soviet occupation in 1939. After the Germans invaded the USSR in June 1941, they entered Białystok. Mass murder of Jews was followed by ghettoization. Mr. M. and his mother and sister escaped by hiding.

When the final destruction of the ghetto began in August 1943, Mr. M. and his family hid in bunkers. He escaped to the forest three months later. His mother and sister were deported. He joined the partisans and took part in bombings, derailing of trains, and other acts of sabotage. In the summer of 1944, he was liberated by Soviet troops and enlisted in the Soviet army, attending officers' school and working as an instructor. At the war's end in 1945, he learned that his mother and sister had survived.

Mr. M. returned to Poland in December 1946. He obtained an illegal visa in Łódź and traveled to Vienna. The joy of his reunion with his mother and sister in Nuremberg, Germany in March 1947, was surpassed only by his elation the year and a half earlier when he learned they were alive. Jay M. emigrated to the United States. He has a daughter and is an avid skier.

melted snow, and cooked it for a whole night. Everybody went to sleep that night with the hopes of having a good meal the following morning. But when we woke up and we tasted it, it was as tough as the night before. Someone had suggested that we simply take one piece at a time and broil it on the hot coals. That helped. It was partially broiled and partially burned, but we were able to eat it.

Joseph W.
Escape from Przemyśl ghetto, September, 1943

So we [my friend and I] waited till he [a Polish peasant] was alone, and we came out, called him into the barn there. When he saw us he was like he saw a ghost. We had to do a selling job, why he should save us. "Absolutely not!" He will not have us here, people come here, workmen come. "Look, boys. I can't keep you." I says, "You must. I mean, you will be rewarded." "How?" I says, "First of all, we have some money. Here, we have money. I'll show you. We have money. Secondly, we also have some gold. Also, we have relatives in America. After the war, if we survive, you will be rewarded."

So he says, "Okay. Come. I'll show you how we're gonna do it." Just like that. And he took us to this root cellar which was maybe a hundred yards from the house. [A] root cellar's a big hole in the ground maybe thirty feet long, fifteen feet wide in the ground, deep, and it has got just a door and the roof, but in it there were several rooms to the sides. One where you keep onions, garlic, another one potatoes, turnips, beets, other root vegetables. He says, "See this room here?" He brought us all the tools: saws, pickaxes, shovels. He says, "First we cut a square here," he says. "Then you dig a deep tunnel taller than you are, straight down. And the earth that you take out,"—he brought us buckets—"you put it over there in the corner of the cellar. And do this at night. Then when you're finished, you have a lot of earth there. When you are finished, take this earth out. There's a ravine another hundred yards beyond.

Dump it over the ravine. When you finish your night work, in the morning I'll come around and cover it with leaves and branches. Nobody will know that any fresh earth was put over there."

So we dug a little bit, and we said, "Okay, we have enough room for the two of us. We can stay here." "No," he says, "You need more room. There's another person." I said, "Who?" He says, "Come, I'll show you." And there she was. He kept her hidden in a pigsty and she smelled like pig and she was bleeding. I later found out she was in a cattle car. There were some boys there that had pliers. They cut the wires, that little window that you have, and they started jumping out from the train. People escaped by jumping, feet first, then you pushed yourself away from the train, and you fell. Some people broke their legs and they couldn't move anymore. Some people hit their heads on stones and they were dead. And they were shooting. There was a machine gun on front of the locomotive with floodlights down all [the] length of the train. But it didn't matter—you were going to die anyway. So she jumped. And a bullet went through, but it was a flesh wound. So we discussed medically how to treat her, and he says, "I'll tell you how. Peasants, we do this when we have a wound. We take stale bread, rye bread, and we mix it with some spider webs. We knead it and we put it on a wound. This is what we do." So we did that, and slowly it started healing, and slowly we adjusted to a life in a bunker.

[He was] a very decent man. We lived on very little. We took a loaf of bread and we cut it three ways, and we had to live on a small piece of bread and water. In January, we had a scary thing. Germans came hunting. You know, there were all kinds of animals: wolves, deer, and foxes. So the Germans came on a hunting party, and they were hunting in those woods. So he was afraid to come to us, and we were locked in. This went on for three days. We ran out of water, we ran out of bread. We were hungry, we didn't know what was happening. We thought, "What? Has he forgot about us? Did they kill him?" After the third day, [he] told us "Come." He invited us to his house and she [his wife] made us a hot meal.

Slowly we saw liberation coming. He brought us newspapers. We saw where the Germans were retreating and retreating, and the Russians coming closer. We knew all what was happening in Italy. I made dots on the map I cut out from newspapers. We followed every move of every army. We had nothing else to do, just survive. And for entertainment we sang, we sang. We sang everything that came to mind, from lullabies to Hebrew songs to [the] latest hit parade from [the] Polish hit parade, German songs. I remember a lot of Hebrew songs, a number of Yiddish songs. I even remember a German song my friend taught me. [He sings.] In addition, poor Anya was practically illiterate. She came from a very poor family. She had two or three years of schooling and she had to work. Her mother died and her father was very poor. She couldn't read, so we taught her the alphabet. She knew nothing. Her math was abominable, yet she was nobody's fool. And we waited [to] be liberated and hoping that nothing would happen. In July, we heard this shooting already. The salvation came on July 27 of 1944 when the first Russian units came. We peeked out, and we saw Russian soldiers in the yard.

Celia K.
Glubokoye ghetto

So the farmer that offered me his home, risked his life. He put on a yellow star, entered the ghetto. Believe it or not, you could enter the ghetto at that time because they were gathering the Jews. He came in and he found me and said, "You're going out with me. I have papers for you." Sure enough, we took off the stars, him and me. And the two of us set off on the main highway.

Now the life on the farm—I can't begin to tell you what it meant to be in hiding. The guy made a hole under the floor in the barn. The hole consisted of maybe as wide as I was, two feet, and as long as I was. You couldn't turn. If you crawled in on your stomach, you remained on your stomach. If you crawled in on your back, you remained on your back. Sometimes, when it was quiet, he would pull me up by my legs and give me a chance to straighten out my bones and give me a little food. But it was harvest time, and the barn was full of workers. So sometimes I remained for a week, ten days in one position, under the floor in this hole. There was no other way. The workers slept in the barns, so I couldn't utter a sound. The rats were so big. The rats are indescribably big. And they used to chew on me. And you couldn't—we learned not to scream.

I used to ask the peasant what's going on. He said, "I don't know." There were no papers. There was no radio. The only thing I would hear, that the Germans at that time deprived people of salt. Salt was such a commodity that they would risk their life for a bag of salt. I used to hear the peasants: "How many did you get today?" They used to pass by the barn that was a main road. For each Jew they used to catch they would get a sack of salt.

[The Polish peasant] said to me, "You have to go because your life is in danger." After lying under a floor for almost a year and a half, I didn't have any muscles. I was soft. I was achy. He told me in which general direction I should go. "The partisans should be here and here and here." After wandering about at night in the dark, cold, my feet swell up something awful. I didn't know how to walk anymore. I heard some footsteps. "Halt!" in Russian. "Who are you?" So I said to them, "I'm Jewish." "What's your name?" I told them. "How do we know who you are?" I said, "Well, I have two brothers who are partisans. Their names are such and such." "Okay. We know who they are. Come with us." They took me and led me to the partisan camp.

Jay M.
With partisans, forest outside Białystok

The life at that time didn't mean much. We knew what the Germans did to us, and sooner or later, we thought, we're going to get killed anyway. So, not putting a great value on our lives, we thought we would do what we could. As soon as the winter ended, the first thing on the agenda was to get weapons. We then met members of other groups. One fellow, a Pole who was also in the partisans, was from a village not too far and he knew that the Russians dumped a lot of their personal weapons in a river when they retreated in 1941. So we decided to go there at night, a moonless night, and that young man led us to the place, pointed it to us. It was probably late March or early April. The river was still a little frozen. We undressed, naked, had to break through the ice and dove into the water. And the dives were successful. Many of us brought out rifles, semiautomatics, bayonets. We could not stay in the water for too long because of the very cold temperature, but we were very pleased with the find. The wooden stock[s] were very heavy, very swollen, but surprisingly the metal inside the chamber was cleaned out exceptionally good. They stuffed it with grease, and it protected it beautifully.

Celia K.

The partisans were getting very well organized by that time, by 1943. They had radio contact with Moscow. They had parachute drops of ammunition. They had personnel, trained personnel, to organize like an army. And the Germans were afraid of them because the war was not going so well for them. They knew eventually they'll have to retreat, and it would be very difficult to retreat with the partisans working in the background. So they decided to exterminate the partisans. We had dugouts, and we lived in those dugouts. From there we conducted our missions of sabotage. How did we obtain food? We used to raid villages. Take a cow, take a pig, or take whatever and kill it.

They wanted me to work in the kitchen, being a Jew and being a girl. I said, "I'm volunteering for the patrol." I was given a horse, I was given ammunition, and I was given an assignment. There was a school that was used for an ammunition dump for

Postwar portrait of Celia K.
"I was given a horse,
I was given ammunition, and
I was given an assignment."

the Germans. We had to go and set it ablaze, this ammunition
dump. I've never been on a horse before. I went on the horse with
thirty people: two girls, twenty-eight men. And we blew up the
school, all right. But the horse threw me off. Some partisan
plucked me by the neck, threw me over the saddle, and rescued
me. From then on I was more careful.

And they taught us how to set explosives on railroad tracks.
We were given orders to make the retreat of the Germans as difficult as possible. When the first German was caught, a seventeen-
year-old, with a wounded knee, the commander handed him over
to me and said, "Celia, he's all yours. You could torture him. You
could kill him." I couldn't. I bandaged his knee, I fed him, and I
turned him over with all the captured. I couldn't do it. I shot a lot
of Germans, a lot of Ukrainians, a lot of Lithuanians in the course
of my work, but not point-blank to take a seventeen-year-old and
kill him. I couldn't do it. Maybe I was softhearted. Maybe I'm
sorry. I don't know. I just couldn't do it.

But we killed. Mercilessly we killed. We used to go into villages
where we knew that people collaborated with the Germans. We
used to kill indiscriminately. We killed off an awful lot of people

we knew that were against Jews. We did a lot of damage. We blew up railroad tracks. We blew up bridges. We blew up roads. We blew up trucks. The Germans had a miserable time.

Jay M.

Then we set out to do some demolition work. We built our own bombs, mines to mine trains. Those were best made out of unexploded artillery shells and mortar shells. Some of them we found in the woods. At various times we used different methods of putting a bomb under a train. In the beginning, we would get to the selected area and put it under the rail with a pressure-type switch. So when the train would get to that area, the rails always give under the weight of the train. It would explode.

In addition to blowing up trains, we also used various ways of burning bridges, cutting down trees, and dumping them in front of an advancing column. They would get disorganized, scared, and just by a few sharpshooters we could pick off quite a few of them. And this lasted until the summer of '44. By that time the Russian army had advanced close enough, and we were liberated by the Russians.

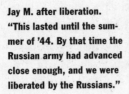

Jay M. after liberation. "This lasted until the summer of '44. By that time the Russian army had advanced close enough, and we were liberated by the Russians."

Helen K.
Age 19, Warsaw, Poland

I was living in the ghetto till 1943, May ninth, May tenth, when the Jewish Warsaw uprising was. I was taken out, almost one of the last people from the Warsaw ghetto. A lot of people don't know, and they feel that we went really very passive. But if you want to look at history, and I'm sure you know enough that countries like France or Belgium or Holland, they went in a few days. The Germans came and took over. The Warsaw ghetto was holding out for four weeks. Even Poland didn't hold out for four weeks. The Germans were really afraid to come into the Warsaw ghetto. They came in tanks when they decided to liquidate the ghetto. This was 1943, Passover, and we were all prepared. We didn't have much ammunition, so we threw Molotov cocktails on the tanks and a lot of Germans got killed. So what we did, we took away their ammunition. We were psychologically prepared to just get killed, rather than be taken to the concentration camps.

My mother was with me and my brother. One day when the Germans came in—this was at the very end of the Warsaw ghetto. [*Long silence.*] I want you to know my mother wasn't even forty years old. Neither was my father. The Germans were coming, and we had to pull ourselves up on that rope, and she couldn't make it. So she went into the bunker below with the resistance. There were several bunkers. We didn't make big bunkers because we didn't want if the Germans will come in, not all the people should be caught. So we had five different bunkers downstairs, and we were hiding upstairs, maybe fifty, sixty people upstairs. My mother couldn't make the rope because the Germans were coming very rapidly. She was hiding downstairs. After they left, the Germans, I went to look for her and she was gone.

A few days later, we were taken out from the ghetto. They came with a fire truck, and with a ladder they took us all down. It was my brother, myself—at that time I was married—my husband, and his sisters. We were all hiding there, maybe fifty people.

The Warsaw ghetto in flames, 1943. Helen K. recalls, "After the houses were burning they came in and demolished them." *Courtesy U.S. Holocaust Memorial Museum*

Everything was burning. You couldn't stay there. They smoked us out. People had to get out from the houses. You couldn't hide. And then not only—on top of this, after the houses were burning, they came in and they demolished them. So even if you were hiding, the people got suffocated underneath. So I was with his [my husband's] family and my brother and we together. My mother was taken a few days before. And then they took us all to Majdanek.

5

"Very Little Windows"

DEPORTATION AND ARRIVAL

The planned systematic murder of Europe's entire Jewish population was called by the Germans the "Final Solution to the Jewish Question." Concentration camps were established for political dissidents in Germany from the beginning of the Nazi regime in 1933. As German rule was extended to other countries, anti-Jewish policies and laws were put into place. Labor, concentration, and death camps were established. The largest was near the Polish villages of Oświęcim (Auschwitz) and Brzezinka (Birkenau). Although more than ten thousand labor, concentration, and extermination camps were built, scholars estimate that at least 1.1 million people, of whom 90 percent were Jewish, were murdered in Auschwitz/Birkenau alone between 1941 and 1945.

The deportation of Jews from across Europe to the camps was a huge operation that required detailed planning and immense organization. So important was elimination of European Jewry to the Nazis that even when trains were badly needed to service German troops at the front, they were often diverted to transport Jews to the camps. Deportations were euphemistically called "transports to the east." Most Jews envisioned hard work, not death camps.

Deportations often occurred with very short notice. Jews were typically told to take only one suitcase and to assemble near railroad stations. Upon arrival at the stations, Jews were packed into sealed cattle trains, often 100 to 150 people compressed into a single car that might be labeled "ten horses." The cattle cars had no sanitation and admitted very little air. Little or no food or water was supplied. After several days in blistering heat or subzero cold, transports arrived at extermination camps with hundreds of deportees already dead.

Arrival at the camps was equally nightmarish: screaming guards, loud noises, barking dogs, beatings, and flames from the chimneys of nearby crematoria. Those who looked older, the sick, the disabled, and mothers with young children were usually sent straight to the gas chambers. A few were selected for slave labor and some for specious medical experiments. Those left alive were not exempt from subsequent selections, which occurred often.

Arrivals were quick, allowing the dazed occupants of the cattle cars no time to comprehend what was happening. At Auschwitz/Birkenau those who survived the first selection were stripped, showered, shaved, tattooed with a number, and given ill-fitting clothing—all meant to dehumanize and undermine the will to resist.

Abraham P.
Deported from Romania to Auschwitz at age 24

[On May 3, 1944] two *gendarmes* [police] knocked at the door. It was a Wednesday morning. They said, "Get up! You be ready in fifteen minutes and go to the school. You can only take so much with you." Everybody—sick, kids, it didn't matter old, young—everybody had to be there within a specific time. And the *gendarmes*, they went over our luggage to see what we have. Not too many luggages were there because they didn't let you. So we just tied it up on sheets, whatever you could do. They kept us there all day long, not knowing what is going to happen, what they are going to do. And everybody was just sitting there, with their own thoughts. Hardly anybody was talking to one another.

All of a sudden, with a loudspeaker they said, "Get yourself ready and go over to the railroad station." They handed us buckets and they threw us into those boxcars—eighty of us in a boxcar. They didn't even write your name or who you are or what you are or something like that. They just threw you into the boxcar. And those people who couldn't get into the boxcars, the younger ones had to help them. And they couldn't help them. The *gendarmes* used to kick them so he should be able to move. So you finally got about seventy or eighty of us in a boxcar, and the minute you got [in] there, they locked us up.

Clara L.
Born Kisvárda, Hungary, 1925
19 years old when deported to Auschwitz

The doctor of the ghetto told me, "I think it is our turn now." And he pointed to a small doctor's bag and he said, "I want you to know, here I have the medical supply of the entire hospital." He showed me small vials, and I knew how to handle an injection because my father had diabetes. So he said, "You know how to handle an injection, so I want you to know this is morphine and this is something else. And all you need is one or two. If you want to use it, I want you to know it is here." The ghetto hospital was emptied. The sliding doors of the cars were locked. We could hear, you know, as they slammed on the bar, the crossbar. There were people, of course, in the hospital wagon, people that died. In the morning they would open the sliding doors. The dead were thrown out. The last night, the doctor who was traveling with us, with a wife and two children, said good-bye to me, and he said, "I have decided to take another way." And I saw that he went to this bag. The children were asleep. I saw as he did his wife. And they went to sleep.

So we came closer to Auschwitz, and I asked my mother [if] she would want to have this way out, and she said no. She was a very religious woman and apparently decided this is what is going to be. Although I blame myself that I should have done it, for her and for my father, and for myself, and for my sister. But my mother wasn't agreeing to it.

And here I will say something that was, absolutely, in all this upheaval and all this tremendous strain, what was absolutely not only an eye-opener, but a shock to me. That my mother very clearly said, "We are going to be separated. It's no question about it. I want to ask you that—you do as they tell you. If they tell you to go to the front where the soldiers are and you have to do them favors, do anything, but [*crying*] save your life." Of course this was shocking because, coming from a very pious and a very perfect mother, it was a shock to me: "You save your life. Whatever you are told to do, do it! Just save your life!" And she said the same thing to my sister.

Abraham P.

I remember about the boxcar it was hot. We were cramped. There was no room to sit. We couldn't even see out of the boxcar. Even that little window that was over there, it was wired up with barbed wire. And when you have old people, and everybody is

Abraham P.'s father three weeks before deportation.

scared, little kids are crying—it was nothing but chaos and pande-
monium. There was absolutely nothing that you can do. I looked
at my mother and father. She was just sitting there, and in her
mind was going—God Almighty, what was she thinking? My
father was just quiet, quiet, quiet. He didn't say very much, and
then we started to *davenen* [pray]. And we *davenen*. And usually the
prayers, some of the prayers [were] "God help us." You know,
somehow they had a feeling that we are like little sheep right now
and they are sending us somewheres, to an unknown place. Who
is going to come back? Who is going to survive? Who is going to
live? What will happen to us? Here are people, religious people,
who always wore long clothes, and their privacy was so—it was—I
can't even find—I mean, here is a man who is a religious man
and then he has to go and—and take care of his personal need
right in front of so many people. I'll bet many of them just held it.
They would rather suffer pain than go out and empty their bowels
in front of people.

Martin S.
11 years old when transferred from Skarżysko-Kamienna concentration camp to Buchenwald

I recall when they were piling us into the car, they wanted every-body to move back so they could put more people in. Eventually people kept going back, but there was no more room. I do recall they fired across, to make more room so [they] shoved another batch of people in. I remember a good percentage of people died. For three days, people defecated on the floor. For three days, we didn't have any food or water. I remember that the thirst was the overwhelming thing. We just couldn't—that is again something that keeps recurring in my mind, this constant thirst! And I remember when they let us off the cattle cars in Buchenwald there was a hose with water, and some people couldn't even make it to the water.

Helen K.
19 years old when deported to Majdanek

My brother died in my arms. My younger brother . . . [*long silence*] and my husband's two sisters. There was not enough oxygen for all those people. They kept us in those wagons for days. They wanted us to die in the wagons. You know the cattle cars with very little windows? He wasn't even bar mitzvah. So you know, when my brother died in my arms, I said to myself, "I am going to live. I must be the only one survivor from my family. I'm going to live." I made up my mind that I'm going to defy Hitler. I'm not going to give in. Because he wants me to die, I'm going to live.

Edith P.
Deported to Auschwitz/Birkenau, then transferred by cattle car to Salzwedel concentration camp

Nobody talked. Nobody talked. We just looked at one another. I remember I was full of life, a young girl, and I said, "What's going to happen to me? I'm just starting. I'm just starting to blossom." I understood that. "What's going to happen to me?" And I just looked around. I didn't cry. Never.

I don't know how long we have been in those boxcars, but it was dark. I still hear it. I still hear the train *tum, tum, tum, tum.* Nobody said a word. We were just wondering, "Where are they going to take us?" One morning, I think it was morning or early afternoon, the train stopped there for an hour. Why? We don't know. A friend of mine said, "Why don't you stand up"—there was just a little window, with bars—"and see?" I said, "I can't. I don't have enough energy to climb up." She says, "I'm going to sit down, and you stand on my shoulders." And I did. And I looked out. And I saw paradise! The sun was bright and vivid. There was cleanliness all over. It was a station somewhere in Germany. There were three or four people there, one woman with a child, nicely dressed up. People were people, not animals. And I thought, "Paradise must look like this." I forgot already how normal people look like, how they act, how they speak, how they dress. But here there was life, and I had such yearning—I still feel it in my bones—I had such yearning to live, to run, to just run away and never come back! To run to the end, where there is no way back. And then I told the girls, "Girls, you have no idea how beautiful the sun is." And I saw a baby was crying and a woman was kissing that baby. Is there such a thing as love?

Bessie K.
In the cattle car after her baby was taken by the Nazis

Actually, I don't recall how long I was in the train because it was a terrible thing to me, because it seemed to me that [I'm] losing everything that belonged to me and it was a hard fight for us. I was alone, within myself. And since that time, I think all my life I've been alone. To me, I was dead. I died and I didn't want to hear nothing. I didn't want to know nothing, and I didn't want to talk about it. And I didn't want to admit to myself that this had happened to me. I don't how long we were going in the train, but

"I was born on the
train and I died
on the train."

Bessie K.
Born Vilna, Poland, 1924
Recorded 1983, age 59

Bessie K. enjoyed a culturally rich childhood in Vilna, marked by celebrations on Jewish holidays and harmonious relations with non-Jews. While she was visiting her aunt in Kovno in 1940, the Soviet Union occupied Lithuania. She could not return home after the German invasion of Lithuania the following year, though her father attempted to have her smuggled back to Vilna.

In 1942, Mrs. K. married. She gave birth to a son. She tried to hide her son in a "bundle" of coats during a deportation, but a German guard heard the infant choking and held out his arms, "and I hand him over the bundle. And this was the last time I had the bundle." In an Estonian concentration camp, Bessie contracted typhus and escaped being sent to the gas chamber with the help of her aunt and a friend. After the camp was liquidated, she was transferred by ship to Stutthof and survived a selection by posing as a non-Jew and with the help of other non-Jewish prisoners.

After liberation by Soviet troops, she felt that she was the only Jewish woman left alive. Mrs. K. remarried a Polish survivor (Jacob K.) in Płzeň, and they emigrated to the United States. It was only many years later that Mrs. K. was able to tell her husband and daughters of her son's death. For years at holiday gatherings she felt, "I'm dead." Mrs. K. is still dismayed over the world's indifference and remains concerned about the future in which her children will live.

to me it was a lifetime. The way I felt is I was born on the train and I died on the train. I actually didn't know why I was there on the train and what was happening to us. I wasn't even alive. I wasn't even alive. I wasn't there.

Arnold C.
11 years old when transferred to Auschwitz

They marched us to a train station, packed us in cattle cars, and we just kept riding the trains for days. There was again a stop. It was late at night. We went through a big town and we stopped at the train station. We must have been there for a few hours, and I looked through the small, little windows in the cattle car, and I happened to look into an apartment. I saw a family sitting by the table eating. There were several children and adults. And I was thinking to myself, "Will I ever be able to find my parents and sit again at a table as a free human being?"

Father John S.
Košice, Slovakia

I heard that the Germans put up a big wooden fence around the railroad station. It was rumors that the Jewish people were being deported. They built a tall wooden fence there and nobody was permitted to approach the fence. The word was out that they had machine guns lined up alongside the fence in the street which paralleled the railroad tracks. But I sneaked up to the fence and I was in my cassock, so I really stood out there. I looked left and right but I didn't see anybody, even soldiers. I found a hole there. It was a raw wood fence. And that was the day when I saw my train, my deportee train. It just must have pulled into the station. . . . It was a cattle train and right in front of me, just about two tracks from the fence, stood one of the wagons. It was opened by an SS soldier. The impression was terrible because it was terribly packed. I literally saw what you see in pictures: mothers with children, old people, and little children. The impression was terrifying. It was really packed, I mean compressed. One man immediately jumped off, and I always remembered his face because he looked a little bit like my father. He must have been something like mid-forties, closing on fifty. I did not hear what he said to the German soldier, but his behavior was polite. My feeling was—what I made out, that he was asking for water. And immediately that SS soldier, with the club of his rifle clubbed him down. And several times—to insensitivity—and then I ran away. I was so scared and I was so upset. I never saw anything like this in my life. I simply ran away.

Arnold C.
On the cattle car to Auschwitz

The train moved on. There was another stop. They opened the door, [and] there was a man standing out there. One of the boys of the 131 spoke Polish and he asked him, "Where are they taking us?" Well, he told him they are taking us to Auschwitz. At that time I did not know what Auschwitz was. When we continued, this young boy—the Polish man must have told him something more in Polish, because he said he is not going to go on to Auschwitz and said he was going to jump from the train. They were able to open up a board in the floor, and he jumped out. Another kid followed him, and we could watch through the little window that the first one that got out, we saw him run. He was able to make it across. The other kid who jumped out must have injured himself because we saw he just did not move.

Edith P.

I remember my sister told him, "Father! We have always been a very God-loving people. How come that God has forsaken us?" I remember that very vividly, she in her anguish. My father said, "You know, we have forsaken him before." And I'm so happy about that, that I heard it. Because my father was such a devout religious man that he believed, really, that he left God before God has left him. That he went and died—not in vain, maybe. I don't know.

Edith P.
Born Michalovce, Czechoslovakia, 1920
Recorded 1980, age 60

In Edith P.'s middle-class Jewish family, which had lived in Czechoslovakia for generations, the notion of someone or some power uprooting them was "unthinkable." The Hungarian occupation resulted in anti-Jewish legislation and a dramatic shift in the attitude of their non-Jewish neighbors and friends. After the German occupation in 1944, she and her family were interned in a brick factory outside their town, then two weeks later deported in cattle cars to Auschwitz.

In the train, her father urged them to "keep the principles that you have been taught." She was separated from her parents and taken to Block 23. Accidentally meeting her sister-in-law, she moved to her block—one day before the extermination of Block 23. "People did not invent an expression what Auschwitz was," she says. The constant smell of burning flesh, and even the sun and moon, reminded her of death. She and her sister-in-law were selected for transfer to Salzwedel concentration camp. There she worked as a cook for the SS until she was liberated by U.S. troops.

Mrs. P. married an American physician, and they raised three daughters. She acknowledges the importance of her husband's loyalty and support in helping her live with her memories. She discusses her ambivalent feelings toward Germans and her frustration and sense of impotence when the genocide in Cambodia became known. She acutely feels the loss of her family: Seders are not the same without them. "There is something missing," she says. "It's not easy to live this way."

We were in Auschwitz already—we didn't know where we were. I never heard of Auschwitz. We just saw people just running around like mad, mad people, no hair and clothes with stripes. I said to my father, "You know, maybe we are going to survive. Look, there are people running around. Maybe they are workers." "Look, my family," he said, "I think we have arrived, and there's one thing I want to tell you. Whoever survives, you've got to go and work right away. Sell your knowledge. Go to work. Keep your sanity. And keep the principles that you have been taught." That was his last words I heard.

Father John S.
Košice, Slovakia

It was summertime and it was one of those very, very quiet nights and I couldn't sleep for some reason. I woke up to a sound of many people. My impression was literally thousands of people crying. I didn't know what it was. It was a terrifying impression, and then I realized this is the sound of people or—crying. I remember even reflecting that must be children, women, men—everybody, because it was that kind of a chorus, wailing and crying. And next morning I talked to several other people who were still left in our Jesuit house. They all said that they heard it, and I think it was the custodian, a gardener [or] a janitor, who told me that those were the Jewish people crying, because at our station the Hungarian *gendarmerie* handed them over to the SS troops to be deported to Germany. And sometimes, when this happened, the people would start to cry. And that would spread through the whole train.

Abraham P.
Arrival at Auschwitz/Birkenau

The train screeched, and all of a sudden they came and knocked at the doors and we heard voices, and dogs barking. Then there were people jumping in, and dogs were jumping in with them. And they were screaming and yelling, "*'Raus! 'Raus! 'Raus!*" And you were confused—there was nothing—and one guy who walked in, who must have been a prisoner, he says to me in Yiddish, "*Host du gold? Host du brilyant?*" Do I have gold or do I have diamonds? I looked at this guy. Is he crazy or something? And then I saw people been thrown out of there. And I saw older people, they had to go and jump out of the train. The platform was low and the train was high. And people were beaten. And then, when you walked out of there, we finally got out of the train, out of those boxcars, all of a sudden there was a stench hit you—and you didn't know what that is. And nobody told you what is going to happen. Nobody told you where you were, what was going on. The only thing that you saw, we saw SS and we saw prisoners in striped clothes, and I saw dogs who were sniffling and I saw people being beaten up. And they tell you to stand in line. And then way in the distance you hear music—a band playing! My God, it was such a confusion. I mean, you didn't know what was going on.

Golly D.
Volunteered to follow her husband from
Theresienstadt to Auschwitz

The train stopped in Birkenau near the platform. A few prisoners with a striped uniform came into the train and said, "Leave everything you own on the train. It will be delivered to you later. Out! Out! Line up! Five in a row! Line up! Line up!" Whoever could grabbed a can of sardines or anything, food, and stuff it in their pocket and then go outside and line up. In front of me I saw this high SS—you know, from a distance, this high SS officer with a big German shepherd next to him—and the women had to step in front of him, one by one. I saw a brief exchange of words, and I saw him pointing either to his right or to his left. And when I looked a little later, I saw all the older people, or mothers and children, or sick or handicapped people were sent to his left. Next to me stood a young friend of mine, a young woman I knew from Theresienstadt, very young. She said to me, "Golly,"—she also

Auschwitz. Golly D. recalls, "I saw this high SS . . . officer . . . pointing either to his right or to his left." *Courtesy U.S. Holocaust Memorial Museum*

observed the whole method—she said to me, "Golly, I'm pregnant in my third month. Do you think I should tell him?" I said, "I think you should because looking at those people, the children and the old people, you'll probably get better quarters and better food." I can't forgive myself to this day, but she probably would have told him anyway. But that I encouraged her to do it—meaning so well—and sure enough, she was sent to that side. Later we knew that those people were exterminated immediately. So was my husband, upon his arrival.

Herbert J.
Born Maine, USA, 1921
American soldier

I was in the Eleventh Armored Division, Eleventh Armored Infantry, Fourth Army. The Germans had their tank barriers, and they called it the "dragon's teeth." They had these structures and pillboxes. We had passed that and had continued on. Two half-tracks of soldiers, of which I was a part, were held in an area to hold prisoners while the rest of the outfit continued on. So we had to wait until the foot infantry moved up to relieve us of the prisoners, which was a few days. Then we continued to catch up with our outfit.

On an evening we came into a town and they had the white flags out. And we should have been cautious because there wasn't anybody out on the street, but we figured the town had been taken. We moved on into the town and started getting ready to occupy a building for the night, and the Germans came from everywhere. There was no shot fired. They just—they caught us flat-footed. After a few days, we were transported in different vehicles, and we ended up in Austria. Then we finally got to camp Gusen. We were in camp Gusen for I'd say about two, three days and they moved us to camp Mauthausen. There were all nationalities. A lot of people think it was only the Jewish people alone. But there were political prisoners and captured prisoners such as I was.

> **Renée H.**
> **Placed on train to Auschwitz/Birkenau to join
> her parents. Train is bombed and rerouted.**

We arrived in Bergen-Belsen. It was at night. I remember spending the early part of the night looking out through an opening in the car, which they had opened because they didn't want people screaming. There was some screaming going on because of the tightness of the air—to let in fresh air. I remember seeing houses and just rims of light, because there was blackout and all you could see was the rims of light from some of the windows. So I knew we were in a town and I thought maybe, just by hope-against-hope, that maybe we had been sent back to Bratislava. It turned out not to be Bratislava but it was Hannover, Germany.

A little while later, we arrived in camp, and then there was a long march. The march was the most horrendous thing I have experienced because after eight days the people were just in no shape to walk from the station to the reception house at the camp, and that march seemed endless. It looked enormously long. In my mind now it seems like three hours. The Germans kept shouting and yelling. There were truncheons and dogs, and they would fall on the people. We finally arrived, and we were assigned a block. I remember thinking to myself, "I'm so exhausted. I must sleep." I remember the first night falling asleep. I had nothing to eat for a long, long time, nothing to drink. Because I wasn't in Auschwitz with my parents, and I remember saying to myself, "I will never stop looking for them." I remember thinking life had played a terrible trick on me.

Clara L.
Arrival at Auschwitz/Birkenau from Hungary

The young and able were sent to one side, and the old and young women with children on their arms were sent to the other side. There, also these Polish people, both Jews and non-Jews, helped because they would say to these young women who carried their babies on their arms, "Give it to your mother, give it to your mother-in-law. Don't be a fool! You can save your life." And many, many women did that. They handed their babies to the older women and they went to the working side and they were saved. Their children perished.

Renée H.

The next morning, I woke up and I immediately started inquiries, finding out everything there was to find out. I asked everything about life in camp and people did consider me a pest, and I pushed my way around, meanwhile always holding on to my sister. We got acquainted with some of the older members. All I was interested in [was] wandering all over, just like I had done in town, asking everybody if they knew anybody who came from Bratislava.

Walter S.
Deported from Germany

It was Auschwitz. It was unbelievable how they had organized to separate the people. The hollering went on, the Germans with guns. [We were told] everybody leave everything what you possess inside. You'll get it later on. We got out of the freight cars in no time. I would say, in a few minutes they had separated one thousand people—women on one side, men on the other side. And it's well known, you know. The one side meant death, the other side maybe going to Hitler camp. But we didn't know. We really did not know. They selected three hundred men to be separated, and we were loaded in trucks. What had they done, they looked at the ones which were not too old and not children, but which were strong. We were taken to Auschwitz III, which was Buna. We were building a big chemical complex where they wanted to make synthetic rubber, the I.G. Farben chemical complex.

Right away [we were] herded in a room where all our civil clothes were taken off. We were shaved, all the hair removed, our bodily hair removed. It went so fast, everything, and all the work was done by other prisoners. See, the guards would stand by, but all the dirty work was done by fellow prisoners. We were naked, we took a shower, and then I did get my number tattooed, which is 117022. This was supposed to be my name. I had no name anymore. That was it.

Joseph K.
Deported from Gorlice, Poland

They shaved us of all hair and this is an extremely painful experience, when men used rusty razor blades and nick you, and then they use Lysol on the cut. That's an excruciating pain. It just burns and some people didn't even survive from that.

Women prisoners of Auschwitz. Golly D. describes being ordered to undress, and prisoners forced to shave other prisoners' heads. "The soldier, the SS men stood right next to it, looked us up and down, and giggled and—and made remarks. It was most humiliating."
Courtesy U.S. Holocaust Memorial Museum

Golly D.
Arrival at Auschwitz/Birkenau from Theresienstadt

We were let into a barrack [and] ordered by the SS to undress completely. In front of us were three large, huge barrels—empty barrels. And then we were ordered to throw the clothes into one barrel, the shoes into the next barrel, and the jewelry into the third barrel. So this way they spared themselves the work of having to sort it out. Then we were led into an adjoining room. There I saw several stools lined up. Behind each stool a prisoner, a woman prisoner, who had a razor in her hand and who was shaving every prisoner's head bare, including the underarm hair and the pubic hair. We stood in line now, completely naked. The soldier, the SS men, stood right next to it, looked us up and down, and giggled and—and made remarks. It was most humiliating.

Martin S.
Arrival at Buchenwald

They were taking us to have showers, to clean us up. Nobody wanted to go into the shower. And there were people saying, "These showers are okay. It's okay." Jews were talking to us, and they would say, "I'm telling you. I'm one of you. It's okay." We ultimately went in. You had no choice. And when finally water came out—but again, you thought this was the end of you. It is impossible to describe the thoughts, the feelings.

Bessie K.
Deported from Kovno to concentration camp in Estonia

And they had a speech we should work hard and we should behave so we'll be deserving for the honor for keeping us there, and they'll be good to us. And we are going now, we should undress, they will give us a bath. They took us into the place and the men were given the water. They shaved us, the men shaved us. Somehow—all my life I was very respectful, because at home, everything was to be honored and respected—and I didn't care, somehow. The men were standing there, and the German soldiers were standing and laughing the way, you know, the women are bathing and the way the men are shaving.

Clara L.
Arrival at Auschwitz/Birkenau

We didn't know how we looked, but we saw each other—completely shaved. Completely! And there, stark naked, we were hustled into a shower, given a bath. And as we walked out each of them were thrown one piece of clothing. The one who was lucky got a long dress, so she immediately would tear off a strip from the dress to cover her head. There was a tall girl, she got this very, very short dress. It was so pitiful. But you couldn't feel pity for someone else because you were yourself in that same situation.

Hanna F.
Age 19, deported to Auschwitz/Birkenau posing as a Polish non-Jew

We got to Auschwitz. I knew that I wouldn't be able to survive. I saw what was going on. Hundreds and thousands of people—[*long silence*]—It's hard for me to begin because it's—They stripped us of our belongings. They cut my hair, they shaved my head, and they took away whatever I had, which I had very little, and they put us in a—what you call it? A block, a cell block, like the rest of the prisoners. And it looked very bad, very grim. [My number is] 50069. I still have it. I'm not ashamed of it. They should be ashamed of it.

I befriended a woman on the train coming from Germany to Auschwitz. She was a doctor. There were a few professional people on that particular train. One was an opera singer. One was a doctor. One was a dentist. I got very friendly with that woman doctor. But the day we arrived in Auschwitz, the SS people came in, the soldiers. We were stark naked. We were waiting to have our heads shaved. And he recognized that opera singer—she was a Jewish woman—and he got very hysterical, a smirk on his face. And he made that woman, a middle-age woman, get up, stark naked, and sing.

Arnold C.
Age 11, arrival at Auschwitz/Birkenau

As they got us out of the cattle cars, they lined us up and started marching us. There was an SS guard next to me, and I asked him in German, "Where are we going?" He did not answer me. As we kept marching, I saw the camp and it looked like something, a place out of the unreal, because this was my first time I have seen women with their hair all shaven off. The barbed wires with the electric fences, the German guards with the dogs—everything was very unreal. And the size of it was overwhelming, the size of the camp. They took us through a little area which was a forest, and

"We all snapped to attention."

Arnold C.
Born Kovno, Lithuania, 1933
Recorded 1983, age 50

Arnold C. was eight years old when his family attempted to flee from the German invasion in June 1941. They returned to Kovno when overtaken by the invading forces and were ghettoized. Mr. C. and his family survived a selection and mass killings and were transferred to a labor camp. His father saved him and six others by hiding them in a loft during a roundup of children.

In 1944, he and his family were placed on a transport. His mother and sister were removed from the train in Stutthof. He and his father were separated in Landsberg. Arnold C. was transferred to Dachau, then to Auschwitz/Birkenau. On the train, some boys managed to rip boards from the floor of the cattle car and escape. He did not want to risk the jump and arrived in Auschwitz/Birkenau. Wanting to appear taller and older, he put sand in his shoes hoping to avoid selection for the gas chambers.

In the winter of 1945, he and other prisoners were sent first on foot, then by train to Mauthausen. Allied forces bombed their train en route, killing and wounding many of the prisoners. The guards removed the wounded and executed them. The train arrived in Mauthausen, where there was little food and he saw prisoners driven to cannibalism. After transfer to Gunskirchen, for a minor offense he was chased by a German officer and barely escaped being shot—just one day before U.S. troops arrived and liberated the camp. Mr. C. was reunited with his mother and sister in Italy and lived in Florence before emigrating to the United States. He notes that his group of friends and the observance of Jewish holidays were crucial to his survival in the camps.

then we came in front of a low, flat building. A high-ranking officer, SS man, which I later found out was Mengele, was in front of us. And another German officer asked Mengele, "Are these to be killed?" And he said he wanted to look things over first. It was interesting. We had a very little boy with us—he was only about six years old—a very lively, beautiful little boy who knew how to give commands, military commands, in German. He jumped out in front, and he said to all of us children the command to stand still at attention. So we all snapped to attention. And he gave the command to take off our hats, and we all did it in unison. Apparently Mengele was very impressed with that group. What he had in mind to do with us was hard to say, but he wanted to look us over at a later date, and he says, "No, let them go."

So here we were, in front of the crematorium, and we were marched off into a big place where a transport ahead of us had left all their belongings, and they were gassed. I could see the treasures on the ground: American money, dollars, gold watches. Apparently they were told they would come back and get their clothing and so on. So they left it there in little piles.

Abraham P.
Deported from Romania to Auschwitz/Birkenau

This man came, this tall SS man, and he pointed with a finger. He put the three of us, the three older brothers, together. And my little kid brother, he was with us. And I told my little brother, I said to him, "*Solly, gey tsu tate un mame,*" "Go with my [mother and father]." And like a little kid he followed. He did! Little did I know that—that I sent him to the—to the crematorium. I am—I feel like—I killed him [*crying*]. My brother who lives now in New York—he used to live in South America—every time we would see each other, he talks about that. And he says, "No, I am responsible, because I said that same thing to you!" And it's been bothering me, too. I've been thinking whether he has reached my mother and father. And when he did reach my mother and father,

he probably told them, "*Avraham hot gezogt ikh zol geyn mit aykh.*"
[Abraham said I should go with you.] I wonder what my mother
and father were thinking, especially when they were all—when
they all went into the crematorium. I can't get it out of my head.
It hurts me, it bothers me, and I don't know what to do. I feel
that I am responsible for that. And my brother says to me I'm not
responsible for it, because he is as much responsible as I am but
there isn't very much that—I guess I will have to live with it.

6

"What My Eyes Have Seen"

THE CAMPS

German concentration camps are one of history's ultimate horrors. Most prisoners who survived initial selection for death spent their waning energies struggling simply to stay alive. Threats to life included exhaustion, starvation, disease, beatings, and frequent selections. Some who could not bear the horror committed suicide.

In some cases, family members helped each other, as did friends from the same town, country, or political party. The Germans and their collaborators, who considered the Jews subhuman, killed whom they pleased, when and how they pleased. Camp guards beat, tortured, humiliated, and murdered prisoners—men, women, children, young, and old. Unimaginable brutalities were part of daily life. Under such conditions, distinctions of gender, age, and social and economic class disappeared, and life was reduced to biological imperatives: stealing another crust of bread, staying alive another day.

Prisoners displayed extraordinary resourcefulness in finding ways to maintain their mental equilibrium. Some witnesses feel these efforts were in fact the reason for their survival. Others are equally convinced that any success bred by internal or external gestures was merely accidental. Religion was, for many of those who speak here, irrelevant. Many survivors, believers and nonbelievers, attribute their survival to luck.

Edith P.
Deported to Auschwitz/Birkenau

Auschwitz, if I would like to describe it, I would say there is—there has not—there has not been—people—people did not invent an expression what Auschwitz was. It was hell on earth. And the silence of Auschwitz was hell. The nights were hell. And the days—somehow we—we got up at three o'clock in the morning, and at four o'clock summertime or four-thirty, when the sun came up, it was not like the sun—I swear to you! It was not bright. It was always red to me; it was always black to me. It never said, never, never was life to me. It was destruction! The sun was never beautiful. And when the moon was out, it meant only destruction. We almost forgot what life was all about. And in the evening, when you dared to go out and you saw the flames of the crematorium—that was disastrous! The smell of the human flesh, which we didn't know it was. We were young kids, inexperienced of such horror. Who is experienced in such ways?

Clara L.
Age 18, deported to Auschwitz/Birkenau
from Hungary

The second night I said to my sister, "You know, it's strange," I said. "You remember if Julie"—we had a maid, Julie—"if she broiled liver, you know, there was a very peculiar smell." Why? Because they broiled liver on an open fire and the blood as it dripped down had a very peculiar smell. And I said to my sister, "You know, Rifi, I somehow smell like when Julie used to fry liver." So she said, "I don't know, you probably think of a good dish what we used to have at home." I said, "No, I smell that." And apparently that was the first sign that we knew that there must be some place away that there are bodies burned. Also there would be in the morning, in the distance, I could clearly see it in the distance that there were chimneys. But we always thought these—these belonged to the neighboring cities' manu-facturing plants. We never knew that would happen. Then slowly we found out.

Abraham P.
Age 22, deported to Auschwitz/Birkenau from Romania

We were handed a couple of postcards to write to our parents. Can you imagine that? A couple of postcards. But you didn't get a pencil to write, but somebody did have a pencil. So I said to someone, "Where am I going to write a letter to my parents?" They didn't give you an address where to write. He says, *"Meshuge afn kop!"* [Crazy in the head!] He says, "Are you kid-ding? Your parents are killed already." "I can't believe that." Then he says to me, "You smell that thing over there? It's probably them." Can you imagine that? Give you a couple of postcards.

Edith P.

Everything went fast. They did not give you a chance to think or to contemplate where you are going, what you are going to do. They brought us there to destroy our bodies and soul. We did not work. We stood in line for six hours—six hours daily. Three hours in the morning and three hours in the afternoon. It's very difficult to stand when you are a healthy person, but when you are hungry and you haven't eaten for two, three days, it's very difficult. And many times we didn't stand. We just fell.

Clara L.

I remember the first night was a crying from every side, an awful lot of crying and whining and pleading with God and cursing God and all kinds of things. And it was a terrible adjustment. Then we were told that every morning we would be awakened at sometimes two o'clock, sometimes three o'clock.

Hanna F.
Age 19, deported to Auschwitz/Birkenau from Germany posing as a Polish non-Jew

You used to get up in the morning, roll call in the morning. I realize that people do go to work, and I figured if I go to work [it] will help because the others [were] sitting around and waiting for destruction. They were taking us out to fieldwork, digging ditches. We marched to music every morning. There's an orchestra sitting in there when we were walking out from *B Lager*, B Camp. We passed the A Camp, and were going outside behind the gates. [The orchestra was] sitting on the left side, not far from the shower room where you came, you know, and you undressed, and you left your clothes there, and so supposedly they gave you a shower. I cannot go into all the details that you want. Some of them are very gruesome and I don't—I really cannot go back so far. It hurts. You had to walk to the, you know, right left right left. And if you didn't, you were hit. You were clobbered.

There were fields. And when I got there, that was the time of harvesting. There was cutting, the beets, raking hay. Some of them had to carry the stones. Make a pile of stones over here. When you got finished with the pile of stones over here, you had to take it from here and put it over there. And that took up a whole day. Sometimes we did get the soup, and sometimes we didn't.

Clara L.

We have to line up outside and wait until the German officer comes to count us. Of course we were told we should not even think of getting out of there, because there were wire fences and the wire fences are charged with high voltage.

Hanna F.

There was a trench, and over the trench there was the electric, you know, the wires were electrified. The electric fence that separated us from the world. Anyway, some of the women didn't know. Maybe they didn't know any better. They were jumping over the water and they went to dry their clothes over the trenches, and they were electrocuted. They were just hanging on the wires. There must have been about six, seven women glued to the wires, to the electric wires. That was a warning for the others, they shouldn't go closer.

> **Chaim E.**
> **Former Polish prisoner of war**
> **deported to Sobibór in 1942**

Now, Sobibór was not a working camp. There were two kinds of camps. There were working camps and camps what was strictly just gassing. Sobibór was one of those camps where the transports came and immediately to the gas chamber. The camp was somewhere in the woods that was between Chełm and Włodawa. In the woods was a small station, a village Sobibór. And next to the railroads, in the woods, they built a big compound round with barbed wires and woven with pine tree branches. And the trains with the people were driven behind the fences. The fences were so that from the outside you couldn't see what happened inside. They took us in this train and unloaded us and they lined us up, and they picked out from the whole group eighteen people. And I happened to be one of the eighteen. Now, what that meant really I didn't know. They needed people to do the work in the camp, just to make it going. Random picking—skills was not the point. So we were taken away, eighteen were taken away to one side. And they took us to the quarters where the people worked already there. The others went away. I didn't see any more.

My job was to go separate clothes from the people what were with our transport what they went to the gas chambers. They brought the clothes back, and we had to separate those things. [That's] how I found out. When I came to work and I start to separate the clothes what they brought in, I found the clothes from my brother, his pictures and everything he had with him.

**"I found the clothes
from my brother."**

Chaim E.
Born Brudzew, Poland, 1916
Recorded 1986, age 69

When Chaim E. was five, he and his family moved to Łódź. Later he served in the Polish army, was captured by the Germans in 1939, and was sent back to Poland eighteen months later. In 1942 he and his brother were deported to the Sobibór death camp. He was one of the very few selected to work. Mr. E. quickly learned that almost all Jews sent to Sobibór were immediately gassed and their bodies burned. He was assigned to sort the clothing of those who were sent to the gas chamber, and found his brother's clothes.

While aware that ten prisoners would be executed for every one of them who escaped, Mr. E. explained, "You try to save your life. I don't think anybody in a situation like that will think differently. It's hard to judge somebody, what he would have done. You really have to be in the same position." An army captain who arrived in a transport of Soviet prisoners helped organize an uprising in 1943. Mr. E. killed a German guard, others cut telephone wires, and with his future wife they ran for the gate and escaped. Using gold and diamonds he had found hidden in the clothing he sorted, Mr. E. was able to buy food and bribe peasants to keep them alive during months of hiding.

After being liberated by the Soviets, Mr. and Mrs. E. returned to Poland. They could not bear the antisemitism they found there and traveled on to Holland, his wife's home. They presently live in the United States, where they frequently speak to classes about their experiences. They have a son and a daughter.

Bessie K.
Age 18, deported to Stutthof from concentration camp in Estonia

Stutthof. This was very bad. In Stutthof, I found the doctor who operated on me in the ghetto. When she saw me there, she was so happy to see me. Right away she said, "Where's the baby? What happened to the baby?" And right there, I said, "What baby?" I said to the doctor, "What baby? I didn't have a baby. I don't know of any baby." That's what it did to me [*pointing to her head in a gesture indicating she's crazy*]. Now she said to me, "You're young. Try to survive." She said, "I can't make it here." At that time I didn't know what she was going to do to herself. She must have taken poison, and she died, right in front of my eyes. So again, it was taken away from me. Everything was being taken away from me. Everything. Nothing belonged to me. And I was alone.

Now from Stutthof. This was a terrible place, terrible place. This is the only place I felt, I looked up to God and I said, "If only I could be a bird to fly out from here." This is the only place I wanted to fly out. If only I could fly—my God, I wanted to fly! And people looked for one another, and people found one another. And I didn't find nobody. So again I was alone.

Martin S.
Age 8, deported to Skarżysko-Kamienna concentration camp

You saw beating and shooting. Immediately you began realizing, "Uh-oh, I have to watch myself." I don't remember, from that moment that I got into camp, that I ever had any other thought than survival. My father, my brother, and I were taken in one direction. My mother was immediately put into another camp. I was particularly attached to my mother, so it was devastating I would say. But interestingly enough, as I said to you, there was a sudden instinct of survival, that quite frankly, I didn't dwell on it. I can tell you honestly, I attribute my survival to this instinct. Because I saw children just falling by the wayside. People dying. As a matter of fact, I trained myself to be very brutal, very cold. And—and often-times I—I . . . sometimes think I was made too inhuman. Because I didn't care about anybody else. How old was I then? Eight years, eight and a half years old? That was a quick, quick lesson.

Herbert J.
Age 23, American POW, Mauthausen

The main thing in the camps was the definite intent to dehuman-ize all the people that were there, to make them feel that they were of no value. This was a definite effort on their part, to take away any semblance of humanness and respect and whatever you might call dignity, to take all that away.

The Jews were marked. They were all tattooed and there was no doubting what they were. Even their clothing, their clothing was marked, you see, and we were told, when we were picking clothes up to cover ourselves with, not to take any clothing off the bodies of any of the Jews because they were marked "*Juden.*" You'd get the abuse. Definitely they were intent on just extermi-nating them.

Golly D.
Auschwitz/Birkenau

Selections were conducted, sometimes outside the barrack, some-times inside the barrack. This selections cannot be compared with the ones at the platform, because at the platform we did not know what the selections were for, while now we knew exactly selection meant certain death. We saw the smoke from the chimneys. It spread around like a wildfire that people were gassed and burned. We knew it all. So if you would stand in line, and then the SS man comes, and all he had to do is point his finger at you and say, "You! And you! And you! And you!"—there was no turning back. You had to go, and you knew you had to go to your death.

Hanna F.
Auschwitz

I took sick. I contracted malaria, and within a few days sick in the barrack they took me to the hospital, so-called. I was very sick with malaria and I thought the end is coming, because every day they were coming in and they made selections, you know. And the first selection I went through I didn't even realize that it was a selection because they put us outside, so I figured they put us out for some fresh air. Dr. Mengele came over with two other guys, two other SS people, and he was pointing: "This one, that one, the other one, the third one, the fourth one." They gathered their numbers. They were put on another block and they went to destruction the following day. But I didn't know what was going on. I was new.

Arnold C.
Age 11, Auschwitz/Birkenau

Then the selections began. Instinct told me that the bigger I look the better the chance I have of surviving, by putting sand in my shoes. And from that day on I always put sand in my shoes. It gave me an extra inch. I was told that if you don't urinate frequently, you may look more adult in a selection. I tried to hold it as long as I could.

I remember a selection when again Mengele—and at that time I knew who Mengele was—he took us all out—131—it was 129, 2 of them jumped the train—he lined us up and made a selection. Being summer, I used to take off my shirt, being on the outside. I wanted to save it. And I developed a beautiful suntan. So he stops in front of me, this Mengele, and he says, "Oh, beautiful suntan." He says, "Turn around." I turned around so he could watch my back. He says, "Turn around again. Okay, and drop your pants." I dropped my pants. He says, "How old are you?" I say, "I'm fourteen." He says, "You're a liar!" and he slapped me. I said, "No, I'm not a liar. I'm telling the truth. I'm fourteen." He looked

Arnold C., age 12,
Italy, 1945.

at me again and my suntan, and again I don't know what he had
in mind. He took the next kid out, and he pulled the next one
out, a very good friend of mine. I should mention their names.
They were two brothers, Arele and Menele Kaplan. We went to
kindergarten together. And at that time, we already had tattoos on
our hands. Whoever was pulled out, their tattoo was written
down. I think it was the following morning, they came with a list
of all the tattoos which they had written down and they pulled
them all out. They were all called out, and they knew where they
were going. There was one boy, he was probably around fifteen.
And as he was told to line up in the group that was selected, he
yelled at the SS officers. His name was Chaim Auka. He should
be remembered. He said, "Jewish blood is not water! You'll get
yours one day!" And they were taken away. They were gassed the
same night. I could see the crematoriums burning. You could
smell it.

Werner R.
Transferred from Theresienstadt to
Auschwitz/Birkenau

There was something like five thousand people in those barracks,
in D Camp. And then they decided that they want to exterminate
the entire camp. So they lined us up. We had to strip, and they

lined us up in a long line. There was Dr. Mengele himself and one other officer, and they were standing there at the end of the table. You marched by, and they used to nod their head in one direction or the other direction. Depending which line you went to, you were alive or dead. You didn't know which one was which. I went through that thing three times in one day. At the end of the day, out of the five thousand people, they chose ninety-eight of us to go to another camp. They needed work done. They were short of people so they chose ninety-eight, and I was amongst these ninety-eight. So we went into that group. The rest of the people were all killed. They all ended up in the gas chamber.

Golly D.

There was not one of us who was not infested by lice. And the lice sort of sucked the last bit of blood and strength out of you. There was no protection against it. One or two of the prisoners still had a little piece of comb that went from woman to woman. So we would take our kerchief and put it on our lap and comb through the hair which had maybe grown this much by then [*shows less than one inch*]. And the lice were raining down like snow, like—like black snow came down.

Hanna F.

In my bunk bed there was a woman. I couldn't communicate with her, but I know that she was from Malta. When she took sick, when she got extremely cold, she took the blanket. I covered her till, you know, the shakes were going away, subsided. And when I took sick, she used to take the blanket and cover me. We had a blanket. A particular Sunday night, she was already sick, and she was covered. She was out of her wits. After the cold, the shakes subside and the heat gets to your head. It's just unbelievable, the 104, 105—you're completely out of your mind. I woke up at night, and I was very cold. When I touched her, she was dead.

Anyway, I felt very sorry for a minute, but I took the whole blanket and I covered myself. I had the whole blanket for myself till about six o'clock in the morning.

Chaim E.

To Sobibór came normally about twice a week the transports from different places. We really didn't see this kind of like in Auschwitz and other, with people starving on the street and things like that. It was a different kind. This was mass murder. The people went really direct to the gas chamber. They separated the men of the women and children. So the men were directly through. Before the gas chamber, they would cut the hair of the women, the long hair what they collected to send back. I had this experience once, too. We were picked out at night, when a transport came. They gave us scissors and we had to go there and cut these women. They were already undressed, naked, ashamed—the people younger, older people.

It's so hard to imagine that things like that can happen. You know, sometimes we ourselves, you were thinking for a minute, "Is it really true that really things like that happened?" You were like in a dream, really. You have to force your[self] to believe what you see. Sometimes I couldn't believe, "Is it true?" But I wake myself, I shake my head. I wake myself and I say, "It happened. It happened."

Martin S.
Skarżysko-Kamienna concentration camp

It was within a matter of months that my father became ill. Very high fever. That was one of the signs. You just touch someone and they are literally burning up. And he could not go to work. Generally the word is you've got to go to work, because if they find you in there—they had a sport. If someone became sick and they took him out and he said, "I'm all right. Just, I want to rest one day," they'd say, "Well, okay. See if you can run a straight line." And what they did—they told them to run in a straight line, but they were firing bullets on either side of that line. So that if they couldn't hold the line—and that's what happened to my father.

```
Perla K.
Born Corfu, Greece, 1928
Age 15, deported to Auschwitz/Birkenau
```

One morning on the way to work I saw my two brothers working, from far away. One of my brother[s], the younger one, he—he wave to me. And he has bread in his hand and he want to give to me. But the SS saw him, and he went near him. First he sent a dog. He grabbed him and he went near him. And he beat him so bad, he beat to death—after I find out he die. After the SS sent the dog to me. And he grabbed me and I fell to the ground, you know, and he started scratching me. When he finish, I get up. And everybody, all the girls are afraid to, you know, to go near me, to help me. I get up and I start to walk again. To go to work.

```
Herbert J.
American POW in Mauthausen
```

Political prisoners were not subjected entirely to the same rough treatment that the Jews were. You see, anybody else could have an excuse and maybe get away with something. But the Jews had no excuse. They were Jews and they were just nothing. I mean, this is the thing they tried to get across to them, and it's hard to make people realize.

There were some guards who treated everybody humanly when they were away from the center of operations, where they were off by themselves and all they had to do was watch out for the men and see that they did their work. But when an officer would come around, anybody with any rank, they would go into a big tirade and kick the nearest guy to them and yell and scream and hit them with a stick, to put on a big show. When the officer went away, they'd go sit down on a rock and just let the men alone.

The same way, in the quarry, there was a place where the water seeped out of the rock. And if you were thirsty, you could go there and suck up a little water. You weren't allowed to do that, but if there wasn't anybody around, the guard wouldn't say nothing. You could go get yourself some water. But if there was anybody around, you wouldn't dare go near it. You'd get shot.

When we were going from the camp to the quarry, the [local] children were encouraged to hit us with sticks and whatnot. The children were every age from five and six years old on up to teenagers, even bigger. They'd hit you with sticks. Some of them had barrel staves. This is what this girl had. She had a barrel stave. She come and she hit me with it, and I was stubborn and I wouldn't fall down right off easy. And she hit me a couple of times, and finally I went down. I couldn't help it—weakened condition and all—and she bent over me, and she's calling me names and whatnot, and she says quietly, "Here! Here!" And so I reach up defensively and she's poking something at me. It was soft, and I put it inside my shirt. *Brotenspeck*—broiled pork fat between German bread. Every day after that she was there and she'd do the same thing—only it didn't take as many whacks with that barrel stave to get me to fall down. I'd fall down a lot easier! I got every day two sandwiches, and I get out to the quarry and I get off in a corner someplace, and I'd get it out of my shirt and eat it. And she never got caught. It would have cost her her life.

> **Abraham P.**
> **Transferred from Auschwitz/Birkenau to Buchenwald, Zeitz, and Schlieben concentration camps**

Every day you must have heard it, about at least five or ten—twenty—who knows how many times, anything that you did, *"Los! Mach schnell! Mach los!"* It was like a pain. It used to get you so mad. I was afraid I'm going to react to it one day, and I'm going to get killed.

Schlieben was the pits. What I used to do was, I used to take the sulfur from a bucket and I used to put it into the missile. And we each one of us had a quota of doing it. And if you didn't do it, you were beaten. And that's when that *"Los! 'Raus! Mach los! 'Raus! Mach los!"* used to be every second, every minute. They were driving you out of your mind. And to top it all off, that foreman, come lunchtime, he used to come in and have a sandwich, a thick sandwich in his hand, with all kinds of wurst, kielbasa and you used to smell—it generates, and it made you—you were hungry anyhow. And he used to eat it [in] front of you. And after he got through with it, he threw it down on the floor so that we could all go and try and grab a crumb out of it.

Martin S.

I remember the hunger, that wrenching, twisting pain that lived with you on a daily basis. All you could ever think of is to get something to eat. You could never fill your belly. It used to be uppermost in your mind. You used to dream of a feast. Just one day, you kept hoping you could go through the day without this twisting pain that you constantly felt. That is an indescribable feeling.

Abraham P.

I sometimes—I wonder how we survived it, with that little bit of food. And then it came, and they used to give us that bread, finally, to eat. They used to give it to us and we had to slice that bread. God forbid if you slice it just a hundredth of an inch in the wrong direction: "What right do you have to do that!" We used to fight. And then you were trying very, very hard to eat it slowly, eat that bread slowly. You know, try to—I wonder if was to enjoy every bite of it or pay attention to every bite of it. As I say it to you right now, I remember sitting there, you know, like in a corner by myself. I don't want anybody to disturb me when I eat it.

Hanna F.

We used to come back after a day's work. Sometimes there was something to eat and sometimes there wasn't. One night I was so hungry, I couldn't sleep. It was a very bad night. They were bringing in people for destruction from two particular parts of the country, from Będzin and Sosnowiec. And the screaming and the hollering was going on, and all three [*sic*] chimneys were lit up. It was like broad daylight. I couldn't sleep. My—[how] would you call it? She was sleeping next to me—my roommate? We were five on a bunk. She saved a tiny, tiny slice of bread and a piece of margarine for breakfast. See, I was still new, because she was already there for some times and that was only two weeks when I got there. That particular night, I stole that piece of bread from her. I never admit it. And she got up in the morning and she was swearing like a truck driver. And I just closed my ears, not to listen to the swearing that she did. And still in all, together we went to work in the morning, and the whole day she didn't forget she lost that piece of bread. I never admitted that I took it. I was very hurt, I was very sore, and I was very sorry because I was hungry and she was hungry. But somehow, once we were outside, there was some, sometimes you picked up a leaf from a beet or you picked up something—there was something always to put in your mouth. But that was no solution. You got diarrhea and you would [be] dying anyway. Once you got diarrhea, that was the end. So this wasn't good and that wasn't good. So, what choice did we have?

Helen K.
Age 19, deported to Majdanek after the fall of the Warsaw ghetto

They put me in a block with five hundred other women. Somebody told me my mother's there. My mother was taken a few days before, as I told you. So I went to see her. You know, my mother was there. So it's like I lost her twice, really. But she was very,

"So this wasn't good
and that wasn't good.
So, what choice did
we have?"

Hanna F.
Born Czemierniki, Poland, 1923
Recorded 1980, age 57. Died 1994

Hanna F. grew up in a mixed neighborhood. In 1942, she and her family were deported to the town of Parczew, where they hid during the roundups of Jews. They were separated and Mrs. F. was captured. She later escaped from a slave labor camp. With false papers that identified her as a non-Jewish Pole, Mrs. F. was able to join a Polish labor transport to Germany. Six months later, betrayed by a fellow worker, she and other Jews were imprisoned by the Gestapo and then deported to Auschwitz, where she saw "a mountain of people" (she does not call them corpses) and chimneys that lit up the night sky like daytime. Mrs. F. "stole" her bunkmate's crust of bread and, when another prisoner was distracted, "traded" her wooden clogs for the other's good pair of shoes.

Mrs. F. credits her survival to consistently denying she was Jewish and to a succession of slipups in the German bureaucracy. In Auschwitz, she lived in a block for non-Jewish Polish prisoners and later in a hospital barrack. She was transferred to Majdanek, Płaszów, back to Auschwitz, then to Germany, still posing as a Pole. In Czechoslovakia she escaped from a transport two weeks before liberation. After liberation she felt, "I am all alone in the world—lost, without words." Eventually, she reassumed her Jewish name and identity.

Mrs. F.'s testimony includes unusually frank depictions of the dehumanizing conditions that she experienced and of the behavior to which she and other prisoners were driven. She was the sole survivor from her family.

very lost. She was lost. She was very passive. She was very lost.
And, you know, they gave you one portion of bread and one por-
tion of soup for the day, and I—my mother became very skinny.
And she was very thin and she was very, you know, lost there. So
I used to bring her my soup to her, and I just cut off a little piece
of bread. And I said to her, "You know, somebody gave it to me.
Eat it." And I use to give it to her and run out, because if she
would say to me, "Eat a little bit," I would eat. I was very hungry.
But I felt that she needs it more than—you know—I was younger.
So I used to give her the soup and run out because I didn't want
to be tempted that I should eat with her. And she was in the camp
with me for maybe six weeks.

Every few weeks they have selections. One day I walked out
with her and she went one way and I went the other way. I had
a friend, childhood friends for many, many years. She didn't let
me. She pulled me back. I said, "How can I let her go?" And
she said, "Helen, you're not going to help her. You know where
she is going." And I stayed. Then we—I went to Auschwitz.
They sent us to Auschwitz and I was the only one left from the
family.

Arnold C.
Age 11, Auschwitz/Birkenau

The life in camp was, you know, you waited for the soup. And
you learned to finagle, to move. You get in line once, and if you're
lucky you eat it real quick and you make a quick turn and stand
in line again. Many times I was able to do it until I was finally
caught by one of the assistants. He was a Russian prisoner of war,
Ukrainian, and not very sympathetic to the Jews. He says, "I've
seen you before. You look familiar. Didn't I give you the soup
before?" I said, "No, no." "Let me look at your plate." My plate
was still wet. Well, he smacked me so hard I flew back to the end
of the line. I was lucky.

Edith P.
Transferred from Auschwitz/Birkenau
to Salzwedel concentration camp

A German officer came in and said, "Who can cook?" They put me to the kitchen. That was very nice, because there was food there and I cooked for—I think it was sixty SS men and women. Every morning at three-thirty they woke me up. At four o'clock I was in the kitchen already—had to make coffee, breakfast. I started to gain weight. I was up to maybe eighty-five pounds in Auschwitz. Of course, I had more to eat here and I gained—who knows—twenty pounds. I became myself again.

I remembered home. I remembered my father, my mother, my family, and I want to conduct myself so that they are proud of me. And I became very religious, in the sense that I communicated with God. Every morning at 3:30 when I came into this kitchen, I had ten minutes talk with God—not from fear. I never talked to Him as a second-class citizen. I demanded it. I demanded what He has done to His people. And I demanded to be liberated, 'cause I want to live. I wanted it so badly.

Hanna F.

I had a dress and I had a jacket to go with it—I don't know how—and I got a pair of wooden shoes. That particular day they decided to delouse us. Hundreds of thousands of women. It was a hot day, we were standing in the sun, stark naked. I said to myself, "If I want to go back to work tomorrow, and if I haven't got a pair of shoes, I cannot go to work. And if I'm going to sit here, I will not survive." A woman was very busy delousing her clothes. She was so busy. She had a pair of shoes standing next to her. I was very brave. I stepped out of my wooden shoes, and I stepped into her shoes, and I walked away. I just exchanged the shoes. Well, those shoes kept me going till I took sick. Steal the shoes? No, I exchanged the shoes. I said, "Well, she's not going to work and she has the wooden ones." I was trying to clear my conscience. I didn't walk away with the shoes completely—she had a pair of shoes.

Arnold C.

Besides selections, the German guards or Mengele and his helpers used to select young boys for experiments. At one time, they said, "All the young boys are allowed to have a glass of milk." I presume it was their reason to see who were the youngest ones. Well, I wasn't going to have any of their milk, even though I was one of the youngest. And all the ones who had the milk were kept in a separate place then, separate bunk beds. I was standing outside of the barracks, and I saw Mengele coming. When I saw him coming, I knew something is going to happen. I ran into the barrack, and there was no place where to hide in the barrack. We had three bunks. The lowest bunk was probably about eight inches off the floor, cement floor. I managed to squeeze myself in underneath that bunk. Mengele came into the barrack. He walked back and forth with his other Nazis, and I could see their boots passing by, and he took out a bunch of kids. It was a cold day and the cement was extremely cold, and from fear and the cement I was shaking so hard. When they left, I got out. And I was lucky—I survived that selection.

Clara L.
Age 19, Auschwitz/Birkenau

There were very, very sad things. There were in the next barrack a young woman who was pregnant, and they tried to hide it because pregnant women were immediately taken to the gas chambers. One morning she gave birth there. Of course the child was killed right away. And she was saved. But as she said, "I will never be the same person again."

Helen K.
Transferred from Majdanek to Auschwitz/Birkenau

[We] were extremely supportive. I remember when I was in
Auschwitz, and at the block where I was there was a girl who had
a baby. She was so skinny, you didn't even know, you didn't even
notice. And the baby died a few days later which was—the baby
couldn't possibly live on that nutrition, what she had. But she
delivered the baby. In the middle of the night she had pain, and
there were women who, some of the women were nurses. The
baby was delivered. I'm telling you—with a knife we cut off the
umbilical cord. We didn't have a drop of alcohol. We didn't have
nothing. The mother lived. It's very hard to explain it to you. We
just did it. What we had to do, we did. Our aim was to defy
Hitler, to do everything we can to live. Because when you live—he
wants us to die, and we didn't want to. We didn't want to oblige
him. This was our way of fighting back.

Perla K.

In Auschwitz they used to take all the girls, the pregnant girls, to
the Block Ten. There was the block for the experiment. And they,
they used to do in the womb three injections in the womb, and to
put in X rays to sterile the girls. And the twin children, too. I
don't know what they did there, but nobody survived from there
[*sic*]. The girl[s], they came back, but they came back very sick.
Because after that the girls was bleeding and with terrible pain.

Clara L.

They came one day, some German officers, and they said they
need for experiment well-bodied and healthy girls. And they would
get in exchange for cooperation a loaf of bread every day. Who
could resist it? Of course, the older ones said, "Don't do it. There
must be something behind it. They don't give you a loaf of bread
for nothing." What happened is they made various experiments on

Clara L.
Born Kisvárda, Hungary, 1925
Recorded 1993, age 68

The youngest of three children, Clara L. fondly recalls Sabbath observance in her home. Her older sister emigrated to England, and her older brother was conscripted into a Hungarian forced labor battalion. She never saw him again. Mrs. L. accompanied her father when he traveled to Budapest for medical treatment.

After the German occupation of Hungary in 1944, they returned to Kisvárda, where they were forced to move into a ghetto, then deported to Auschwitz. On the train, she witnessed another family's suicide and was shocked by her mother's advice that she "do anything" to survive. Their separation on arrival at Auschwitz was the last time she saw her parents. She remained with her younger adopted sister.

Mrs. L. recalls a young woman in the barrack who gave birth to a baby and the selection of women for medical experiments. She later exchanged four days' worth of bread for a psalm book that she credits with having strengthened her resolve to survive.

She was assigned to a slave labor commando digging trenches in Silesia, and in January 1945 was sent with her younger sister on the death march from Auschwitz. They stole pigs' food to survive, and when her sister collapsed and could not go on, Mrs. L. carried her so she would not be shot. They arrived in Bergen-Belsen, from which they were liberated by British troops. After her sister's death, Mrs. L. left for England to join her older sister and in 1948 emigrated to Canada. Her experiences persist in nightmares and suddenly recurring memories. She expresses the hope that perhaps now, fifty years later, she will be able to discuss those experiences with her daughter.

them. You must have heard. Some of them, for example, they looked for girls with beautiful eyes, and we couldn't understand why. Apparently they were experimenting [to see] why women with beautiful eyes had very healthy eyes. Those who came back from this experiments, they said they just butchered them. They would cut their spine and take out fluid, and—and gynecological experiments. And what happened to these girls, in a very short time shriveled away and they were taken out. Within a couple of weeks.

Renée H.
Age 11, Bergen-Belsen

My sister was being watched by the camp doctor. He would come by the children's barracks all the time, come to my sister, pinch her cheeks, pull her ears, and try to be very friendly with her. And then one day he said to me that he would be able to give us oranges and chocolate if I allowed my sister to go into the hospital for a few days. And my sister was perfectly well, so I couldn't understand why he wanted her in the hospital and I was just very sassy. And I said, "No you are not, because if you are I am going to kick you." And I went up and sort of said, "I'm serious! I'm

Renée H. (left), age 13, with her younger sister in Sweden.

really going to. I mean it!" And so he laughed and then forgot about it. Later on the *Blockälteste* [German-appointed prisoner in charge of barrack] told me that he [the camp doctor] had hoped to be able to use my sister for scientific research. At that time I had no idea what it meant, but later on I realized that he was very interested in the fact of her deafness.

Helen K.

In Majdanek, one of my husband's sisters was with me. She was such a strong girl, a beautiful young woman, maybe twenty-five, twenty-six. We slept on the same bunk, and she developed diarrhea. She was very, very cold, and she only wanted me to lay next to her to warm her body. She had—I don't know what you call it—dysentery or something. It was just awful. I had to lie next to her because she was dying. And she said, "Helen, please stay next to me. You know, warm me." And—and she was the last one. She went, too. She [lay] in my arms, just like my brother did. The smell was so awful I was dying, but she was so scared. She was—that's all. She was crying, and I should stay with her. So I did. I stayed till—till she became cold and stiff in my arms. She was just the most beautiful girl you could ever imagine.

Renée H.

It was the beginning of the typhus epidemic. One thing I did receive from the woman in Sered' was a small bag of tea which I was able, during the time of the typhus epidemic, to exchange for a vaccine for my sister. I was told it was a typhus vaccine. Whether it was one or not, I'm not sure, but the fact is my sister never did get the typhus. I did.

Abraham P.

You got accustomed to the stench. You saw people, you saw fires. You saw carts, two-wheelers, and then you saw some carrying corpses. And it becomes a natural thing to you. You know, you didn't see them anymore. How one can adapt himself to a situation like that so fast, I couldn't believe it. I couldn't believe how selfish you could become.

Martin S.
Skarżysko-Kamienna concentration camp

My brother and my mother were painting. That was their job in a different area, painting walls, painting the German barracks and so on. They did something. I don't know what it was. They didn't get up for the—in time for work, or they took too long a break, whatever it was. So my mother and my brother—remember, that was the whole world to me then, I had nothing, nobody else—my mother and my brother and about twelve, fourteen other people were being taken into the woods—that was common—to be shot. When they were putting them together, someone came running to me and told me that they're being taken to be shot. I ran over to this guy who I thought was my best pull, and I began pleading and begging him, "The only thing I've got left in this world is my mother and my brother. Please! Help save them!" All I remember is asking him, begging. Oh, I remember begging. Next thing I saw, they were already shooting two or three people and I saw my brother and my mother. And I guess as they started shooting—see, what they would do is one at a time—that's what I meant about the brutality. He yelled out a command, *"Halt!"* Halt. And they stopped. And he said to me, "Which ones are yours?" And I pointed to them. He just pulled them out of the line. I just went back to work, they went back to work. That was it. Do you see this matter-of-factness?

Edith P.

I had terrible dysentery. After a few months, naturally, I maybe weighed eighty, ninety pounds. Food was terrible, and I had to go to the bathroom. There was still some humanity in me. I was embarrassed in the block. So I said [to myself] I will go to the latrine—who cares? But there was a *Blocksperre* [barrack lockdown], as they said. The camp was closed. It was like a curfew because two prisoners were missing. Who knows? Maybe they committed suicide. We don't know. So I went. I figured I'll take that chance. And when I came out, a German—a very famous one, and I am not proud of it—Irma Grese—confronted me. She was the devil, the bestial devil of Auschwitz. She was beautiful. Absolutely beautiful blond woman. Impeccably dressed, with high shiny boots. And she confronted me and she says, "You know there is a curfew. What are you doing here?" I said, "I'm sorry. I have dysentery. I just had to go. I have terrible cramps." She says, "Turn around." And I did And she hit me about ten times on my back with a whip. And she said, "Now you go back." I didn't cry. I did not cry! The humiliation pained me terribly. Not the physical—one can survive physical pain. But how does one survive emotional pain?

Martin S.

I don't think there was ever a week that went by when you didn't feel "This may be it." It was one of those situations that you always kept looking over your shoulder. You always had to think ten steps ahead. You always had to plan, "What if? What if?"

Werner R.

I did something awfully stupid that day, when I think back on it. Somebody gave me a cigarette to smoke and I don't know where they got that cigarette, because the stupid part was this: if anybody caught you smoking a cigarette you got shot. This used to be a standard joke by the Germans. The German officers used to walk down the camp, smoke a cigarette, and drop it. Then someone, you know, used to pick it up. They turn around, pull out the gun, and shoot him.

Walter S.

They had some funny things in their mind. They would take one prisoner, just by chance, and take his hat and throw it away. Now, you had to have a cap on. The man would step out of the line to retrieve his cap. That was the end of the man. The man was shot. Now this was just—for them it was—it was a game.

We did work twelve hours a day, seven days a week. When you were in a concentration camp, I think the most critical time of your life at that time was the first six weeks. I would say in the first six weeks, I would guess that 60 to 70 percent of the people died, of the newcomers. The chances were so slim that you could survive the first six weeks. It's hard to tell. You could be the strongest person, it didn't make no difference.

Helen K.

If you survived in Auschwitz or in Majdanek the first few weeks, somehow, it was easier. Most of the people who died, died the first few weeks. I remember, you know, being there a year and a half, the transports used to come from Holland, from Hungary. Beautiful, big women, strong and husky—they went like flies. Like flies! They could not. The shock of this, you know, affluent society, and then to come into this concentration camp, with the dirt, the—the lice, the—the food, and no facilities—they just couldn't survive it. They were dying like I have never seen anything like it.

Chaim E.
Sobibór

Life in camp was really, for the people I'm talking about what worked there, at times was the routine work. You know, you went to your work and things like that. You separated clothes, whatever you had to do. But many times—many, many time[s], it didn't go routine. If something just not happened the right way, you immediately felt it. Like, for example, was a group of ten Jews. They worked outside the camp, and they went with two guards, two Ukrainian guards with them every day. Now, one day they killed this guards and they ran away. So the Germans later caught some of these people, and they brought them back. And they got—they went to *Lager drei* [Camp Three]. The camp was divided in three sections. *Lager* one, that was where the Germans, Ukrainians lived. *Lager* two was where we lived and worked, and *Lager* three was a section separated from us where the people got gassed and burned. If it is mentioned the word that you go to *Lager drei*, that meant you're dead. So these people went to *Lager drei*, *Lager* three. All these people what worked had to line up, and they picked every tenth one of the line. I happened to be number nine. All these people they picked out went with them to *drei Lager*, *Lager* three. Things like that happened very often.

Every individual acts differently, I guess. Maybe the people, I don't know what they were thinking, but I assume everybody wants to save his head. He didn't think that maybe they would pick every tenth if he ran away. You try to save your life. It turned up to be somebody got punished for it. But I don't think anybody in a situation like that will think differently. It is really hard to judge somebody to being in a situation like that, what he would have done. I would resent that, if somebody would say, "I would have done it differently." Really not. Because you really have to be in the same position, have the same feelings.

In *Lager* three, about fifty, sixty Jews worked there. They did the dirty work there. The gassed bodies, they threw on the fire, and all that kind of chores. They were guarded all the time. They came sometimes over to our *Lager* to bring the clothes or bring things like that, but they always [were with a] guard. We were never allowed [to] talk with them. No any contact because of the simple reason, the Germans still believed that we in *Lager* two don't know what is going on. If you went near the *Lager* three, then they caught you, you never came back.

I remember a transport came and it was just all naked people.

A whole train full, loaded with naked people. And we had to unload it. There was mostly dead, half-dead, very few could walk. And already the half-dead and dead ones, they piled them on this lorries, like the coal-mine lorries. And they piled in the people half-live and live and everything. I still see in front of me an older lady, very gentle face, and I think to myself, "Don't throw her on the pile of dead bodies!" And that went straight to the ovens.

Martin S.

The inhumanity! There was a period of time that I walked around, I would say that was the first year, I just kept asking, "Why?" And I couldn't get the answer [*crying*]. I remember I walked by a spot and a guard hit me very hard over the head. After I recovered—because he put me to sort of semiconscious state for a few minutes—I turned around and said, "He doesn't know me!" I wasn't even thinking of the fact that I was a child. "He doesn't know me. I don't know him. Why does he have such a hatred for me?" Those things used to gnaw at me. The brutality of killing. There was clean way of killing and there was a brutal way of killing. I could not understand the brutality. They did turn me into an animal for a while, because when I got out I was told by some of the other prisoners, "You can't behave this way." I said, "They made me an animal and I'll act like an animal."

Renée H.
Bergen-Belsen

When I came to look [for my mother] at these transports, I noticed that one of the soldiers who used to be very irritated with me all the time, especially when I started to ask in perfect German, "Could I please call out my mother's name?" I knew my mother couldn't hear me, but I thought maybe somebody who knew that she was deaf would tell her that I had been calling out her name. By doing that for the fifth or sixth time, the soldier so lost his temper he just picked me up and flung me against a stone. And I lost

"They made me an animal and I'll act like an animal."

Martin S.
Born Tarnobrzeg, Poland, 1933
Recorded 1986, age 53

Martin S. enjoyed a happy childhood until the German invasion of Poland. He was eight years old when he was deported to Skarżysko-Kamienna, a slave labor camp where he was immediately separated from his mother. "I was particularly attached to my mother, so it was devastating. But there was a sudden instinct of survival that, quite frankly, I didn't dwell on it. I trained myself to be very brutal." He decided he would be a "model prisoner" as a means of surviving and produced more shells than anyone else in the munitions factory.

He and his brother were later transferred to Buchenwald. To "make light," they would sing songs written for them by poets among the prisoners. After liberation they returned to Poland and were reunited with their mother. Mr. S. had hoped the Polish people would feel sorry for them; however, there were two violent anti-Jewish episodes shortly after his return.

He emigrated to the United States in 1947. In the beginning, he felt compelled to recount his experiences to teachers and students at the yeshiva he attended. One day a student asked him, "Why don't you tell one of your bullshit stories?"—after which he did not speak of his experiences for thirty years. He describes the consequences of keeping his experiences bottled up inside and ends his testimony with a bleak outlook on the nature of man.

consciousness at that time and the immediate result was that I lost, for temporarily, my hearing—which was in some way to me a sense of tremendous worry because I had to be my sister's ears. I had to hear for her. After about five or six days, my hearing came back. But I have, since that time always had a loss of hearing.

Herbert J.
American POW in Mauthausen

I worked in, I suppose you would call it like a carpenter shop where they were working with wood. But I was anxious to get out of there because one of the men made a mistake cutting a piece of wood. And he tried to hide it, but he was seen. And the officer that was in charge there walked up, and he picked up the piece of wood and he looked at it and he looked at this guy. Then he grabbed him by the arm, and run his arm into the band saw and threw the hand over in the corner. Of course, the man run over and he picked up his arm and he's trying to put his arm back on. He died because—bled to death. You know, nobody helped him. Just bled to death.

Renée H.

When I was in the camp, I managed to find a roll of toilet paper. And I managed to also barter something I had for a pencil. And I started to write and I was writing down everything that was happening to me, about my longings, my fears, conversations I overheard, things people had said. And at one point, this roll of toilet paper was found in one of the searches by the soldiers. I remember coming back from the *Appell* [rollcall] seeing a soldier with the toilet paper, and rolling it and reading it to someone else—and laughing and finding it very amusing. Suddenly I rushed up to snatch it. He pulled it away and he said, "No! This is too good for you." And he took it with him and, of course, I heard the conversation. I heard what they were describing. One of the things that I remember him saying to the other was, "She has a wonderful

185
KL.: Buchenwald   Jud -Jugendlich   Häftl.-Nr.:
                                        68333 P

Häftlings-Personal-Karte

Fam.-Name: ▓▓▓▓▓   überstellt   Personen-Beschreibung:
Vorname: Menek   am: an KL.   Grösse: 127   cm
Geb. am: 6.5.32 in: Tarnobrzeg   Gestalt: schlank
Stand: led. Kinder: —   am: an KL.   Gesicht: oval
Wohnort: W.O., Kr. Jaraslau, Distr. Krakau   Augen: grau
Strasse: Ul. Mickiewicza 14   am: an KL.   Nase: klein
Religion: mos. Staatsang.: Pole   Mund: gew.
Wohnort d. Angehörigen: Mutter: am: an KL.   Ohren: gew.
    Sara Sch   Zähne: vollst.
    Schönwald b. Leipzig (?) am: an KL.   Haare: dunkelbraun
Eingewiesen am: 5.8.44   Sprache: poln., deutsch
durch: RSHA   am: an KL.
in KL.: Buchenwald   Bes. Kennzeichen: keine
Grund: Polit. Pole - Jude   Entlassung:
Vorstrafen: am: durch KL.:   Charakt.-Eigenschaften:

                                  mit Verfügung v.:   Sicherheit b. Einsatz:
              Strafen im Lager:
   Grund: Art: Bemerkung:

                                                              Körperliche Verfassung:

KL.I3/6.44-800000   53.

Martin S.'s prisoner ID issued in Buchenwald.

sense of humor!" And I didn't remember writing anything funny in it. I remember feeling, saying, "You may have taken that toilet roll, but you haven't stopped me from writing." And that was when I vowed to spend the rest of my life writing.

Martin S.

They used to call them *Kapos*. Those were guys that worked for the Germans but they were really prisoners. I remember one pleasant time some of us took revenge on them. Because once they got to Buchenwald, they were no longer the big shots. So some of them were eliminated, by the prisoners. People just beating on him until he died. He was begging us. "Let me live!" And one of the things that they said, "Let the kids decide." We were the kids. And all of us put our thumbs down on him. In my own private thoughts I say he deserved it. As a matter of fact, he was responsible—he knew my mother from Poland. And she came over to ask him [for] a favor, and he hit her with his full fist. Just that she dared come over and ask a favor. She was bleeding from her mouth. And I remember when I saw him that way, I couldn't feel but sweetness.

Arnold C.

I can say that the group of boys who were with me were really a tough bunch. We were very much together, very Jewish. We resented other Jewish kids who did not speak Yiddish. Zionistically inclined small group. There was one boy in particular who managed to hide his *tefillin* [phylacteries], and he used to *davenen* in the morning. We knew of the Jewish holidays. I remember Rosh Hashanah, I remember Yom Kippur. We knew when Yom Kippur was going to be, and I saved a small piece of my ration for days. I hid it in my pocket, so that when Yom Kippur came, Yom Kippur eve, I should be able to have a festive meal. And we all did it—all the children did it. Fasting was no problem for us—we were fasting practically every day. I remember Pesach. Someone had found a small piece of matzo. It was an older man. He gave it to us and we all put it in front of us. We all looked at it, and we knew it was Pesach, so we looked at a piece of matzo.

Clara L.

These Polish men who are working on the other side of the fence, I asked them once, "Can't you get for me a prayer book?" I wasn't very deeply religious before. I mean, I was religious, but not—I said, you know, "I would love to have a prayer book." So he said, "Collect about three, four days of bread, and I bring you one. You will throw it over the fence, and I will throw you back the book." And I collected it. I had four days, four slices of bread and my sister said, "I'm not going along with it." I said, "It's all right. You don't have to." I saw him working on the other side and I said, "I have the four slices of bread." He said, "I have the book for you." I said, "Who throws it first?" because I was worried, you know, he would take the bread. He says, "I trust you." He threw over the prayer book, and I threw over the four slices of bread. And it was—it wasn't really a prayer book. It was the Book of Psalms.

And there is one girl—she lives somewhere around New York—who says she remembers me, that I used to stand out, when we were waiting for the Germans, to be counted, and I would start saying the Psalms. And the Psalms, you know, it's a long book. But every single day I said the entire Psalms. It helped, sort of. From then on I used to say to my sister, "You will see! We are going to survive. You will see." And she kept on saying, "I don't think so. It's impossible." And I said, "You will see!" It's not because that I became so religious now that I believe in God more than I did. But I said, "I—I know I'm going to survive." And it did help me.

We were just herded and put into cars, wagons again and shipped out. Now, I was afraid to take that Book of Psalms, because I was afraid we did go through again the delousing, to go to the shower, and go change the clothes. We got different rags. I was afraid that if they will discover it, I would be shot on the spot. So very reluctantly I left it there. And I very often said there would be no money which I wouldn't spend if I could get that ever back, because that was something that I would have held on all my life. For months and months this Book of Psalms was—my life.

Rabbi Baruch G.

The fact is that in my circles a dependency on faith, I mean a lot of faith, that God will help, was a part of the psyche that I was familiar with. Whether this was [what] kept me going? Possibly. I don't know. We knew some who didn't have that kind of faith and still survived. Many who had more faith than I did, I'm sure, and did not survive. There's no rhyme or reason, no explanation of why one survived and the other did not.

Arnold C.

They had brought in a transport of Polish Catholic children in our barracks. These were children of high-ranking Polish officers or

Rabbi Baruch G. photographed after the war in a camp uniform.

government officials. They were apparently shot, and they took the children to Auschwitz. They were accompanied by a Catholic priest. They were on one side of the barrack, we were on the other side. And even though we were in the same boat, I can assure you, they hated us. They used to beat up on us. There were many of them and very few of us. Then one day they took them away. Where they were taken, I don't know.

Martin S.

Obviously, you don't always keep your head downtrodden. You try, just to survive, you have to make light. So there would be times that I remember we would make some jokes. You'd try to lighten things up. For example, when we were in Buchenwald, I remember that my brother and I began to sing. To entertain people. Now, we didn't see much of each other because we were in different compounds. There were some poets and writers amongst the Jews, and they began writing songs for us. And we'd sing them. And you say, "How can you do this in—in this inferno? How can you do this, in all this?" You had to find moments. And we did.

Edith P.

Our morale? I don't know how to call it. I'm not talented enough
to give you an expression what the morale was. We stuck together.
We were even singing sometimes, would you believe? I remember
I was talking about Hungarian goulash. I used to tell my sister-in-
law's sister, "Esther, if only my mother will make me once a Hungarian goulash, I don't care if I die." We used to talk about our
boyfriends. And there was something very interesting. We became
very intimate with one another. I told people—women—things
about myself which I would have never told in a normal circum-
stance. Never. We had not deep secrets, because we were supposed to be so-called decent girls—but we had secrets, like every
human being. And we told that to one another. We had to. I
don't know why. Maybe to console one another that we had a
beautiful life. That we were loved and we loved, and we were well
dressed, and we were smiling, and we were laughing, and we were
joking—that once, we were alive.

One day, two French prisoners arrived to the camp. They were
POWs and we saw *men!* Beautiful, two young men. And I said to
my sister-in-law, "You know, I think I am alive!" I haven't
thought, for a year I haven't thought man, woman, sex, to be in
love. It's the first time I saw a decent man. And I thought—
believe me, he was not a handsome fellow—I am sure he wasn't—
but I thought he was an Adonis! He was the most beautiful person
on earth. They came to ask the *Kommandant* whether they could
give us some food that they have received from the Red Cross—
and the *Kommandant* said no.

Arnold C.
Age 11, Auschwitz/Birkenau

Christmas and January, we were given days off. It was very
strange. I used to see the Christmas tree in front of the camp. The
German officers were all in very good spirits. And that's one day
we were not beaten. A day later, they started over—over again.

Helen K.
Auschwitz/Birkenau

I was working in [the] ammunition factory. The name of it was Union Factory. We were making hand grenades for the Germans. Whatever sabotage we could do, we did. We kept together. We really needed each other's support. I was sleeping with five girls on my bunk. Two of them were twins from Warsaw, and we became very, very friendly. In this ammunition factory, there were five or six girls who were working the *Pulver* [gunpowder] room where they put actually the ammunition, the powder into the grenade. So they were every day searched from head to toe naked when they were going into work and when they left work. But they were able to smuggle out some of the *Pulver*—in the vagina, in the mouth. We were able to smuggle out some of the powder, in a capsule, very small capsule which were inserted into the grenade. Then we gave it to the men. And we blew up one crematorium—in Auschwitz. So I want you to know that there was in the camp, in the concentration camp, with Germans surround[ing], really the impossible, we did blow up one crematorium.

When the Germans were looking through the ruins of the crematorium, they were able to find the shells. And they saw it was

Three of the women hanged for sabotage in Auschwitz. Helen K., who had bunked with one of them before their capture, describes: "The whole camp had to watch. And they were hanging there for three days." Left: Esther Wajchblum. Center: Rojza Robota. Right: Ala Gertner. *Courtesy U.S. Holocaust Memorial Museum*

"We did blow up
one crematorium."

Helen K.
Born Warsaw, Poland, 1924
Recorded 1979, age 55

Helen K.'s family was ghettoized with more than four hundred thousand people in a small area of Warsaw. After her father disappeared, Mrs. K. and her family moved to Mila 18, headquarters of the Warsaw ghetto uprising. When the Germans and their collaborators came in to destroy the ghetto, her mother was captured and deported. Shortly thereafter, Helen K. and her remaining relatives were removed with others from the bombed-out building where they were hiding. They were deported to Majdanek.

During the journey her brother died in her arms from lack of oxygen, as did her husband's two sisters. In Majdanek she found her mother, only to watch as she was taken to her death in a selection. Mrs. K. was transferred to Auschwitz, where she worked in a munitions factory. Women friends smuggled out gunpowder used in the October 1944 uprising in which a crematorium was destroyed. When the shells were found in the ruins, the women were identified and hanged in front of the entire camp.

Although she and her husband were not the same people after the war, they somehow managed to stay together. "I don't know if it was worth it," she comments. "Did we really learn anything?" she asks. "I don't know."

from our factory. They took the five girls or six girls who were working in this ammunition factory, and they hung them. Those were all eighteen, nineteen [years old]. One of them, I told you, I slept with her on the same bunk. I just never got it out of mind. It was so painful. And the whole camp had to watch. And they were hanging there for three days. You know, when I talk about it, I just have [*long sigh*] such pain.

One morning we heard that there was a blowup of the camp. The rumors, too, were kind of taken probably as kind of a figment of one's imagination. [We] used to call it a "*yivo*" news. "*Yivo*" news was the acronym for "*yidn viln azoy*" [The Jews want it thus] news. In other words, if anything good that we had the rumor, that's not true because we just made this up. So it was put in proper place. We heard of the attempt of the assassination of Hitler. But that, too, was put into a perspective as not really affecting us.

From the very beginning, there were already ideas to escape and things like that. But that was very secretive. Really it was only a small group, like organizers. If they [camp guards] knew a little bit that you even think about, then they didn't fool around with you. Just to *Lager* three, and that's it. I was not in the group, but I happen to have friends there, so I knew what's going on. In the camp itself, where we lived, there were also separate workplaces like a silversmith, a tailor, a shoemaker, and other kind of trades that was for the Germans, what they need. If they need a suit, the tailors make them the suit. So they had a little more freedom. There really was not any definite things that people were talking about organizing. It became in a way a routine. The courage was missing there. You need somebody to give the push.

The way really it happened is, from Russia came transports. They brought Jewish prisoners of war—Russian, Jewish prisoners of war. One of them, this Pechersky, happened to be a captain in the Russian army and when he came, we told him what's going on, so he wanted the first night to run away. We said, "Wait a minute! You just cannot run away. It's not so easy as you think." He had these military skills, and he happened to have the courage, too, to do it. So that was decided. With some pretense, they called in [a guard] to show him something, whatever. The only weapons we had was kitchen knives. They killed him, one and then the other, and put them under the clothes. And the same thing were happen[ing] in other groups. So, for example, in this places where the tailors were, the Germans were having their suit made. So they asked them to come and that time [the suit] will be ready for fitting. So they killed them there. So were going on all over the camp. That's the way they killed them, but still [we] kept working till the five o'clock. In the meantime, were also people assigned to cut the telephone wires and things like that.

There was one German was in the office. Three people were assigned to go in there and do the job. And one of them got afraid, the last minute. I figured, "Now is the end. Either we go through all the way, otherwise we're all gone anyway." Not that I'm a big hero. I'm not a hero at all. We have to finish our job. So I went with those two, and we all jabbed him with knives and said, "That's for my father, for my brother, and for everybody you killed!" and things like that. My knife slipped, and I cut myself and I was full with blood. So when we came out of the office, it was five o'clock and Selma [my future wife] was waiting already for me there. So she wiped my blood up and had some handkerchief put on, my bandage.

The tension was so high, there was not any control anymore. It was not organized anymore. It was just a wild situation. We start to run all different directions, to run away. We ran to the front gate. Somebody already exploded the front gate. We had to pass

where the Germans lived. At once, when the Germans heard what
was going on, they came out [with] machine guns and things like
that. Some of us had some guns so were shooting. I grabbed
Selma and I say, "Let's go!" So we ran. A lot fell. And we got out
of this gate, and we ran in the woods and whoever did—made it,
made it.

We also saved a lot [of valuables found in the clothing of the
dead]. So when we expected the day of the uprising, we put on
our bodies, with bandages, some money, gold, and jewelry and
things like that. We ran the whole night and we came [to] the
edge of the woods and we saw a separate house there somewhere.
And we went in and we asked if, for some money, he can keep us
over the day. We were afraid from both sides, from the Germans
and from the Poles, but that doesn't mean there were not some
people for money they might do things. So when we approached
these people and we said we would give you some money, and
hold us the day, he agreed on that. In the evening, he told us that
in the same village they caught a lot of people from the camp and
they took them back. They got shot and things like that. So, we
were one of the lucky people. We just made it and he didn't
report us or didn't turn us over to the Germans.

Walter S.
Auschwitz III (Buna/Monowitz)

I did get ill. Diarrhea. I had a fever. I didn't want to go in the
hospital. It's really not a hospital. All they had to treat you with
was aspirin, more or less. People were afraid to go to the hospital.
There was a rule, at that time in 1943. If you were longer than
two weeks in the hospital, a truck would pick you up and take you
to the gas chambers. My fever got so bad, I couldn't walk anymore, and I was taken to the hospital. Fate was in my favor. My
illness more or less saved my life. I belonged to the Maccabi ha-
Zair, a youth group. It turned out that the main nurse was a phar-
macist, but he was also one of the leaders of the Maccabi ha-Zair

Walter S.
Born Steinbach, Germany, 1924
Recorded 1979, age 55. Died 1995

As a child, Walter S. developed a strong sense of German identity that created a feeling of shame in him when Nazi law forbade Jews to attend school. After *Kristallnacht*, learning his father had been deported to Dachau, he moved to a kibbutz near Berlin, hoping to emigrate to Palestine. When the Gestapo took over the kibbutz, he was forced to harvest crops, starving yet forbidden by the Nazis to eat any of the vegetables.

Mr. S. was transferred to several camps and eventually deported to Auschwitz. There he was shaved, tattooed, and selected to work for I.G. Farben in Auschwitz III (Buna/Monowitz). He became sick, entered the infirmary, and discovered that the head nurse was a man who had led his Zionist group in Germany. With his help, he survived. Mr. S. witnessed a public hanging of prisoners who had attempted to escape and was among those ordered to remove the bodies. Another escape attempt resulted in more hangings. No physical strength, no degree of faith could help one to survive, he remarked. It was pure chance. For him, the worst part of being in the camps was not the torture or hunger but not knowing when his turn would come.

In 1945, Mr. S. was evacuated to Buchenwald, then to Altenburg, where a female guard offered to help him escape in exchange for his promise to speak on her behalf after the war. In April, he and the guard fled into Allied territory, where they were interrogated by American troops and later freed. Walter S. met his wife in a displaced persons camp in Germany. Disabled by multiple sclerosis, he lived in a nursing home beginning in 1976. Although he had not spoken about the Holocaust for forty years, he spent his last years meeting with students to combat racism, bigotry, and discrimination. He received many honors for that work.

in Germany. He knew that we belonged to a special group by the numbers when we came. You see, you could tell by the number what time of month, where you came from, and I got in this hospital. He saw my number. He said, "Don't you belong to that group?" He said, "Don't worry." He knew exactly when the trucks would come, because the German officer would tell him already, "Now let's prepare the people which have to go out." He took me off the list. He had taken me from one room to the other. So after six weeks he found a job for me in the same hospital. It's really something unbelievable how other people died. For me it was just vice versa.

People have asked me, "How did you actually survive?" I can tell you one thing. You could be the strongest man. You could have the strongest even will to live. You could be very religious and prayed all your life—it really didn't help. It couldn't help, because the malnutrition and the sufferings you had to go through—somehow wouldn't help you to survive. You had to have luck. And this was in my case the system. My illness was my luck.

Werner R.

So, I was there in Auschwitz, and—I don't think I want to—the usual stuff, the usual horror stories that you are familiar with, that you've heard from other people that happened in these camps. For me, it was a question of—first of all, I was on my own, so to speak. I didn't have any friends. A lot of these people had friends. They came from the same town and so on. I didn't. I was very much on my own, I was constantly, sort of, on the outside of things. In Auschwitz, it was a question of, really—if you wanted to survive, it was a question of resigning yourself to your fate. You know, because you couldn't do anything about it.

There were lots of people there who were elderly—elderly! People who may have been in their forties or even fifties, you know, who could not take the injustice and who felt that they couldn't take it. Emotionally, they couldn't take it and who threw

**Werner R., 1945,
approximately age 17.**

themselves against the electric wire, you know, committed suicide
that way. People who—just to whom this whole thing was just
too much. I have never been—I could not be involved in a situation like that. To me it was a question of survival. The trouble
was you got weaker, and there were things that you could not
control and things that you had a fear of. Once you got dysentery in the camp there, you know, it was like the kiss of death.
Once you had a sickness, a disease there in the camp, you know,
that was it.

Walter S.

You know, sometimes a human being doesn't think he can go on
anymore, and might give up. But somehow you get used to
hunger. It's unbelievable, because you hardly had anything to eat.
You had to work very hard. But you do get used to hunger. You
also get used to pain. The one thing you don't get used to . . . is
what's going to happen the next day. You just don't know how the
next day goes on. A funny thing is also, I think, as long as time
goes on, you get to a point that you don't have the real feelings
anymore of a human—human being. You feel somehow completely different.

Martin S.

That was the day, and night, day, and one day ran into the next day. And people would always say, "Will ever the Messiah come?" And then after a while you don't want to hear anybody talking that way. Rumor would come around, "Did you hear this guy had a pair of *tefillin* [phylacteries], put them on. They caught him and they killed him." You say to yourself, "Why do people do that?" That was the typical day. . . . If it was a typical day, it was a good day.

What do you remember? You remember those days when [there] was a garbage can, and you knew you weren't supposed to go there. But you said, "Hang it all. I've got to." And I remember going over to that garbage can and pulled out a bone that had a little marrow on it. And I got caught, and I was brutally beaten over the head. He must have hit me thirty, forty times. He kept hitting and hitting. . . . I was so conditioned—I hated him, but I said, "Thank God he didn't shoot me." I remember the day when a man was caught with a belt, a very defiant man who wasn't going to go down like a sheep. And the German officer, an SS, kept firing at him and he kept walking towards him. He fired about five, six bullets before the man dropped. By the way, when they did that we had to watch. That was one of the rules. They had to teach a lesson. So everybody had to be lined up. "This is what's going to happen to you."

So when you say "a typical day," you cannot pick out a typical day. What you pick out is the horrors. What I remember is the methodical nature of the goddamn German. They had three people that had to be killed, for whatever reason. I can't remember. But they wanted us to see it. There [were] boxes [for] the bodies. Well, it would be too messy and too much work to kill them in the center and then have to carry the bodies over. So right in front of the box, they lined them up and they shot them.

Herbert J.

And this one American, we kept telling him, "Be quiet! Be quiet!" But he was very insolent and he was giving the Germans a lot of talk, a lot of language and whatnot. And he could speak a few words of German. And so I didn't speak any German at the time, so I didn't really understand what was going on. But the Germans were talking among themselves and pointing to him and laughing. They took us to Mauthausen and they staked him out, they stripped him and staked him out on the ground, just his arms outstretched and his feet outstretched. But they didn't put any pressure on him or anything to hurt him, but they staked him down good and tight. So we went out and we asked him if he was cold, and he said he was. And so we got some old clothes and whatnot off some dead bodies and we come over and covered him over to try to keep him warm a little. But other than that, he wasn't in any pain. We didn't think much about it. If this is the kind of punishment you get, it wasn't too bad, you know. We went back inside, and come nighttime of course we went to sleep. And all of a sudden we hear screech, screaming and yelling and whatnot. We jumped up and we go rushing out. It's dark, and we're bumping into each other. We went over—and a lot of the Russians had been there, like I say, for a number of years and had turned to cannibalism. We didn't realize it then, but they had so badly torn at his body that he died from the effects. He was bleeding to death, and nothing much we could do. This was why the Germans were laughing, because staking him out just left him available. After that, we used to watch each other's back.

Renée H.

Right across from us was a charnel house filled with corpses, not just inside but overflowing all over. There were corpses all over. I lived, walked, beside dead people. And after a while it just got to be so that one noticed, and one had to say to oneself, "I am not

"So they put me with the fresh bodies."

Herbert J.
Born Maine, USA, 1921
Recorded 1989, age 68

Herbert J. enlisted in June 1944 and served in the U.S. Army Eleventh Armored Infantry, which fought in the Battle of the Bulge. He was captured by the Germans and transported through several holding camps to Gusen concentration camp, and finally to Mauthausen. There he observed a prisoner hierarchy in which Jews suffered the worst punishments and atrocities. He learned, when taking clothes from the dead, to avoid wearing those marked *Juden*. He recalls filth, inadequate sanitation, starvation, and cannibalism among some of the Soviet prisoners.

From Mauthausen, dogs were sent out after escaped prisoners. Captured escapees were executed, their bodies left where they fell, and only the dogs were brought back. Among Mr. J.'s duties were the care and feeding of those guard dogs.

Marching to the stone quarry for forced labor, he would be harassed by local children who were encouraged to strike the prisoners. To his great surprise, one day a young girl pretended to beat him in order to clandestinely hand him sandwiches.

After the war, nightmares and violent outbursts forced Mr. J. to sleep separately from his wife. "It doesn't leave you entirely."

going to see who it is. I am not going to recognize anyone in this person who is lying there." It got to the point where I realized that I had to close my eyes to a number of things. Otherwise I would not have survived even at that time, because I saw people around me going mad. I was not only having to live with all these things, but with madness.

Herbert J.

At the last end of my time in the camp when I was too sick, I was told not to go on sick call. And I asked why and they said, "You don't come back from sick call." And I was pretty sick. So when the Germans made their inspection after everybody had gone out to work and found me there, they started beating on me. I crawled out of the barracks and I crawled underneath. Underneath the barracks it was all muck and slime and human feces and whatever. I got down there. They tried to chase me out from under there. That night when I crawled out, some of the fellows in my outfit who were still alive brought me some soup. The next morning they piled me with the dead bodies, and I stayed with the dead bodies until nighttime and they'd bring me back in again, at nighttime. Because they would bury from one end, the oldest bodies first, and they couldn't catch up with the amounts. They were cremating. So they put me with the fresh bodies.

Hanna F.

I got a job carrying people's waste out from the barracks at night. I was very sick. I got diarrhea. That was already recuperating a little bit from the malaria. I walked out with two pails of human waste and I was going towards the dump. I walked out, and between the barracks was a mountain of people as high as myself. The people died at night, they were just taken and on the dump— you know, a big pile of people. And I said to myself, "Oh God.

Must I walk by?" But in the meanwhile, I couldn't hold back, and I just put down the two pails and I sit down because I had a sick stomach. And the rats were standing and eating the people's faces—eating, you know, they were having a . . . [*long silence*]. Anyway, I had to do my job. I was just looking, what's happening to a human being. That could have been my mother. That could have been my father. That could have been my sister or my brother.

Helen K.

Sometimes at night I lay and I can't believe what my eyes have seen. I really cannot believe it. You know I was in—in Auschwitz. Whenever I got up in the morning the lines were unbelievable. The kids used to come stay in line waiting to be burned. Whenever I used to get up in the morning I said, "Mine God! How can God allow this?" The kids were standing in line! There were lines—every day, there were lines of people, of kids. Such little kids they were, waiting there. I just wanted God should strike me dead! I couldn't bear—I have nightmares about those lines, waiting to be cremated. And the world allowed this to happen.

7

"Too Good a Fate"

DEATH MARCH

Even as certain defeat loomed in late 1944 and early 1945, the Germans were determined to fulfill at least one of their war aims: to exterminate the Jews. As Soviet troops approached Auschwitz and other camps, the Germans began forced marches of prisoners toward the west. Some walked to the nearest rail terminals and were transported by open freight cars to camps in Germany and Austria. Others struggled for days and weeks in snow and bitter cold, sometimes covering hundreds of miles. Those who lagged were shot. Their corpses littered the countryside, leaving stark evidence of the death marches.

Prisoners were forced to endure unspeakable agonies during the journey. Some managed to escape in moments of darkness or confusion, but most who tried were caught and shot. Starved and frozen, the majority presented a nightmarish spectacle to people in the places through which they passed. Some watched the columns of skeletons with sympathy and tried to offer food and water. Others scoffed contemptuously. When those who survived the death marches finally reached Germany and Austria, the camps were overcrowded and unprepared to receive them. Having endured the agonies of the march, large numbers died of starvation and disease in the cramped and filthy quarters of their new "homes."

Rabbi Baruch G.

I would say it started perhaps in the middle of 1944. Knowing that the Germans are being attacked from both sides, we knew about the war, that eventually—that they are running scared. But on the other hand, there was a thought of Germans being too clever to let any evidence of us survive. So there was this mixed emotion: "They are getting it, what they deserve. But what's going to happen to us?"

Abraham P.
En route from Auschwitz, June 1944

They opened up the door, the gate from the boxcar. I was sitting next to the gate and the guard who was sitting opposite from me saw a soldier reading the newspaper. And he asked him, "What's new?" He says, *"Die Alliierten haben gelandet."* The Allies have landed. Oh my God! And I kicked the other kid over there. Oh God! I think things are coming to an end! I mean, we are going to be out of here soon. Yeah, but it took another—almost a whole year before we were liberated. And then we were taken to Buchenwald. I was still together with my brothers—we were in the same boxcar. And we were kept there for about a week until they started sorting us out where to ship us. Finally we were shipped to Schlieben.

Golly D.
Gross-Rosen concentration camp

January [1945], word spread around that Russian troops are coming close from the east. So our hopes were on the rise again, because we thought the Germans will just disappear or run away and leave us there to be liberated by the Russians. But that would have been too good a fate for us, too good a solution for us. Instead, on January 20, they lined us up again, threw each of us a quarter of a bread, and that's when the death march started—the march started. We didn't know then. Later, it became known as a death march in the truest sense of the word.

Helen K.

The Germans evacuated Auschwitz. This was in 1945 in January. And all the people, everybody who could walk they just took. And I said, "No! I am not going! I don't care!" We were made [to] believe that the whole camp is mined. That once the Germans will leave, they will blow up Auschwitz. I didn't care. I told you, after I saw those girls hanged something happened to me. I really was— this was already—I was so close to those girls, I just—it was just very, very, very terrible.

I had a friend of mine, who we lived through the ghetto together. So she came to say good-bye to me 'cause she was leaving, she was going to Germany with the Germans. And I said to her, "Frania take [my] shoes. You know, they might save your life. Take them." You didn't leave [your] shoes under the bed. You were sleeping on them, because if you didn't sleep on the shoes, somebody will take them. And I was so weak already, I said to her, "Take the shoes." And she took them.

Walter S.
Working in "hospital," Auschwitz III
(Buna/Monowitz)

Winter 1944, we knew already something was going on, the end of the war might be very shortly due, because we found out that the Russian army was closing in on Auschwitz. January 1945, the camp was liquidated. Now I believe if we stayed in the hospital part, we would been freed the next day because all the sick prisoners were left behind. And later on, we found out they were liberated by the Russian army. Our luck, that the work detail of the hospital, we were all put together in one freight car, bitter cold, and those freight cars were open. We were about three and a half thousand prisoners. While the train was moving, we would throw the dead bodies overboard. But before we did that, we would strip them of all their clothes because we needed the clothes for our own protection. After five days, two-thirds of the prisoners

were dead. We arrived in Buchenwald—and there it started up
again. We were new prisoners in a new camp again. It was
unbearable.

Arnold C.
Age 11, January 1945

They decided to liquidate Auschwitz and move us again. So one
fine morning they lined us all up and we were marched out of
Auschwitz to where, I don't know at that time. And this was a
very difficult forced march. We marched all night, we marched
all day. I remember I had shoes, wooden shoes, and was a lot of
snow on the ground. The snow used to stick to the wooden
shoes, and all of a sudden I was five inches taller. And I had to
stop and break it off and walk again. I had a long pair of pants,
wrapped with a string, and they kept falling down on me. I was
cold, miserable. We just kept walking. They never stopped! I had
rations. We were given a piece of bread for two boys and a can
of meat for two boys. So I carried the bread, my other partner
carried the can of meat. There was nothing to open the can of
meat with.

Werner R.

We were lined up, and we were each given a chunk, a loaf of
bread—sort of a loaf of bread about [this] size [*measures with his
hands*], and a chunk of margarine. And I had got myself some
shoes. Other people managed to get some rubber boots from
somewhere. Don't ask me where. They got themselves rubber
boots, which proved to be disastrous. Having worked for this German, cooking occasionally, I filled my pockets with sugar. And
that was it, finished. So they started. They lined us up and said,
"Okay, let's start marching." So we marched. And step by step,
things got bad.

"So we marched.
And step by step,
things got bad."

Werner R.
Born Berlin, Germany, 1927
Recorded 1987, age 60

Werner R.'s mother, although born in Germany, was an American citizen through her father. She was a nurse in World War I and received an Iron Cross for saving the lives of German soldiers. Werner R. was six years old when his father lost his job because of the rise of Nazism and moved the family to Zagreb, Yugoslavia, where Mr. R. attended public school. In 1940, a year before the German invasion, his father died.

His mother could have gone to the United States but would not leave Werner R. and his sister. To guard against deportation, the children were baptized and lived apart from each other. His sister escaped to Italy, and Mr. R. joined the partisans and was arrested at age sixteen. He was jailed in Graz and Vienna, then transported to Theresienstadt. In 1944, Mr. R. was transferred to Auschwitz/Birkenau, where he experienced selections, slave labor, and executions.

In January 1945, Mr. R. was forced on a death march from Auschwitz to Mauthausen. On arrival, Yugoslav prisoner-doctors amputated his toes to prevent gangrene. Prior to the arrival of Allied troops, there was no food in the camp and he witnessed cannibalism. Disease was rampant. "It was a concentration camp at its worst." Liberation by U.S. troops came in May 1945. Mr. R. returned to Zagreb, where he was able to contact his sister and uncle and learned of his mother's death.

In 1947, he emigrated to England. Eight years later, he married and emigrated to the United States. He is skeptical about the value of testimony to guard against such horrors occurring again and volunteers his remembrances only as a way of documenting what happened. In Auschwitz, he bunked with a famous magician and now performs a magic act. "I owe the world more than the world owes me," he comments.

Death march. Werner R. remembers, "So this whole bedraggled group was marching, and people were dying left and right." *Courtesy U.S. Holocaust Memorial Museum*

Joseph K.

The conditions we were under at that time were so—I don't know how to describe it. They started to march us five abreast. When we left the camp, they gave us a half a loaf of this bread, and this was finished right away, because we couldn't trust each other. To keep bread on yourself you invited death, because we would kill for a piece of bread. So, you had to eat it right away. As we started to march into the woods, it must have been late in the night when they made us stop. We lay down on ice, 'cause I remember in the morning we woke up in water. Our bodies had melted the ice.

Clara L.

I must say we came through really German villages that women would open their windows and, as we were passing by, they would hand us jugs of hot water. It happened in a number of villages. They—they had the expression on their faces that they can't believe it. You know, rag-tag army of women. By then, you know, then we were walking about two weeks.

Joseph K. photographed
postwar in a camp uniform.

Golly D.

At this time, the American forces entered Germany from one side
and the British forces from the others. The Russians came from
the east. They [the Germans] were taking us away from the Russians, so they didn't quite know anymore where to lead us. Most
of the time during these three months we slept outdoors. We slept
outside without a blanket, without clothes, without shoes. Because
the shoes we had gotten had wooden soles, and from walking so
much the soles wore all off completely. Also, when the snow fell,
the snow would stick to the soles, so you couldn't walk with them
either. Anyway, the shoes dissipated, and at that point we would
just rip a piece of cloth off our—whatever we had, coat, dress—
and wrap it around our feet.

Joseph K.

The soles were made out of wood, with no break in them. It was
just a piece of wood with some leather over it or canvas or what-

ever. And we couldn't bend our knees or the ankles. [We] just walked like robots, just drag, step by step. But we knew the minute we fall down, that was the end.

Werner R.

It was cold. It was bitter, bitter cold. It was subzero temperature there. That was bad. And as we got up, there were people sitting there. They couldn't move anymore. They were just frozen, you know, half-dead. So this whole bedraggled group was marching, and people were dying left and right, you know. It was just—it was absolutely—and there was nothing you could do. I mean, if you tried to help somebody, you would stay there. It was totally hopeless. And so you stopped, and then we marched on a little bit, and there were people staying there, and as we marched off, you heard so many people with a gun shooting these people who stayed behind.

Arnold C.

I got very tired of walking. I just wanted to go to sleep. I couldn't continue. So I began to fall back. And as I was almost to the end of the thousands of people who were marching, I saw the Germans were shooting people who were falling down. I can't do that! I got to continue. So I started to speed up and came back to some of my friends who I knew, and they held on to me. We were all holding hands as we were walking. And then I had to relieve myself. I have to stop. I ran off to the side, I dropped my pants, and as I dropped my pants the German guard slung his rifle off and he pulled the rifle to load his bullet. I said to him, "I am not tired! I can continue! As soon as I relieve myself, I'll catch up." Well, it gave me a few seconds to do what I had to do. I pulled my pants up again—I didn't have time to tie it—and I ran back. And he didn't kill me.

Clara L.

It became more and more difficult walking. You see, people were becoming very weak. And my sister kept on saying she cannot do it. I said, "You have to!" It came to one point that I had to take her on my back and practically carry her. And those who couldn't walk, the German would say once or twice, *"Geh! Du musst gehen! Geh weiter!"* [Go! You must go! Go farther!] But some of them just resigned themselves and we would just march on. Then about five minutes later you would hear a sound of a gun. We heard this all the time and we knew what happened. We never looked back. We knew those who didn't want to carry on, they were just left on the road, shot. And that's it. For one part of the trip we took a train, and we were told we arrived at a place called Bergen-Belsen.

Golly D.

I remember a young woman, a little older than I, from Berlin [who] couldn't anymore. I remember [her] walking up to an SS man and pleading with him, "Please shoot me. I cannot go on anymore." You know what he said to her? "You're not worth the bullet. Get back into line." That was the attitude.

Joseph K.

It started to rain. And it was like a cloudburst. Thunder. Lightning. And it was pouring. And they just kept shooting all night. They decimated us that night. This was one of the most unbelievable experiences any man can even visualize. And this was going on all night.

Golly D.

I always tried to walk on the outside of the column, which had certain advantages. When snow fell, sometimes you could—did I tell you, we got no food? No food! None whatsoever, as of January 20. That was the last piece of bread. If we could maybe pick up a little snow to wet our mouth—but God forbid the SS man saw you. I was caught once picking up snow and was beaten up so severely with the wooden part of the rifle that I never dared to do it again. When the nature came back to life, say March or so, and things started to sprout, they [the prisoners] would run into the field and pick a blade of grass or a bud from the tree, to eat, to eat, to eat, just to eat. This went on for months.

We were not aware, even though we could look at each other, we were not aware of our horrible appearance. Not because we had no mirror [but because] I think the drive to survive another hour, another day, was so great that we didn't even look at each other. But I remember walking past this one village in Saxonia. We looked upstairs and thought, "Does something like that, windows with curtains, still exist?" Maybe it was even warm in there. We couldn't imagine anything like that anymore. And the curtain was pushed aside, and an older lady looked out, and I looked up. And then I saw her expression. She saw us, and I saw her expression. She went, "AHHH!" She went like this [*grabbing her face with both hands*]. And that's when it became clear to me what we really looked like. Many people looked at us and laughed and giggled. Maybe it was embarrassment, maybe it was pleasure. I really don't know, but that's the way it was. It was more painful to be laughed at. I felt ashamed for them. I felt ashamed for myself because of my appearance. I can't explain those feelings.

Arnold C.

We marched the whole day, and it was again beginning to be night. And there was an air raid. So everyone was told to drop. I dropped, I fell asleep. It didn't take me long to fall asleep. And I remember the dream that I had. I arrived in a beautiful camp with lots of lights and there were a lot of people standing—a beautiful kitchen. They were handing out soup and bread—and then I was nudged by my friends [on the march]. "We gotta go again." I said, "I don't want to go! We're in a new camp!" "No, you're not in the camp. We have to move." "I can see it! I saw it! It's right here!" Well, they helped me up and we marched again.

[From another camp] the following day they marched us again to trains, put us on trains, and again, I didn't know where we were taken. We stopped at a railroad junction and there was another train parked right next to us of German troops. They were wounded troops moving away from the front. All of a sudden, we heard sirens. It was an air raid on that railroad junction. I think they were Russian planes. They had no idea there was a train of prisoners, and they were shooting up the entire railroad yard. I remember crouching myself down as low as I could get, and I covered my head with a blanket. It must have lasted about ten minutes. And when I lifted my head up, there were holes all over the cattle car, with splinters of wood and blood on the walls. There was a boy who was sitting next to me. He was sitting upright and I moved my hand against him and he just fell over, and as he fell over I could see the holes in his head. There was another friend next to me. He had a little fur hat and he took it off and said, "Look at this!" he says. "There's a hole right through it—but," he says, "I'm alive!" We banged on the doors to have the guards open up the doors. They opened it up and they took all the killed and the wounded. The wounded that they took out they shot them right outside.

Then we continued on. I think we were on that train for about six days. No water, no food, nothing, nothing. They did not open up for us to be able to get out to relieve ourselves. Nothing. Everything was right there in the cattle car. It was winter. The only water I could get was by scraping off the frost from the walls.

There were little icicles that formed. Whoever managed to grab an icicle, it was a delicacy. We had a stopover in Prague, Czechoslovakia. And I remember yelling through the little windows, "Water! Water!" and some of the Czech people who heard us ran up with little cups and tried to give it to us. And the German guards just knocked it down and wouldn't allow them to give us the water.

Christa M.
Age 15, Christian German student

Towards the end of the war, we're scared to death whether the Russians or the Americans would get there. We didn't know anything about the Americans, much. But we knew enough about the Russians, and we were scared to death. They were approaching from both sides. Of course, there weren't any more schooling because of the bombing. Food was becoming short. Even so, we didn't really suffer—well, it was getting really short because I stole then. I used to go in the fields and steal potatoes and sugar beets. And I herded some cows in exchange for bread here and there, some eggs. Because there was no more help. I mean the fields were going rotten, so we worked the fields, too. There was no more farm help. [They were] all in the war. And my mother had heard that there was free cheese given away. So she said, "Tomorrow morning, you get your rucksack, and you go over there and get all the cheese you can put your hands on."

The town was bedlam, filled with SS, loudspeakers all over the place. Hitler screaming, I mean, like he screamed. I couldn't stand his voice. He always screamed and screamed, "We're winning the war!" You don't have to be very bright. You look around you and then you hear this, "We're winning the war," and you're in shambles.

I was walking east. There was a school [that] used to be used as a private girls' school, that had big walls surrounding the property. When I turned the corner, I saw—it's still, now, it's just hard for me because there are no words. There really are no words. There are no words. I can't find words. Well, there were people leaning against that wall, sort of hunched, quite a few, and there were some few standing in the middle of the street in little clumps. And they all had the blue and white striped uniforms. We had seen uniforms like that in the paper so I thought—I knew they were prisoners. But I didn't know what prisoners. But, my God, they are skeletons. I mean skeletons! I'll never forget the eyes. The eyes were three times the size because there were no more faces. Skeleton hands. And I see all these people. And the ones that were against the wall, they couldn't even walk. They could not walk, and so I immediately went towards them—I don't know, it was just a reaction. I really don't know what made me do it. Human compassion or whatever. I had food. These people, the first thing was these people must get food. And all I had was this cheese. So I started opening my rucksack, and the minute I reached in and got the first piece, these people came literally crawling. If you can imagine, people crawling, as much as they could, on hands and knees towards you. Just looked at you. To this day, I see those eyes. I see those faces. And just for the cheese.

So I gave the cheese out. I had almost given it all away, and a little bit left. And I feel like a bayonet in my back. It was an SS guy. And that's the first time I've really seen an SS guy close up, [with] the insignia on. He's got the big German shepherd. And he screamed at me—again, that screaming—"If you give those bastards one more piece of whatever you got there," he said, "I'm going to make you join them! You're going to go right with them!" And I started running. I got away from that guy.

I see the columns marching as far as I could see. . . . The people had wooden clogs on and rags around their feet, and they couldn't—their feet were bloody and they couldn't walk anymore. They were just shuffling, and it was drizzling and raining, and they didn't have any hats. I remember the little soup bowls, but I never saw anybody giving any soup out there at all. And they had them on their heads, and I thought, "Oh, my God. They're putting them on their heads because they don't want to get their

"To this day,
I see those eyes.
I see those faces."

Christa M.
Born Saarbrücken, Germany, 1930
Recorded 1987, age 57

Christa M. grew up in a Nazi home. They moved to the Black Forest in 1938, then lived in Frankfurt and Ammerland. She saw Nazis humiliating a rabbi on the streets of the city, forcing him to beat a drum and chant, "I'm a filthy Jew!" In school, she was taught to see Jews as less than human, dangerous to children, and the cause of all woes. When she chose "The Lorelei" for a recitation, she was slapped and reprimanded because the author was a Jew. If she did not greet people with the "*Heil Hitler*" salute, she was reported and punished. She was compelled to watch Nazi propaganda films that depicted Jews slaughtering animals, and was told that if she were bad she would be sent to "the camps." Jewish teachers disappeared without explanation.

In April 1945, with the Allies approaching, Mrs. M.'s school days ended. Food was scarce, and on the way home from getting cheese she witnessed an evacuation from Dachau. She ran home, but her mother refused to believe the description of what she had seen.

After the war, she felt she could no longer remain in Germany and emigrated to Paris, then to the United States. In 1985, she returned. "It was the same stuff. Nothing has changed."

heads wet." You know, you're a kid. Meantime it didn't occur to me that they didn't even have food. And the SS was pushing them and shoving them. And anytime, anytime somebody fell out of line—because they're exhausted, they couldn't walk—so anybody who could not keep in step, they shot them! I saw one directly in front of me. He fell. He could not move—he or she, I don't remember, I couldn't tell, they were all skeletons—and he let the dog loose. The dog went right for the jugular and he [the guard] just stood there, took his revolver. He just shot him. I'm standing there, I couldn't—just shot him. Then yelled for the others to move on.

Rabbi Baruch G.
Spring 1945

Between April tenth and my liberation, which was within three, four weeks, I probably suffered more than in the years before, physically. I remember being on trains, on cattle trains, losing my strength. I remember my breathing was becoming very heavy. I can see myself, think of myself as I have seen others in the last days of their lives—reaching a point where I didn't even want to go down from the train. Because you had to jump down from the cattle train, which is high, in order to get some food or whatever. I just

Rabbi Baruch G., July 25, 1945,
Budapest, Hungary, en route
from Theresienstadt to Italy.
"After liberation I suffered
probably more from the loneliness and the isolation, more
than during the Holocaust
period."

didn't want to go down there. It was too much effort. I just wanted to be left alone, lie there. I remember feeling distinctly a sense of resignation, heavy breathing, and nothing—no feelings at all.

Abraham P.
Schlieben concentration camp

Then they picked us up and they put us into boxcars for ten days. We were locked in, and I don't know where they took us to. We were traveling with hardly any food. I'll never forget it. Once we were raided by the Americans. The train stopped, the guard ran away, and they left us over there in the open. I saw—now it'll give you an idea what we were like and what level we were in—I found there eight plum pits next to a piece of manure. I took them out of there, I wiped it off with whatever I was able to wipe them off with, and I took out the pits and I ate them. We were left over there in the open. We could have gone any place, anywhere—but then you didn't know where to go. You didn't know where you were!

We finally arrived in Theresienstadt, and there, too, rumors were going around. "The war is practically over. The Germans are going to kill us off—machine-gun us."

Golly D.

Heidi and I—the Czech girl and I—had talked about escape many times. But we were so scared, and I'll tell you why. Once we were resting during the day, because the SS also had to rest. We rested at the edge of a forest, and right in back of us was a thick forest. About five girls ran off deep into the forest and the SS saw it, went after them, caught each and every one of them, pulled them back in front of us. We had to circle around them. They beat them bloody till the blood was running down from head to toe, and then shot them dead. *After* they beat them severely, then they shot them. So we were afraid to escape [but] I realized I had no choice. We have to escape because I knew I was near death.

You know, when you die from hunger your legs fill up with

water. Under your eyes you fill up with water, and you become—
virtually become stiff. I could not lift my feet higher than two
inches off the ground anymore. I could not move my arms. And I
had seen many die, and I realized when I saw my legs that is the
end. Anyway, now I'm back in this little village called Annenberg,
where the girls—there was a whole commotion. They [the guards]
had to get the girls back in line. And Heidi and I—it wasn't
planned, we did it more by instinct—we went to the right of the
road and we hid behind a farmhouse, a big farmhouse. We cow-
ered together behind the house and just sat there, not knowing
what to do next. But we waited. It was all instinct. We waited till
the column was lined up again and marched off.

Joseph K.

They started to march us off again. They brought us into this forest area. We're marching, and we hear this German on a motorcycle pulling up to the head of the convoy. And the word passed
on that the Americans [had] surrounded the forests. The German
guards were marching up forward. By then there were already
more guards than prisoners. As the last guard walked by me, I
started to run. I ran away from the group—and I just kept running.

Werner R.

We continued marching on. And the same story again. The group
became smaller and smaller. So we ended up in Mauthausen. They
took us into these big shower rooms and they turned on warm
water—and people were just keeling over. Suddenly the shock was
horrible, was absolutely awful. I know that, for instance, some people who managed to get hold of these rubber boots, they had the
boots removed, and they removed the toes as well because they
froze in this rubber stuff. It was just horrible, and I just passed out.
We left, I was told, something like five or ten thousand. By the time
the trip was over, there were only a few hundred of us left.

Christa M.

A classmate of mine came up on his bike. I was so glad to see a
familiar face. I went up to him, and by then I started crying. I
couldn't stand it anymore. I was falling apart and I said, "What's
going on?" I wanted to jump on the back of his bike, to ride with
him for comfort. I wanted to be close with someone I knew. I was
afraid of everybody. He barks back at me, and he said, "You're
such a stupid ass. Don't you know what's going on?" I said, "No, I
don't know what's going on." He said, "Well, they're emptying
Dachau. Those are all the prisoners from Dachau. They're going
to march them into the mountains and they're going to shoot
them. They already shot twenty thousand. They're going to shoot
the rest—and they should have done it long ago." And that did
me in completely. He took off. And he was the one who I thought
I'd get some comfort [from]. I found out later he was the son of
an SS officer.

Some sort of small supply truck came by. They threw the door
open, and somebody in there motioned for me to come in because
I was crying so bad. So I think they felt sorry for me. I don't
know. I went in, and it turns out they were German soldiers who
had taken off their uniforms and had put on their fatigues or
something, because people were then stealing already civilian
clothes. The biggest thing then was to get rid of your uniforms so
you don't get caught. He had stuff on the truck and there was a
tarp over it. I said, "What have you got in the truck?" "Oh, it's
stale army bread. We're going to dump it to lighten the load
because we're getting out of here. We want to get into Switzerland
as fast as we can." So I knew they were deserters. I said, "You're
going to dump this bread? See this hunger out here? Can't we
give it away?" He just sort of shrugged his shoulders. But he
reached back, he brought a loaf and I sort of broke off some and I
handed it out the window. Oh, my God. A prisoner way in the
back, he just fell. And the others fell like dominoes. They just fell

over each other to get to that piece of bread. People were so desperate just to get that little piece of bread.

I just ran home the rest of the way. I was in *fine* shape when I walked in the house [*sarcastically*]. I tried to tell my mother. Of course, if a child of mine had come home looking the way I did, I would have done it differently. But the first thing she said was, "Where is the cheese?" I could have hit her. I could have hit her. "I gave it away." Of course, she got so mad. "You and your stories! Here you go again! What'd you do now?" This whole line of questions. "There are people out there," I said. "They're not even people," I said, "They're skeletons!" "You are so full of it! Get to your room!" I tried to get her up then. I said, "Walk up there with me! I'll show you!" But she wouldn't go. "No, no!" She didn't believe me. "Don't make things up." And it wasn't till much later, when she saw pictures after the war. But it was never discussed. And she would never say anything.

8

"Lost, Without Words"

LIBERATION

As the German defeat became evident, so did awareness of the enormity of the catastrophe unleashed by Nazi Germany. Allied soldiers, stunned by huge mounds of corpses and living skeletons, were among the first to confront the atrocities in the camps they liberated. Germans from all walks of life, former citizens of Hitler's Thousand Year Reich, were compelled by Allied forces to view the unprecedented mass murder that had been carried out in their name in nearby camps. Those still alive among the victimized had to redefine the meaning of freedom in a world where their families, their homes, and their towns, villages, and religious communities had been destroyed forever.

For most of those who survived the camps and death marches, "liberation" offered little solace. Most were alone. They were ill, weak, and malnourished, facing a bleak and uncertain future. Those of us who today celebrate the "triumph of survival" overlook the burden of survivors' painful memories and their sense at liberation that "I'm not alive, I'm dead" and "I'm alive, but so what?"

Some camp survivors recall responding to the entrance of American or British soldiers with elation, scarcely believing that their ordeal had come to an end. The elation soon gave way to recurring nightmares and painful memories. Those who returned to their homes in Poland, hoping to find family, reclaim property, and resume their lives often encountered hostility, indifference, and violence. Many therefore chose to leave their former homes and traveled to displaced persons camps in Germany, Austria, and Italy, where they spent months— sometimes years—before being allowed to settle in other countries.

Colonel Edmund M.
Born Baltimore, Maryland, circa 1919
First Lieutenant, Sixty-fifth U.S. Infantry

I was in my, I guess, mid-twenties [and] I was an infantry officer in General Patton's Third Army. We had fought our way through most of Germany, and a few days before the liberation of this camp we had fought our way into Austria. My particular unit was one of the first units to gain entrance into Nazi-occupied Austria at that time. So at that time, we were waiting—by "we" I am referring to my specific unit—we were told to stop and wait for the advance of the Soviet army that was coming from the east, from Vienna, that they had recently captured, and approaching us. The Soviet army was approximately a hundred, a hundred and ten miles away farther to the east.

This was the spring of 1945. It was beautiful. The country was picturesque. We were admiring the flowers. Things were now more relaxed. Two or three tanks then stumbled upon Mauthausen concentration camp. There was no prior knowledge, as far as we knew, to the existence of this major concentration camp. The effect, I think, was pure chance that our American tanks found these. So quickly, then, the airwaves were filled with the radio messages going in all directions about this particular camp having been found. I jumped out of the jeep to head in towards the main gate. Even though it was a beautiful day, [a] very, very beautiful day, I felt a brief chill. I don't know what caused the chill. Perhaps a premonition of what we were about to see.

Werner R.
Age 18, Mauthausen

The trouble was that the American troops advanced from one side and the Russian troops advanced from the other side, and they had an agreement that "This area is yours and this area is ours," and everything was fine and dandy. Unfortunately, nobody

counted that the Russian forces would be held up in Vienna. So
the whole thing got delayed. And in the meantime, while the
squeeze was going on, there was no food in the camp. I mean, it
was sort of a—a concentration camp at its worst. The camp was
overcrowded. There were maybe in one of these bunks four or six
people sitting, crouched together. They were giving us a spoonful,
tablespoon-full of moldy bread per day. Sometimes twice a day.

I'll never forget. There was a huge pile of corpses—huge pile
of corpses, which were moving. They were still alive and breathing, but they were just piled up there. And this pile was actually
moving, this whole pile. You know, the moment somebody sort of
fainted or passed out, you simply used to drag them and put
them on there. There were cases of cannibalism in the camp at
that time. There was a little bit of grass, or some stuff like that
growing out—it was all eaten up. There was nothing there. People were getting diseases. You name it, a disease, within about
two or three days, gone. Things were totally hopeless. If somebody died next to you, you were lucky. What you could do is ask
the food for this person who is dead, and then you took it. But
there was just so long that you could keep a corpse next to you. It
was a bad time.

Arnold C.
Age 12, Mauthausen

I remember I used to pick grass to nourish myself. The portions
of bread that they used to give us—if you just blew on it, it just
disintegrated. It was all mold. There were big tents where we
were kept. I wanted to leave my tent and go to a different one
because most of my friends were there. It was about six or seven
o'clock in the evening. I walked out, and as I was walking toward
that tent a[n] SS officer saw me. He says, "Where are you
going?" I knew I was not supposed to be outside of my tent. I
just turned around and started running. He pulled out his pistol
and he emptied his pistol after me. And he missed me. I made it

WITNESS

back into my tent, and I said, "The SS is after me!" So I
dropped down on the ground and some kids threw a blanket over
me. And he came looking for me. There were many people in
that particular tent. Thousands probably. He couldn't find me.
That night, I remained in that tent. That same night there was
an air raid. The planes dropped bombs all over the place—and
one of the bombs landed in the tent where I [had] wanted to be.
Many of the children were killed. In the morning, there were
arms and legs hanging all over the place. I must admit, it was the
first and only place where I saw cannibalism. I saw two people
take a piece of meat from a body and try to make a fire and
cook it. The German officer who walked by, who saw it, shot
them immediately.

From there, again a forced march, another camp. We were
taken to Gunskirchen in Austria. I slept on the outside. There
were too many dead bodies inside the barracks infested with lice. I
had decided to run away. I made arrangements to escape from
that camp. On the night that I was supposed to escape, the Germans disappeared and saved me the escape. The following morning I saw the first American troops. They drove in with the jeeps.
We marched out of the camp—and we just walked!

Christa M.

We were preparing, you know. Then we heard always the artillery
coming in, and we expected all kinds of horrendous things.
There's a jeep, and two Chinese Americans in it. We didn't know
what an American was. So on my own I got up and go across.
"Oh, you're Chinese?" They were furious. That was my first lesson because they said, "No, we are Americans." Only two? That's
it? We were expecting—the propaganda was dreadful! "The Americans are coming in! All the women are going to be raped! And
we're going to get shot!" Two lovely guys are offering you a stick
of chewing gum.

Edith P.
Salzwedel

That morning, it was the fourteenth of April 1945, early in the morning. Evidently the Americans broke through and broke the water lines and we had no water. And he [the Nazi boss] wanted to shave or needed water. He said to me, "Come here, Edith. You are going to go with this [woman] officer and with two pails and one mile, you are going to bring some water from the well. We need water." So I did. And when I came back, the water was very heavy, so I just put it down. So she slapped me. This woman knew that the Americans—it's only minutes, only hours that the Americans, their enemy, will be here. But she still had the control over me. She slapped me. She says, "Don't you dare put this down! Let's go, fast!" So I did, and I brought in the water. And he came to me and he said, "Now you know I was a good boss to you, wasn't I?" Oh, sure. How else? Of course! "So, you see? You survived. The armies"—he called the Americans "armies"—"I know the armies are here," he said, "and within one hour they are going to be and I'm going to stay here." He did, because there was nowhere for them to go. Not because he was so brave. As soon as he saw the first American he started to run.

Werner R.

On May 5, a couple of American tanks rolled into Mauthausen accidentally. They didn't even know there was a camp there. And suddenly they find themselves with this huge camp of starved and uncontrollable people there.

Col. Edmund M.
Mauthausen

I jumped out of the jeep and then proceeded into the camp, looking around at this horrifying picture of stone, barbed wire, machine guns that encircled the whole camp. It was a very, well, frightful thing to look at. Just the appearance of the place, not just an open field with barbed wire around it. Far from it. [There was] a very, very large wooden gate that undoubtedly would require many men just to push open. There were guard towers every perhaps seventy-five feet or so that had machine guns in them facing the inmates. Scary, to say the least. The SS at this time—many of them had disappeared, put on civilian clothes and disappeared, whereas some SS were still in hiding within the place.

Edith P.

We heard lots of commotion all over. It was tremendous pressure all over. The gates were closed. I want to emphasize that Salzwedel did not have only Jewish prisoners. We have been with a lot of Danish and Dutch prisoners, and Gypsies. The gates were closed and everybody was standing in the yard like one man. And about eleven o'clock we heard a tank, stopping at the gate. Two shots fired and the gates opened. And as we ran, there was a white and a black American [*crying*] standing side-by-side in the tank. It's the first time I saw a black man. I loved him for it all my life. And he stood there erect, maybe because he understood. And the [Nazi] boss was running and he [the American] shot him. I still see him lying there, with his beautiful shiny boots that I was shining an hour before. And I had no pity on him. And we were liberated and he said, "Everybody goes!" And everybody went crazy. Crazy!

Martin S.
Age 12, Buchenwald

It was April eleventh, four o'clock in the afternoon. I remember this clear as a bell. I remember the Americans coming in. I remember we almost killed one of them because we kept throwing him up in the air and he just couldn't take it—his body couldn't take it. But first there was that—"Is this really an American soldier?" Don't forget, we heard the front coming up. You hear the bombardment and you hear the heavy cannon fire in the distance. So we knew they were coming. And when you see the skeleton crew, you begin to realize something is happening. You walk around and you just say to yourself, "Is this really happening?" It's a feeling that is elation, but at the same time you say, "Don't get carried away because it might be a letdown." So you don't know if you want to jump or whether you want to be happy or not. When they finally came in and you saw the jeeps roll in, you saw the different uniforms, you realized it's over. Tremendous, tremendous high. As a matter of fact, I don't even remember being hungry!

Renée H.
Age 11, Bergen-Belsen

One of the saddest things in my life has been that I have no recollection of the liberation because I was totally ill with the typhus. I have no recollection of what happened when the English came to Bergen-Belsen, none of the things that people told me afterwards about the joy and the sense of being moved from where I was to what was converted into a hospital which was outside—right in the place where the Germans themselves were billeted. One of the men who was liberating us was a Dr. Collis, and he told me later on that I was very near death. Had I had to wait another two days for the English, I would not have survived.

Perla K.
Age 17, Dachau

In Dachau, I tell you the truth, I don't know too many things because I start to be very—They put me to one room. I think was the death room, laid in the floor and I don't remember nothing. I was almost dead, you know. The only thing that I remember somebody picked me up, you know, in his hand. The American, in his hand, and put me to the car—ambulance and took me to the hospital.

Colonel Edmund M.

The thing that impressed I think all of us almost immediately was the horrible physical condition of most of the inmates whom we saw. Some of them undoubtedly looked in fairly good health, but these were in the minority. Most of them were in very, very bad shape. Some of them actually looked almost like living skeletons. I took a look at some, and I would estimate the average weight probably might have been eighty, ninety pounds or so.

I walked into one of the barracks, and the first thing that almost literally startled me was the terrific stench of the barracks. It was just unbelievable. The odor of excretions, et cetera, that were in there, that the inmates could not help over a period of time. It was just so much so, that I first just wanted to grab my breath and maybe walk out immediately without going any farther. But I took a deep breath and went in a bit farther and looked around. The bunks were roughly about, I'd say about six feet long, probably about three and a half or four feet wide. And they were triple-tiered, sort of like young children would be having, except one would be sleeping in them. Here we had three to four inmates sleeping in each of these bunks, just squeezed together, literally, like almost sardines. A few of them were lucky enough to have some straw.

Many inmates, including some whom I met later, were in very bad situations physically from diseases. Typhus, for example. I would estimate that the majority of the inmates within this camp had typhus. In addition to typhus there was diarrhea, dysentery, typhoid, pneumonia, diphtheria—you have it, any—almost any disease mentionable.

"I took a deep
breath and went in
a bit farther."

Colonel Edmund M.
Born Baltimore, Maryland, circa 1919
Recorded 1989

Colonel Edmund M. was a first lieutenant in the Sixty-fifth Infantry, which liberated Mauthausen concentration camp. On May 5, 1945, Colonel M.'s unit stumbled upon the camp with no prior knowledge of its existence. What struck him immediately was the pervasive stench and horrible conditions of the prisoners. He saw the quarry where prisoners were forced to carry heavy stones up 186 steps. He saw the gas chambers and recorded the inmates' stories of the atrocities they had endured.

When rations were distributed to the prisoners, hundreds died because their emaciated bodies could not digest the food. Colonel M. spoke with people from the nearby town who denied any knowledge of the camp. As an intelligence officer, he later took part in the war crimes trials at Dachau. Colonel M. was invited to attend the first International Liberators Conference at the U.S. State Department in 1981. He received a scroll of appreciation from the U.S. Holocaust Memorial Museum and was active for many years in his local Holocaust awareness programs. A research pharmacologist, he published more than sixty articles in scientific journals.

Abraham P.
Age 21, Theresienstadt

I had diarrhea there. I had typhus, and I was put into a hospital. I had, I lost—I was eighty pounds. I couldn't sit down. I lost my hair. I just couldn't walk. I couldn't sit down. I was just bone. Period. There was not even a piece of flesh.

Helen K.
Age 21, Auschwitz

I weighed maybe fifty, sixty pounds when I was liberated. You'd be surprised how much a human being can take. It's just amazing. I think it had more to do with your mental ability to survive than with the physical.

Colonel Edmund M.

One problem that we had there with the inmates immediately, it was brought to our attention by the medical personnel, was that because of the very incapacitated physical condition of the inmates, that they would be unable to tolerate any large amount of food, particularly rich food. They had to be very, very careful that they did not eat too much food at once. Otherwise, it could kill them. It was difficult, I'm sure, for the inmates, having been on starvation diets, not to want all the food that they could get. This was understandable. It was also difficult, I am quite sure, for many of the American soldiers there not to want to give them food, seeing their suffering.

Werner R.
Age 18, Mauthausen

So they bring up these K-Rations—a can of chopped ham in it, you know, and a couple of biscuits and three Chesterfields with a little can opener—and they distributed it throughout the camp. Now this produced a tremendous death rate, instantly. People were eating that stuff and got diarrhea, and there was nothing in the world to stop it. I mean, you know, it was like poison. So I don't know how many hundreds and hundreds and hundreds of people just died right there from that food which was given to them.

Martin S.
Age 12, Buchenwald

They cooked a lot of pork. They made pork soups. And I remember there were doctors in camp, prisoners [who] kept going around saying, "Don't eat this! Your bodies can't take it." I don't remember whether I paid much heed, but I know I overdid it. Thank God I didn't die, but oh, I was sick, I was deathly sick because our systems were not used to it. Now I understand it.

Robert S.
Former Hitler Youth

As I went into those postwar years, day after day, everything remained the same from what I could see. I didn't come across people who said to me, "Do you realize what we have done?" No. There were former Nazis whom I had known who were standing in line to be *"denazifiziert"* [denazified]. Okay, and that was it! Once you were *"denazifiziert,"* then everything was really, "Well, Hitler wasn't all that bad, you know. He had bad advisers." This was the first wave of rationalization that came. I can't tell you—I don't know what I expected people to do. I really do not know what I thought should happen. I just thought things couldn't go on the way they had been, and the way they were going on. I couldn't look at people of my father's age and not say, "Why didn't you talk to me when there was time? Why did you—were you silent?" And I could say the same thing about my mother, and she never said anything about that. It was as if it didn't happen.

Colonel Edmund M.

Well, of course they [the nearby civilians] all denied knowing anything about it. The town itself is about roughly little less than two
miles, maybe a mile and a half, mile and three quarters from the
camp, down at the bottom of a hill. We talked with some of these
civilians. What they in effect were saying was that up at the top of
the hill where the camp was, that this to them was just a training
area for the German troops. They admitted no knowledge whatsoever of the concentration camp. They just basically lied to us
because when one analyzes the records of what had actually gone
on at that place—[prisoners] had come down into the town, come
off trains there, or come in by trucks there, and then had to walk
up the little less than two miles up—the people could not help but
know that the camp was there.

Golly D.
Age 23, escaped from death march

We walked along the path and from a distance saw a young
woman approaching us with a little girl on her hand. The first
thing we said to each other, "Don't forget, we're Germans." So we
met each other, we came close to the woman, and the first thing I
said to her, "We are Germans! We escaped from the east!" She
took my hand. She was all shaken up. She says, "You don't have
to tell me anything. I just passed that column." She couldn't
believe what she had seen, but she realized right away that we
belonged—we belonged to them. She said, "Listen to me. The
American[s] are twenty kilometers"—about fifteen, seventeen
miles—"away from here. You just spend the days, try to stay in
this area and wait till they come, so they will be able to help you."
Next she says, "Up the hill, on the other side of the road is a little
chapel. When after it gets dark, go up there and you will find
some food." She never gave us her name. I have no idea. But she
must have been—she was a lifesaver. We stayed in the area and
every night we went up to the chapel for about three or four

nights, and the fourth night we again found some food, and on top of the food was a little bunch of forget-me-nots.

In the meantime, we heard the artillery shots, and we knew from her this can only be the approaching American army. So we walked toward the sound of artillery. Again we passed a little larger village, from which each and every German had escaped into the woods. They were so frightened of the Americans, thought that the Americans would do to them what they did to us. Nonetheless, they were so frightened that they sometimes forgot even to lock the door, so fast they ran into the woods.

We passed, Heidi and I, a nice-looking house with an open door. Naturally, we walk in. Cabinets full of clothes and sacks full of food. The farmers had everything. So in our craze, what we did—the first thing we did, we ripped off all of our lice-infested clothes. We took clothes out of the closet. Each of us put on three or four dresses one on top of the other. Then the Germans have shopping bags with zippers on top and two handles. We each took one or two bags and we put in rice and sugar and whatnot— everything we did was crazy, but that's what we did. Then we went into the adjoining kitchen. The kitchen was off the hall. And Heidi was still in a little bit better shape—as it turned out later, after we were weighed, I weighed seventy pounds and she weighed eighty pounds, which means she was still a little bit better shape, strong enough, I suppose, to busy herself at the oven. Whatever she could find she cooked together: eggs with carrots, with what- not, whatever she could find.

Suddenly, while we were in this situation, the door was jammed open with force. And two American soldiers walk into the kitchen. Now, fortunately, first of all, we were prepared more or less that the Americans were approaching. Secondly, we recog- nized at that point by their language—and fortunately both of us knew English also. So first thing we told to them, in our fear they shouldn't think we are Germans, we told them, "We are Jewish girls from concentration camp." And he said. "We have liberated so many concentration camps," he says, "You don't have any explaining to do." He said, "Stay in this house. I will give order further back to the officers, and you wait here until the officers come here. In the meantime," he said, "EVERYTHING IN THIS HOUSE IS YOURS!" He had such a warm heart. He didn't know what to do, so he wanted to console us and said everything in that house belonged to us! Sure enough, about an hour and half or so later two very distinguished-looking young American officers walked in. They didn't say much. One of them literally took me in his arms, carried me in his arms. The other one carried Heidi on his arms, and carried us into their quarters. So, typical Americans, I mean they meant so well, but they couldn't also fathom what was really going on with us. So one asked, "Would you like a whiskey?"

Arnold C.

We went to the first town, a German, Austrian town. We went into a home. We demanded food. There was a group of us. They gave us all the food we could eat. I was never so sick in all my life afterwards. We were allocated by the U.S. army, barracks expropriated from German troops.

One day a group of Jewish soldiers from the Jewish Brigade showed up and they said, "Do you want to go to Palestine?" Yes, I wanted to go to Palestine, but I was thinking of where do I find my parents. I found an American soldier. He was a black man and I asked him if he could write a letter to 1819 Wesley Avenue in Evanston. He did. I then decided to go with the Jewish soldiers. They took us to Italy in trucks. Then there was a correspondent from Israel who came to interview the children. They asked me where I was from, I told them and so on. It was published. My mother happened to read that newspaper in Austria, that I did an interview in Italy, and I am alive. She came looking for me. And one day, I saw her coming on the street. I saw her from far. I was standing on top of a hill and I saw her coming. And I ran down the hill and she ran towards me, as we hugged and met each other.

Chaim E.
Escaped from Sobibór with his future wife

We saw in a field a stack of hay somewhere and we figured let's stay over there, because that's the only place we could find. And what happened, some kids came playing there and they crawled up and they saw us. So we had, the middle of the day, to go away. Some farmer with some horse and wagon came around, and I talked to him and he said, "Yah! Sure!" And I got suspicious, so I jumped off and I say Selma, "Jump off! It's not safe!" The way he talked or whatever. And we ran away. We always kept near to woods.

One farmer, we told him we'd give him everything he wants if he wants to keep us here. Just give us once a day to eat and keep or whatever. And one day we talk with him and he says, "Listen. I cannot do it because it is too obvious. I live crowded with people. But I have a brother what he lives very isolated. He might be willing to do it." [We] dressed up Selma as an old lady, and me put on the wagon, covered me with straw and brought us to his

Chaim E. and his wife, among the few to survive the revolt and escape from Sobibór, shown here postwar with their baby.

brother. Now that was a terrible dangerous thing to do because the Germans all over. His brother agreed. So we gave him everything we had. He put us in the barn, a cow barn, on the top, an attic on straw. He put us there, and once a day he brought us something to eat.

He kept us there for quite some time till the Russians came—about six months. A few days before the Russians came, a little nephew from this farmer was chasing birds. And the birds happened to fly in the direction where we were there. And he saw us. So, it was a secret—no one in the family knew about, just he and his wife. So we were in danger already because probably he wouldn't want to keep us. So luckily, two or three days later, the Russians came and then we got freed. So that is really the end for us, the end of the war. So we was really very lucky that these people kept us—at least they didn't kill us. It was a rarity to have people like we met by accident. Very rare. Very rare.

Joseph K.
Liberated, age 19

We came across a group of Americans guarding German prisoners of war. And there was this American soldier who spoke Polish and he asked us who we were, and we explained it to him. He interpreted to the American boys, and one of them took off a submachine gun. He handed it to me, motioning to kill the German prisoners. I became very frightened and I gave it back to him. I just walked away.

I couldn't believe it, that the Americans were real. I couldn't believe it, that the Germans were actually defeated. It took a long time to understand that there was a stronger power than Germany. To us, they were the all-powerful and they brainwashed us [to] such an extent that we had no belief in ourselves. We had no understanding for right and wrong at that particular point in time.

Renée G.
Age 12, Soviet troops enter the area where
she and her family were hiding

The biggest thrill was when we started hearing shooting and we
knew that the Russians are approaching. One day, we saw
planes coming overhead and we were rejoiced. We knew we
could get killed again, because many of the barns were burning
all around us. But as long as were being killed by the Russians,
it wasn't so bad. The only thing we were afraid of [was] that the
barn would start burning and we would have to run out into the
fields and be killed by Germans, if they see us come out. Luckily, our barn was not hit and we saw German soldiers coming
back. And what a joy to see German soldiers coming back
depressed and just dragging back, instead of the ones we saw
marching with full force and pride towards the east. Now they
were really dragging back. On the road we saw them just moving back. We saw the Russian planes hitting the road. We still
didn't know how soon all this was going to happen. And the
next morning we heard a strange language outside. It was no
longer German. We heard Russian spoken. And we said, "This
is it! This is it!"

The farmer didn't want to let us out during the daylight. He
was more afraid of his neighbors than the Germans themselves. So
the next evening, when it was all clear and there was nobody
around, he opened that gate and he said, "Walk out." So we
walked to the highway and we waited. A Russian truck came by
and asked us who we were. We told them we were Jews who were
hiding out. They picked us up, took us to our town, let us in to
our own homes, gave us food, and treated us very well. My father
tried to get some of the goods back that he had before the war.
There was a lot of resentment. The Polish peasants, some of them
didn't want to give it back.

Herbert J.
American POW, Mauthausen

When we were taken prisoner, it wasn't known by anybody
because the two halftracks just disappeared. That's all. Twenty-
seven men. They [concluded] that something happened to us
because they couldn't find us anywhere and we were reported as
missing in action. Then they liberated the camp—it was my own
outfit that liberated the camp, the Eleventh Armored—and when
they liberated the camp and I was able to identify myself and
those who were still alive, I was right back in my own outfit again.
They said something about prisoner of war and whatnot, but, you
know, I said I'd just as soon forget about it. That's about the way
it ended up. The fact that I was in the camp was something that I
wanted to forget at the time.

Joseph K.

For the longest time after liberation, I didn't want to live. I had
nothing to live for. Somehow, in my deep recesses, I was hoping
to live to see Germany destroyed. And I did live to see that. After
that, there was nothing.

Rabbi Baruch G.
Age 22, Theresienstadt

Loneliness has various aspects to it. I remember after liberation, I
suffered probably more from the loneliness and the isolation, more
than during the Holocaust period. And I thought about it the
other day, I suppose it has to do with the fact that after, life
around you seems to be normal—but you are abnormal. Well,
why? In concentration camps, in labor camps, there was a preoccupation with survival, a preoccupation with being thrown around
and how I can make the next day. But then after what was called
"liberation"—actually the realization of liberation was not vivid
with me, was not real with me for a long time.

But I remember during the years '45, '46, '47, even up to '48, I would find myself crying, and quite frequently, feeling there's no one—there's no one around me that cares what I do and what I don't do. There are many other aspects to it that I suppose has to do with loneliness. Feeling of, yes, I'm alive, but that's it. The rest doesn't matter. No ambition. For what? For who? No initiative. If I am to stand, I'm standing. So I am standing. If you tell me to sit down, I'll sit down. That was real for a long time.

Perla K.

I remember one day General Eisenhower came in the hospital. He was walking, you know, in the hospital, walking every bed, and he stopped in my bed and he was talking with the doctor. And he was, you know [*nodding*] his head. After, the doctor told me, he say, "You'll be all right. You're going [to] Greece again." But I say to myself, "Going [to] Greece? To do what? Who is there? I don't know who is going to come back, I don't know anything."

Rabbi Baruch G.
Displaced persons camp

For shoes we were given those wooden clogs and they used to make loud noise when you walked. I was afraid that somebody, that I'll disturb somebody. I was so afraid for people. I was so much afraid to do any harm to anybody, to make anybody displeased with me. Terribly afraid. I remember we had to go to the kitchen to get my soup, you know, for the first few months. I would drag the shoes, not to lift them up, so they wouldn't make much noise. I remember at times going over to the place where I had my dish with a spoon. Take it—take it off the shelf and sitting down and going through the motions of eating, then catching myself—"What am I doing? There is no food there."

Joseph K.

When I went back to Poland after the war to find out if any of members of my family had survived, I was in a train of repatriates. As we left the Polish border, going towards Katowice, which was the next main town, I heard a group of Polish people talking amongst themselves, saying something to the effect, well, whatever Hitler did, at least we are grateful to him for having solved the Jewish problem for us. Now this is *after* the war. This is *after* what has happened to our people!

Martin S.

After liberation, after the war, we went back. We didn't even want to lay claim to anything. We just wanted to look for our families. We were in Kraków. In that two-week period we were there, there were two pogroms. It was so shattering. I cannot find the words to describe the feeling. The incredulousness! It is impossible to eluci-date! Here I'm coming back from what I call hell, and I remember saying to myself, "You know, when we get back to Poland, they're going to feel sorry for us. They'll open the doors for us." And we

Martin S. (center) with two friends at a displaced persons camp after the war. "After lib-eration, after the war, we went back. We didn't even want to lay claim to anything. We just wanted to look for our fami-lies. . . . In that two-week period . . . there were two pogroms."

arrive in Kraków and we're waiting in one of those holding areas for DPs and they're attacking with guns, knives. It was terrible. The *Russians* were protecting us.

After things settled down, quieted down, and they're standing there with machine guns, two other Russians walked by. And one holler[ed] up to one of them, "What are you doing up there?" He says, "Oh, I've got duty. I've got to watch these kikes." That jolt was another one to tell me, "There's no way, no place." After the two pogroms, plus this. It was worse than camp, those instances. The utter helplessness, the feeling of despair. Is there any place that I don't have to fear? Is there any place that I can feel comfortable?

Joseph K.

Some of the survivors came back—and they were killed by the Polish people. There's no excuse. They were not under the occupation by the Germans anymore. They were not forced to do it. The Russians did not tell them to do it. But obviously they felt that they had to help Hitler in the annihilation of our people. That is inexcusable, unforgivable. I will never forgive them. I can't. I don't have a right to forgive them.

I ask a question now, as a survivor. Why was a country like Denmark—Christians, with a Jewish people—Christians having taken upon themselves to save something like 95 percent or upward of that number of the Jewish population, and only a couple hundred kilometers to the east, Christians, too, were cooperating with the Germans to annihilate us? I may sound bitter. I am.

Jacob K.
Age 22, liberated from a death march

When I came back after the war to Poland, we were looked at—we don't belong there anymore. The Poles didn't want us. That's a fact of life. Whether it was just a number, whether or not every Pole was bad or not every German was bad—that's immaterial.

Precisely the pain is even more [that] the few who followed Hitler—if all Germany says now, "We didn't know," or something, that not all Germans are bad and that's true. But the few who were bad—it makes the pain worse, because the few who are bad could do so much damage while the rest was standing by. That's what makes it so bad.

Hanna F.
Age 22, posing as a Polish non-Jew

What I felt when the liberation came? That I am alone in the whole world. I escaped from the transport. I ran away two weeks before, two and a half weeks before the liberation. I ran away in Czechoslovakia—[*sigh*]—I had no desire to live. I had no place to go. I had nobody to talk to. I was just simply lost, without words. I know that everybody is killed. It took me a while till I met my husband after the war. I still had my assumed name. And afterwards, I went back to my own name, to my own identity. And to my own Jewishness. And I am Jewish, all right. I had determined already to survive, and you know what? It wasn't luck. It was stupidity. There was no guts. There were just sheer stupidity.

Edith P.

I recall the same afternoon, I sat down on a big stone and said to myself, "And what's now? What's going to happen to us now? We're all free—are we really free? Where's the family? I'm a young person who had a sheltered, innocent life, and what am I going to do now? Who's going to take care of me?"

9

"It Started with Dreams"

AFTERMATH

Witnesses confirm that "liberation" brought new problems. In time, they reclaimed a place in the world; but the ordeal they had endured pervades their memories and dreams. Often, as they built new lives and families, their experiences affected relationships with their children. Each family found its own way of coping. Just as no simple formula can determine how traumatized a particular witness has been by his or her experience, no simple blueprint exists for judging the impact of parents' Holocaust experiences on future generations.

As witnesses' private lives blend the joys of expectation with the pains of memory, so their perspectives on public affairs combine the hope for a better future with a sober, wary view of human limitations.

Chaim E.
Escaped from Sobibór

I believe the story really cannot be told. If you take ten people, listen to the story, and ask them to tell the story back, you will get ten different stories. Why? Because—I am not so strong in the language to explain it, but even the one what is strong in the language, he knows the expression, has the talent and everything—he still cannot tell the whole story. It is just impossible. Only the one that lived it through knows really what happened. Because the feelings what are involved with this story, they're not the same. Feelings, you can bring to a certain degree, tell what it is—but you really cannot, I cannot tell what I felt when—when I found the clothes of my brother, for example.

Now, if you ask what I was thinking of, I wasn't thinking at all. I was horrified. Things like that, you know, I can tell the story, and it sounds well I know the story—but it is more than the other story. It is more some feelings what you cannot bring out. I see the picture in front of me. You have to imagine something; the one what listens has to imagine something. So it has a different picture for me than for the one what he imagines it. I hear telling back a story, it doesn't sound at all the same what I was telling.

Abraham P.

Oh God, when I came over to the United States I remember seeing—we arrived at night and I saw all those flash[es], you know those lights and I says, "What's this? What's going on over here?" So the other says to me, "You dummy! Those are automobiles!" "That many automobiles? Every second an automobile? It's too many! How is it possible?" Well, then in the day we started to see them. I saw there were a lot of automobiles going by there, which was great. So then we were processed and as we got off the boat they assigned me at a hotel. And I stayed in a hotel in New York. Then I went out for a walk. I don't remember the name of the street or anything. I looked in the windows and I see those big hams, beef—it must have been a butcher shop—and bread, and all kinds of stuff. Oh my God! So much food! After I looked in that window, I started to proceed a little farther down the street and I saw a tall policeman coming in front of me. I immediately went into my pocket and I was ready to take out my identification card to show him that. "Look! I'm here legitimately!" Coming over here, it was a daze.

Coming in from hell, and all of a sudden you're in paradise. That's the only way I can put the two things together.

Renée H.

In July of 1945, my relatives in Brooklyn, who were listening assiduously to the radio, heard my name called out. They immediately got in touch with the Red Cross, but it was still too chaotic for them to do anything about it. I was finally sent to Sweden, where I was for three years. I was given over to a doctor in Sweden who immediately decided to fatten me up, because at the age of eleven I weighed as much as a three-year-old child and had a big pot belly. I slowly recovered from the experience. My sister was with

Renée H., age fourteen in Brooklyn, 1948, where she lived with relatives. "I was determined to tell everybody about my experiences. . . . They couldn't bear to listen to it. . . ."

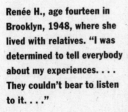

me. She had curiously survived the experience without illness, having turned into a very quiet, silent child and whose sense of the world was totally cut off. My sister came to New York with me.

Coming to the United States was a great shock. I happened to come in August of 1948. It was the hottest day. I had come from Sweden. I walked out of the plane and remember turning around and saying, "I'm going back." Because not only was it very, very hot in the airport, but at the airport greeting this plane, which had taken me twenty-four hours, I was suddenly faced by a whole panoply of black faces. Nobody in Sweden had told me that there were Negroes in the United States. I knew that they were in Africa. But to suddenly come to New York and see all these black faces I was sure I had come into the wrong country. I was supposed to come to the United States. Here was this hot place with all the black people. I thought I was somewhere in Africa. It was my having in some way sensed that life is playing tricks on me all the time, that I wasn't going to the places where I thought I was going to. And then at the ramp were my relatives, waiting for me—none of whom I knew. I had never met them. They had all left long before I was born. They were yelling and screaming, "Renée! Renée! Renée!" So I knew that I was where I was supposed to be. But what was strange was having to get adjusted not only to a totally different milieu but to relatives I had absolutely no inkling of.

It was a very strange thing because not only did I come to the United States, which was visually, humanly, culturally so different from anything I had experienced—[but also] the plentifulness that I saw! I remember going through the streets of Brooklyn and seeing the vegetable stands, the food stands! I couldn't believe that after the war, after having come to Sweden where, obviously, there was no war but there still were shortages, there were still things on rationing—to come to the United States, where everything just was hanging out on the streets! All the food, everything, the ice creams, the things that—seemed like such a strange contrast to what I knew. And then to come through an area of New York which was totally black, where you saw very few white people, and then coming into Brooklyn, which was Hasidic. It was Williamsburg, where all the religious Jews were. And I suddenly realized that this was a very, very strange world.

Arnold C.

My sister married one of the Jewish soldiers from the brigade and went to Israel. And my mother remarried an old friend from Kovno. He had lost his wife and daughter. He was a boyhood friend of my father. He knew us well from before, and the three of us came to this country. Family to me has a tremendous meaning. When I came to Chicago and I met my mother's family, it was quite large. She had four brothers and two sisters. Some came to this country before she was even born. I wanted to have that family, but the feeling was not reciprocal. "So what?" "I'm your cousin!" "So what?"

Arnold C., United States Air Force, Oklahoma, 1960. The first American he saw at liberation from Gunskirchen concentration camp was a lieutenant. At the time he felt, "One day if I can wear that uniform and also be an officer—Well, I made it."

We adjusted well in this country. It's a great place. My biggest achievement was being an officer in the United States Air Force. I remember when I saw the first American. He was a lieutenant from Washington, D.C. He wanted to adopt me. And at that time I felt, one day if I can wear that uniform and also be an officer— Well, I made it.

Martin S.

We came to the United States. We arrived in June. It was the twenty-seventh, I recall, and on June the twenty-ninth a group of children were going to a camp and my uncle said, "We're going to send you to a camp." [*Laughs*] We said, "Nothing doing!" "No, this is a good camp!" "Nothing doing! Nothing doing!" We wouldn't go.

One of the things I remember as a child coming out, I felt I had to tell the world what was happening. That was the highest priority. So I remember the first few months in the yeshiva, I would speak freely. I would tell the kids everything. I would tell my rabbi what happened and so on. Then one day we went out on recess and one of the kids got a hold of me. We were all in a circle and he said, "Why don't you tell one of your bullshit stories?" And from that day on—this was 1946, 1947—I did not say a word, I would say, till about five, seven years ago. The hurt was almost as much as being hurt by the Poles and the Germans because the realization, "My God! My own, they don't believe me."

Rabbi Baruch G.

I do remember the first years that I had a feeling that nobody really wants to know. Nobody has time to sit down and nobody cares. That, too, maybe now, maybe a sense of guilt on the part of those who were miles away and did nothing about it. So why talk about it? Kind of deny it. It didn't happen.

Renée H.

Now the thing that I find, of course, which touches me most about the experiences—the sharing it with my family. When I came to the United States, I was determined to tell everybody about my experiences. I was shameless, telling everybody in my family. And I'm afraid that they were not—being very religious people, they felt that I had to move my own experience into the general experience of the Jewish people. And I found that it was a way in which they were telling me they couldn't bear to listen to it. It was very hard for them to listen to it. The one thing which I discovered—that I ended up by being very protective of my family. And I would say, "They can't stand it? I won't tell them." And I would search for other people to tell it to. But, there were no other people.

Martin S.

I couldn't help but open up [to a business associate]. And when all was said and done, [he said], "I used to read about that. Isn't that interesting." It was a superficial interest. This hurts so much inside me that I can't allow it to be a passing interest. So I don't talk. I've tried in these last few years. People don't give a damn. And I tell you, maybe I can understand it. Because when things are happening in the world, I don't take—I don't feel their pain.

Martin S., portrait as a 13-year-old. "One of the things I remember as a child coming out, I felt I had to tell the world what was happening. That was the highest priority."

I was interviewed with my brother, and he wanted to tell something, and I frankly stopped him. And I cannot bring myself—there certain things that we saw or that we did that made us so inhuman, that I said—I remember speaking to him. I said, "Paul, they'll never believe it." I said, "If you ever tell this, the rest of the story that you have to tell, we'll lose credibility."

There's a strange thing with my brother. He doesn't remember most things. He just blotted out. We recall details of home now. In the beginning he used to say, "Oh, what are you talking about?" He wouldn't believe that he had blocked it out. He blocked out moments where he was on a death march. He blocked that out. He blocked out an instance where he was lined up and they were going to shoot him. [He] doesn't remember he was caught in an inferno, in an air raid, in a barrack. He was sleeping while the whole place was on fire. Doesn't remember that. Nothing. Maybe he's better off, because I don't think he carries the scars that apparently I seem to be carrying. I've had terrible, uncontrollable high blood pressure.

It started with dreams. There was a period of dreams that I would say for about five or six years. There wasn't a single week that I didn't have a dream. The interesting thing was the dream was always the same. I'm being chased and I'm being shot. The dream, the recurrent dream I was back in camp, I was in camp and so on and so forth. Lately there's a new dream. And I think it's when I began opening up. By the way, I did not open up at all until about five years ago. My children would ask me. I—I thought I was shielding them. Now I have a new dream that I am back in the camp, and everything that I enjoyed in the United States was a dream. In other words, in the dream, reality is the camp. And everything that has happened to date, with such unbelievable details, and it shatters me, it really does.

Clara L.

What is, again, very strange, I find that now, forty-nine years after
all these experience, I have more nightmares than I ever had even
in the immediate events. I very often dream and see places which
I have been to.

The other day I have seen a strange—I have seen a very beautiful—you'll see why I bring this subject—I have seen a very beautiful alligator handbag. And as I looked at the bag, I said, "What
does this remind me of?" I couldn't think of it. But I think I just
didn't want to remember. You see, when Bergen-Belsen was liberated these people were let loose. So we were wandering. We were
wandering from one place to another. And there were warehouses.
We came to a building, and we walked in, and I still see rows and
rows and shelves of handbags, ladies' handbags. As we were walking over there to reach those shelves, I sort of stepped on something. And I said to my friend, "Look! There's a body!" You see,
somebody, one of these inmates who wandered to these warehouse
and dropped dead from exhaustion or something. And she says,
"What do you want me to do about it?" I said, "Let's carry it
out." She said, "Are you crazy? You can't carry that out." And
she took a few packages of these linens and dropped it on [the
body]. And then we went to the shelves, and she wanted a handbag. And I wasn't in the mood anymore for the handbag. She
pulled out one handbag. It was an alligator handbag. She says,
"Take this one." I took it, and she took another one, and we
walked out. And I remember, as we left the place, I just threw
back the bag. I said, "I don't want it"—and walked away. And
this only came back. I never thought about it.

Herbert J.
American POW

It took me a number of years to get straightened out. I didn't dare
sleep with my wife after one bad incident where I had a bad

dream and she happened to strike me just right. I come to, I was strangling her. So after that, I had separate bedrooms for years so it wouldn't happen again. My children were brought up [to] never enter into my bedroom but to call me from the doorway. And so that's the way I've been. Even after all these years, there's things that you forget, but something happens and you go to bed at night and you don't even thinking about it, but you'll have another one of those nightmares. It doesn't leave you entirely.

Perla K.

The dreams, the dreams. You know for few years, in the beginning, I didn't have any dreams. But now, all dreams. Two week[s] ago, I was dreaming the Germans, they try to find me. And I went inside of the ocean and I hide inside of the ocean of the world till the German leave. All kind of dreams. They never stop. Believe me, never, never, never stop. Sometime, you know what? I wish to be dead, too [*crying*]. I wish to be dead. Because I can't anymore to cope with this thing.

Celia K.

I was a pampered child from a wealthy family. We had maids. I never did anything and I really was a helpless creature. I didn't know how to take care of myself. So I started looking for a husband. It's just like you go out and you look for a horse in the market, I was looking for a man. And the first man that wanted me, I got married. I didn't know him. I knew him only three weeks, that's all. We had no way of surviving any other way. You couldn't earn anything. I began working at a very prestigious job. I was a secretary, but you couldn't buy a loaf of bread. So what good is it? And my husband was a tailor, and right away he started working, and he earned bread and eggs and milk and things. And I said, "Gee, at least I'll eat." So you didn't look for romance or compatibility or anything like that. You just got married. A lot of marriages were made like this in '44, '45.

I knew that on my own I wouldn't have been able to do it, because I was too helpless. I could take care of myself in the partisans, but then when it was all over, all initiative, all energy, everything left me. I was just a nobody. I was weak. I was soft. I was just sick and tired of taking care of myself. Really. So I said, "If I marry a man he would at least provide for me"— and that was it. Marriages made in heaven. This is what happened.

And it was very hard to start a life, after the war was over. I was pretty suicidal, I must say that. It was very hard for me to get adjusted. I gave birth to a son who worked out very well right now, but my son had a very difficult time, for years and years. I was sick. I had no business giving birth to a child in the state I was in. I admit it now, I could see it and I know it. And my son really suffered for it. I knew that something was lacking in my personality, and that the wounds are not healed.

I did look for help. I went to professionals when I came to America. I thought this baby would be definitely mentally deficient. He didn't have any mother's love. He didn't have any atten-

Celia K. with her husband and son, approximately 1947. "It was very hard to start a life, after the war was over. . . . I could not adjust to a life of a wife and mother."

tion paid to him. Anyway, after I got out of the hospital, finally after almost a year, he didn't know me. He didn't want to go to me. He didn't acknowledge me at all. And my struggle began with relationship with my son and family.

I could not adjust to a life of a wife and mother. I was really, I would say, three, four personalities. In one instant, I would be a young girl. I dreamed about going back to school. This was my foremost dream. I wanted to go back to school. I dreamed that I am a little girl. Then I would think that I'm back home, and then I would know that I was a wife and mother. And then I would know that I am not normal. Something is lacking. I couldn't relate. I didn't have any emotions. My son didn't have any emotions, either. It was a very uphill battle. I didn't hide my suffering. I didn't know how to hide it. I was miserable. So he was miserable.

Bessie K.

Our daughter was sitting in our house and we were discussing with a few young people. And she came over and she said, "Mother, what hopes do I have for my future?" And what can mother tell her? What did my mother tell us? She always said, "We hope that you should not know from any wars, from any bad things," because any mother shelters their children. And what can I tell a young woman? Don't worry! Things will be better! Things will be good! Be hopeful! But this is not the real saying from a mother's heart, "Don't worry." I *am* worried.

Rabbi Baruch G.

When I became aware that existing means more than just simply eating and existing, I would cry and cry a lot. Just anything. If you would just talk to me, just talk to me, I would start crying. Why? Because I said to myself, "Is it true that you're talking to me? Why should you talk to me? It's probably not true." There was a whole confusion around the whole thing of existence. Obviously, at least to my way of thinking, that they got us, or at least they got me, to think of myself so little that nobody should to talk with me.

Of course, I met my wife, which was just marvelous. We were married rather soon right after, but as I look back, I say, "How dared I? How dared I?" I was not well mentally. By mentally I mean I wasn't crazy, I wasn't doing anything outlandish. At least I don't think so. But, but inside—my inside was—definitely still is—scarred.

Of course there are other issues involved in there in relation with my son and myself. We have a good relationship, but not as good as I would like it to be. Without even realizing, you know, when he was growing up, that there was a block. There was a block. In trying to remove it, he has gone to therapy. I did not. He has urged me to in the last few years. I have not. I suppose—I say I'm busy. And I am busy.

[I watched a documentary] and what comes out of that is that mother was afraid to love her daughter because all her loved ones were taken away from her. Did it happen to me? I don't know. Looking back, I missed—I miss it terribly now. The fact that I was too busy and he wanted more of me and I wasn't there. Now, which is it? Is it fear to come close to him? Is it wanting to be normal, so much so that I immersed myself in my work, all kinds of hours, or what? But I suppose these are some of the scars that I mentioned before, that are with us, and I suppose we'll be buried with them.

Perla K.

I was very sick. All the time, you know, I have, my nerves so bad. I was walking the street. I was scatterbrains. I was walking, walking in the street alone. They never let me alone, but sometimes when I was alone, no matter how many car was behind me, I didn't hear nothing. I didn't hear anything. Because my mind, all my mind was in one place. Always in my mind I was

Perla K.
Born Corfu, Greece, 1928
Recorded 1990, age 62

Perla K. was a teenager during the benign Italian occupation of Greece and the subsequent invasion by Germany. When the Germans demanded registration of all Jews, her father decided to separate the family in several hiding places. Later they came out of hiding and were deported to Auschwitz/Birkenau. There her brother, attempting to pass some food to her over a fence, was attacked by dogs and beaten to death by the guards. Mrs. K. learned of experiments on pregnant women. She was transferred to Bergen-Belsen, where she slept on the ground surrounded by corpses. She was transferred to a forced labor factory, then to Dachau, where she was liberated by American troops.

In August 1945, Perla K. returned to Greece, where she was reunited with relatives in Athens. Her only surviving brother returned three weeks later and after a brief visit to Corfu, he emigrated to Palestine. Mrs. K. has never returned to Corfu. She met her husband in Athens. They emigrated to the United States in 1951 and have two daughters.

with my brother, the time they beat him to death.

Sometimes I wish to have a grave, sometime to go there, you know, to cry, to talk and to cry. In that way, we don't have nothing. We say sometime, "Where to cry?" Even after forty-five year[s], believe me, I walk and I'm alone in the house. I walk all the house and I cry. I talk [to] myself like crazy, because I miss them so much. I try to hide myself from my children, you know, and from my husband, because I don't want them to know what I go through. Because you never can forget. How can you forget all these things?

I don't want to forget anything. Believe me. Sometime they tell me, "Why? You know, you have to forget, to enjoy yourself." I say, "No, I don't want to forget." How do I want to forget? How? And you know, for many, many year, even now, I see people laughing, dancing, laughing, and I get very mad. Very mad. I say, "Look! You know, how they laugh? How they dance? You know, these people? How?" When I think my mother, my father, my sister, my brothers—and six million Jew[s]! You know, they are dead! How do I want to laugh? How do I want to dance when I think all that? I was very angry. And I used to go places, and I go places. I'm very sad, you know. I sit down in one place and I look and I don't like. You know? I don't like to go to dance. I don't like to go to anywhere. Because always I think, "My family. My family."

Bessie K.

I had to come out alive by myself. Maybe I did make mistakes. And I have regrets, I have regrets. Because I tried to deny something that no person can. I had a child. I had family. I had a life. But in order to survive, I think I had to die first. That's what I told our two daughters and I didn't know the damage what I was doing to them, to my husband, and to myself.

This is very, very strange to say. I feel I'm in touch with myself, with my feeling, through the therapy. I know myself now. I know what happened then. I'm alive now. And this is why I said through all those years, whenever a holiday came, and we have no family. So our two daughters and ourselves, and the holiday's there—no grandparents, no aunts and uncles, or whatever. I kept saying, "But I'm not alive. I'm dead." And this was doing great harm to them and great harm to me. Maybe I wasn't supposed to be alive, and I live maybe with the guilt that everybody is dead and I'm the only one alive. If I would have been with them, maybe it would have been different. There are a lot of maybes. And there's no questions to ask.

Rabbi Baruch G.

We mentioned a sense of guilt. Yes, sometimes I do feel, "Why have I survived?" Have I fulfilled a basic obligation that one should carry with him to tell the world about it? Why did I then shy away from it these years?

Clara L.

[A psychiatrist said to me,] "Whomever I interviewed, they felt a tremendous guilt feeling that they survived—that they survived, which I don't find with you." And then and there I said, "No, this is the case. This was the case all along. I believed in it. I was one of those who was destined to survive. And I felt no guilt. I did whatever I could for my parents. I did whatever I could for my sister and whoever was around me. More I couldn't do. So I don't feel guilty about it, to remain alive.

Jacob K.

And the scars, the German behavior toward us, the tortuous days and nights, it's something that we have. It is in our minds. You can't forget about that. Six million people is just women and children? I can't tell you everything in an interview. I couldn't even describe one day in the ghetto. I don't want to live with that pain, but it's there. It's there. It forms its own entity and it surface whenever it wants to. I'll go on a train and I will cry. I will read something and I'll be right back there where I came from. And I can't erase it. I'm not asking for it. It comes by itself. It has formulated something in me. I'm a scarred human being among human beings. And they were instrumental in my being scarred.

It hurts because at the time when it happened we thought that

"I'm a scarred
human being among
human beings."

Jacob K.
Born Zwoleń, Poland, 1923
Recorded 1983, age 60

Growing up in Poland, Jacob K. had no illusions about the vulnerability of Jews. Still it came as a surprise when, with the rise of Nazism in Germany, classmates who had been close friends began singing antisemitic songs. After Germany's invasion of Poland, German soldiers burst into their home, forced his entire family to strip, and terrorized them. Mr. K. and his brother avoided the mass deportation of Jews from Zwoleń when they were assigned to clean up the Jewish sector, burying bodies and catering to the demands of the German police.

Mr. K. was deported to Skarżysko-Kamienna, Buchenwald, and Schlieben, from which he was forced on a death march. He was liberated on May 8, 1945, in Sudetenland. Liberation did not end his ordeal. "When I came back after the war to Poland, we were looked at [as if] we don't belong there anymore." He lived in displaced persons camps in Feldafing and Landsberg. He met his wife, Bessie K., in Płzeň, Czechoslovakia, and they emigrated to the United States in 1949. He takes satisfaction in having raised two children, in leading a creative life, but emphasizes that nothing erases the scars of the Holocaust. "The twentieth century crumbled—for one man? Is this what we are capable of doing? Am I part of that human community? I don't think so."

nobody knew, that we were alone. But they did know. They didn't want to listen. People didn't want to listen because people don't care. I'm not making myself in front of you out as an angel, that I don't have the same traits. But I was the one who was persecuted and I have the scars. And it hurts me, and I am vulnerable. And why should I be vulnerable? Why should I be the victim of somebody who doesn't understand themselves? Somebody who wants to hate me because I'm—that, I'm this, or that?

Abraham P.

I didn't know what I really wanted. The only thing I do remember, I wanted to go in a corner and cry, cry myself out. But I wasn't able to do it either. I was drafted in 1948. Somehow I found, as they say, a home in the army. Then they found out that I was in a concentration camp, they turned me over to a psychologist. He asked me about my experiences. I didn't speak English well at the time, and he didn't speak Yiddish. So there was a frustration between—it was frustrating for him and it was frustrating for me. And he picked out that I was a *yeshive bokher* [yeshiva student]. They really needed someone should be able to *davenen* and conduct services. So they made me an acting chaplain, and I managed.

Abraham P., 1950, Korean War. "They really needed someone should be able to *davenen* and conduct services. So they made me an acting chaplain, and I managed."

I was very religious in the concentration camp. In fact, while I was in Buchenwald we had access to some paper and pencil. We wrote down the prayers, and I remember many people who were not religious at home said to me, "Please, say some prayer with me." We did. We always used to *davenen*. After we got out of the concentration camp, that's when we started to question. While we were there, we didn't.

Celia K.

Even [for] well-educated people who are constantly working with the Holocaust survivors, it's hard to comprehend what it is really to go through and feel what we went through. It is hard for a person who really didn't experience it to really put it in the proper perspective. It's hard. My husband couldn't. After so many years, he still asks questions. When he saw *Holocaust* [the television series], he couldn't watch. I said to him, "To me [this television series] *Holocaust* is—what can I tell you? It's a Pollyanna story. It's a Pollyanna story compared to what really happened. It's nothing. This is ridiculous. It's fiction!"

Martin S.

I went to see a film and I really didn't know what it was about— that one about Cambodia, *The Killing Fields*. Had I known what I was getting into—that had a profound effect on me! I got out of there and I said, "My God, nothing has changed." It makes me— My wife says I am the epitome of cynicism, and I agree. I don't trust anyone. I don't tend to believe people.

Helen K.

I do what I can. I feel if I survived—I guess, maybe it's a rationalization which doesn't make sense to me either, but the only way I can justify that there was a special purpose for me to live. And if I shouldn't live out my life as a decent human being, and do something worthwhile—You know, I try to do something useful. Whatever I can do as Jew, I do. I'm involved in Jewish living, and I guess I overdid it with my son because I gave him such conscience—my son is so religious now that it's unbelievable—that he somehow, in his own way, has to pay back something.

Jacob K.

I don't have any bitterness, but let me live with reality. I don't want to live in a world of make-believe. It took forty years to start talking. I couldn't speak to you ten years ago. Bessie couldn't speak to me at all about her past. And it hurts. We perceive life as a precious thing, and then Bessie gives birth to a child and a German takes away the child and kills it. What are we, superhuman to just brush it aside and say to the world, "Thank you for liberating us"—and that's all? We wash the hands clean, like nothing happened? Like if the Nazis die out, nobody is responsible anymore? "Somebody did it. Hitler did it. A maniac and a few Nazis did it. His co-workers. His government, Himmler, others." And that's all? And that's all? I can't—I can't make peace with that. Maybe other survivors can, I don't know. I myself, if you ask me, I can't.

And yet I go on. I'm creative. We [are] both creative. We contribute, we work. But this is not the issue. There's another issue. There's a deeper issue. You cannot brush away the pain by giving something else. In my way of thinking, it is the human responsibility. Everything crumbled. The twentieth century crumbled—for one man? Is that what we are capable of doing as a human race, to let one man crumble the whole—the whole moral structure? The poetry, the music, the culture, everything. Is this what we are capable of doing? And who's going to be next?

I didn't think that was possible to do it. We didn't think that. We thought, "We [are] in a war and war is hell, and somehow we survive." Hitler needed trains for other things, but yet he found trains to drive Jewish people to the slaughter. Everything was

punctual, with the German punctuality and with the German pre-
ciseness. Everything. Am I part of that human community? I don't
think so.

Chaim E.

One day they said that Himmler comes to our camp [Sobibór].
Himmler was the head of the extermination of all the Jews. So a
few days ahead they had a transport from about a hundred girls.
Only young girls. And they kept them in the barrack. When he
came, they took this hundred girls to the gas chamber, that he
could see how they gas them and burn them. Sometimes I'm
thinking, "What kind of a people is that?" There is really not any
different creatures. And later on, when we saw him like on the trials, we saw him in Germany, they do like nothing happened, nothing unusual. Some got free already, they had their families, they
were in business—and they look like your next neighbor.

Jacob K.

You don't run away because somebody hates you. You have scars,
you know. But then there is a difference. You can hate me—you
don't have to love me—but if you kill me, there's a big difference,
you know. All of a sudden, I'm—I'm not even a person. I'm a
nobody. And the Poles saw it. They didn't help. They took advantage. I saw they caught people, Jewish people from the woods that
they escaped, and they brought them to the Germans, and I told
you that the Germans shot them and they got a reward: two
pounds of sugar and a bottle of vodka. I saw it with my own eyes.
The irony of it, the bitterness—that they didn't have to do it.
Nobody forced them to hate. It's a natural—it's a natural behavior. Of course not all Poles do it. Of course, not all Germans are
bad. But what of it? What of it? Isn't it more painful that a few
Germans could instrument a whole nation to stand by while they
did the killing? It says in the Bible for everybody, "Thou shalt not

kill." It says for everybody. You don't have to love me, but don't kill me. I want to have an option to be a human being, not to have to be afraid of somebody, another human being.

Father John S.

I see it, personally, as the greatest tragedy of my life that Jewish people were deported all around me, I didn't do anything. I panicked—not even panic, not even fear. I just didn't know what to do. Nobody told us. Nobody prepared us. I was not ready to act. I was a young seminarian. I lived under the discipline. I had no idea that I could have an initiative of my own—or I should. Today, maybe, I would be ready to run in front of the train and lay down, and I don't want to sound dramatic. Maybe I would have—today I would call out or protest or risk being shot down or clubbed down. At that time, I was immobilized. It was just, you know, a feeling—not even a feeling of what can I do. There's nothing to do—just running away, simply running away. It was beyond my experience. I was utterly unprepared. And there was no leadership—not the bishop, from the city, nothing from the church—absolutely nothing. There was no leadership from the church, I am sorry to say, not in my area. People just were disorganized, scared, panicky, confused. And a good number were antisemitic.

Robert S.
Former Hitler Youth

I'd like to believe, as a person who has learned to think in later life, and as a person who is a native German, that the Germans would not have been able to do all the total madness, the destruction of Jews and other nationalities, if it had not been sort of tied up in this madness of the war. I think this was the real beginning of the downfall of Germany as a civilized country.

I feel my father has failed me in this regard. I have met him a couple of times after his return. He never said anything to me that

"If . . . these are
Germans, and I am
German—am I *that*?"

Robert S.
Born Weissenstadt, Germany, 1927
Recorded 1989, age 62

As a German child in a pro-Nazi family, Robert S. was excited by the Nazi military spectacle. "War! I'm going to be a hero!" he thought, and joined the Hitler Youth along with other children his age.

Robert S. believed the Nazi propaganda. When a liberal relative who opposed the Nazis dared to ask him why he wore the uniform, Mr. S. lectured him about "the whole propaganda spiel." In the environment he inhabited, "the people I knew . . . [were] all for the war . . . and whatever stood in its way to be destroyed."

When he arrived at the Soviet front, he saw German officers hanging their own soldiers from lampposts when they did not prevail despite the freezing cold and lack of food. His convictions began to crumble after he saw what the Nazis did to their own people.

After the war, having learned of the Nazi atrocities, he confronted the silence of family. Neither his father nor his mother would speak of what had happened, of what they had supported and done. Nor did any of the people he knew of their generation, many of whom had been officers. In Germany, Robert felt it was impossible to ask the questions he needed to ask about himself. "I just really felt I had to get away from that in order to look at myself." He emigrated to the United States and did not return to Germany for many years.

was in any way remorseful of anything that he had been involved in. And he had been an officer at the time. . . .

I didn't feel it was [only other] people in my country. I really felt it was me, too, and this was what was very hard. I just never could really say to myself, "You didn't do that." I'm a product of that culture. And I think many of the things that were brought out in their most negative form were—I was a part of that. And I just really felt I had to get away from that in order to look at myself. I couldn't do that in Germany. I couldn't do that, asking these questions. "How? Who am I?" This then became a question in my mind. "If this is Germany and these are Germans, and I am German—am I like that? Am I *that*?"

Clara L.

I was taken by some friends to a luncheon in London [in] a very elegant restaurant. The next table was full of very loud Germans, and it annoyed me. I was upset that they are again on top of the world. Then I looked at them and they were maybe thirty-plus-year-old youngsters, and I said, "What do they have to do with that what happened to me? That wasn't them." In all fairness, it wasn't them. Do they know what happened? Some of them weren't even alive.

Herbert J.
American POW liberated from Mauthausen

[The girl who gave me the sandwiches on the way to the quarry], she says, "I'm a German." She says, "I'm not a Nazi." And it seems that there was a distinction between Germans and Nazis. So I mean this helped me later on, because I was so filled with hatred and whatnot, that I don't know that I could have continued on. The doctors told me it would eat me up if I kept it up. But I come to the realization that not every German was a Nazi, and not all of them were agreeable to what actually went on.

Edith P.

I have given a great deal of thought how I should conduct myself vis-à-vis the Germans. How I should feel? Should I hate them? Should I despise them? Should I go out with a banner and say, "Do something against them?" I don't know. I never found the answer in my own soul, and I have to go according to my own conscience. I cannot conduct myself what my husband tells me, what my children or what the world has said. The only thing I can say is that up until now, I ignore them. I don't hate them. I can't hate—I feel I would waste a lot of time in my life. But sometimes I wish, in my darkest hours, that they would feel what we feel sometimes when you are uprooted and bring up children—I'm talking as a mother, as a wife—and there is nobody to share your sorrow or your great happiness. There's nobody to call up and say, "Something good happened to me today," or "I have given birth to a beautiful daughter," or "She got all A's," or "She got into a good college."

I have tried to preserve the holidays as I saw it at home, transfer it to my own children. We have beautiful Passovers, like I saw it at home, but the spirit is not there. It's beautiful, my friends tell me, but I know it's not the same. There is something missing. I want to share it with somebody who knows me really. My children are all grown up, and there's nobody but mom and dad. There isn't even a grave to go and cry to. And I sometimes wish they would feel that. It's not easy to live this way.

Werner R.

I'll be honest with you. I am making light, as far as the family is concerned, for what happened to me. I resent it, number one, people making money out of their own misfortune or misfortune which befell others. I think I have to be grateful to be alive, and I am grateful. I don't have a guilt feeling like some people say, you know, "Why me?" You know, "How do I prove myself?" But I very much don't want my children to feel that—I didn't want to give them any feeling of fear. I don't want them to get a feeling of horror. To talk about the camp and so on from an educational point of view is another thing. I don't believe that by telling what has happened will prevent anything, will prevent a future disaster.

I don't blame anybody for whatever happened. I don't have a chip on my shoulder. Really, I'm telling this for a historical, you know, as a historical documentation, if it contributes anything at all. But not in order to—how do you call it—to cry on somebody's shoulder. I can assure you, the world owes me absolutely nothing. I owe the world more than the world owes me.

Renée H.

What is left is the sense that—that one can really never totally reconcile cultures. That one does make peace, but it's still the fact of the two cultures that exist in my mind—and I'm sure that in other people who have had experiences like me—that the two [are] separate units in one's experience. So that there is the me that is the wartime and pre-wartime me, and the me that is the post-wartime. It's like having an era before and after. And that while they are all connected in myself, they are not reconcilable. And it took me a long, long time to realize that not only are they not reconcilable, I don't *want* them to be reconciled. That I wanted them to be separate, that I wanted this other experience not to get lost.

Renée G.

People would ask me to talk about my experiences or what had happened, and I would talk about it. But I felt as if I was talking about somebody else. Not myself. I felt as if I were talking about this little girl, somewhere in the background, whose name was Rivka, [who] had gone through all these things. And when I would talk about it, [it was] completely dispassionately, as if it weren't me at all. I naturally knew it was me, but I—I didn't—I

Renée G., 1953, when she became a U.S. citizen, with her parents and two brothers. At center: New York Governor Thomas E. Dewey.

could not believe that this really happened, that such a thing is even possible to happen, even [though I] knew that it must have been me.

I had a compulsion to go back to Poland. I felt I owe it to myself, to my parents, to my people, to my town, to my grandparents, to really go back and touch reality. Really see the house I was born in. My whole family thought I was absolutely insane, that I was a traitor. They couldn't understand how I could possibly take it emotionally. And I knew it was something that I had to do—that I couldn't, you know, move away from this world without doing this.

I rented a taxi, and I told [the driver] I wanted to go to the town where I was born and raised in, to see the house. And somebody told me, "Oh no! Don't go there. It doesn't exist anymore. You wouldn't recognize it. It's all changed." But I was determined. So I went back to the town—and there it was. There stood the house, the same way as it was before. And when I looked at it, that's the first time I broke out crying and it was because I had mixed feelings of joy to see the place where I come from, where I was born, where my grandparents were. And of course, it was like a ghost house, but still, there it was. It was real! It stood there, and it all began to have meaning, a beginning and an end. Sure, they're not there anymore, but this was a reality. I did have grandparents. I did have uncles and aunts and cousins. It was true that I was running up and down and played with them, and my grandfather at Hanukkah gave me five cents, you know, and all the grandchildren had to line up and get it. So it was a bittersweet experience that was just great. It was terrific. I felt so much better than I had before, when I was sort of shoving everything into a corner, like a dirty corner. Sure, it was painful, but it was real.

I was trying to recognize, touch upon spots that I knew I had lived through before, that I enjoyed. I still remembered smells, certain smells that drew me to the Polish forest, for example. Because I did have a very happy youth. And I remember [after] coming to the United States, very often I'd say, "No, this forest doesn't smell the way the Polish forest does, or the way the Polish strawberries do." And sure enough, I went to that whole area and smelled the wheat and the forest, and I said, "This is it! This is what I remember."

Then my other stop that I had to go to was the hiding place. I wanted to know if the farmer was still alive. Again I was told that you can't go there. First of all, there's no road. You can't go by taxi. You have to go by horse and cart. And I said, "I don't care." I told the taxi man I would pay him whatever is necessary. "Get there somehow." So he drove on plain fields through mud, and finally we arrived there. And there she was, the lady, the old lady. And I threw my hands around her and I started crying. And she says, "Who are you?" And I finally told her. I said, "*Yankele's córka, Yankele's córka.*" You know, Yankel's daughter. She said, "No! No! It couldn't be!" you know, and she started crying. The old man

Photograph of the widow of the Polish farmer who hid Renée G. and her family, taken by Renée G.'s brother on a return trip to Poland.

wasn't alive anymore. He was dead for about seven years. But we had a great reunion, and she was so happy. She started talking how she risked her life so many times, and she thought she would never be alive or certainly not see anybody from this family again. I left, you know, very, very excited. I accomplished my mission. I touched—I touched reality.

I wanted still to touch upon one more spot which was very important to me—Treblinka. That's another place where I broke down. As I came upon it, I felt as if I was walking on my own intended grave. And also that's where all my family was buried—all the little cousins that I had remembered—uncles, aunts, grandparents. Every town had its own tombstone, and finally we found it. There it was, a tombstone with the engraving of "Losice." I had my last cry, and we left.

Helen K.

You know, the man I married and the man he was after the war wasn't the same person, and I'm sure I was not the same person either when I was at sixteen and later on. But somehow, we had a

247

need for each other, because he knew who I was. He was the only person who knew. You know, you feel like you come from nothing, you are nothing, nobody knows you—it's a very strange feeling. You need some contact, some connection, and he was my connection. He knew who I was and I knew who he was. And we stuck it out! We are married I don't know how many years—thirty-five or whatever. We had two children and he's very different. He copes differently than I do. And we're here. We're here to tell you the story.

Martin S.

When I see these hijackings and the brutality with which they kill people, I say to myself, "What's new?" I often see films of what happened during the Crusades, what happened before the Crusades, and I can't help but say to myself, "It's never going to change." Man must go through a characteristic change, a basic change in character to make him different. And that's what hurts so much, that I say a thousand years from now, someone will sit somewhere and tell a new story about more brutality. Maybe someone viewing this tape, years from now, can develop a program to find out what makes man tick, to make him so brutal! Otherwise, all this is for naught. I would hate to think that my sitting here is just an academic exercise, because someone may be given a grant so that he may do additional research and thereby make a living. This is too painful. We must [*crying*] do something to change man. Because I am a very bitter man.

Joseph K.

Yesterday, I made a list of members of our family. In 1939, there were 117 people of our family. In 1945, 11 survived. Out of these, 2 survived as non-Jews on Aryan papers, 5 survived in Russia, never having been under the German occupation, and 4 of us survived the concentration camps.

Composite photograph, left to right: (top) Joseph K., his father, his brother-in-law. (Bottom) his two sisters and his mother. His parents and one sister were killed in Belzec death camp. "Yesterday, I made a list of members of our family," he reported in his testimony. "In 1939, there were 117 people of our family. In 1945, 11 survived."

Edith P.

When I heard about Cambodia [*crying*], I went into a depression, because the world has not learned. I felt guilty that I'm living in a beautiful home with all the comforts—and I am impotent. I do nothing. It pains me, terribly, that the world has not learned that don't kill your brother or sister, no matter what the reason is. I share the guilt today. I do.

Rabbi Baruch G.

It is common knowledge, the realization that time is running out. Every year less and less survivors are around. Do we have the right to bury this with us? We have no right to do it. It's got to be told. It's got to be—it's got to be recorded. For one reason and one reason only: not so much to know what happened, but rather what assurance do we have that it's not happening again? Actually, it is happening in one way or another. As a society, as a people, as a community, we must know these subjects. These subjects are real. They may start from a little prejudice or name-calling or whatever it is, and can blow up into the most horrifying experience, either for a whole community, for a whole nation, for a whole people, or for an individual. And this must not be permitted to go on if we—if we are humans. And I hope we are human.

Helen K.

I don't know. I don't know if it was worth it. I don't know if it was worth it. Because you know, when I was in the concentration camp, and even after, I said to myself, "You know, after the war people will learn. They will know. They will—they will see. We will learn." But did we really learn anything? I don't know. I don't know if we learned anything. Or if we ever will. I don't know.

ABOUT THE YALE ARCHIVE

The Fortunoff Video Archive for Holocaust Testimonies at Yale began twenty-one years ago as a grassroots community effort in New Haven, Connecticut. Laurel Vlock, a television host and producer, initiated a "Holocaust Survivors Film Project," with the help of Dori Laub, a Yale psychiatrist (himself a child survivor from Czernowitz), and William Rosenberg, head of the Farband, a local Labor Zionist organization with a large number of survivors. Soon many other citizens gave their support. Using makeshift studios, raising funds for each taping session, overcoming technical problems, and persuading the witnesses to come forward, this group worked under difficult conditions in various Connecticut communities and occasionally in other places. Almost two hundred witness accounts were taped in two years. Recognizing the historical and educational value of this oral documentation, the late Yale President A. Bartlett Giammatti agreed in 1981 to the establishment of a video archive at the university. In 1987, a gift by Alan Fortunoff of New York City assured a permanent basis for the archive, and it was named after his parents, Max and Clara Fortunoff.

It may have been the first time that Yale accepted a local effort by making it an integral part of its main library. The Charles H. Revson Foundation provided start-up funds and has remained a major and enthusiastic supporter. But all beginnings are hard; and I can remember the stage when each taping seemed a triumph against odds. It was still a time when one had to proceed one by one by one—it took over five years to gather a thousand testimonies.

The Yale Testimony project, which has collected four thousand personal histories amounting to ten thousand hours of video testimony, was the first systematic effort to recognize the importance of this audiovisual medium for the purpose of documentation and education. Established as an Archive of Conscience, it encouraged survivors and other witnesses (hidden children, liberators of the concentration camps, bystanders with significant information) to testify by coming to the university's studio. But we also created affiliates to tape survivors throughout the United States and abroad. The countries represented in the archive are England, Israel, France, Germany, Belgium, Slovakia, Yugoslavia, Poland, Belarus, Greece, Argentina, Ukraine, Czech Republic, Canada, and Bolivia.

To make sure that the video testimonies would not become inert, or sit decaying on the shelves of a library, an integrated process was put into effect. In addition to instituting careful storage and preservation measures for the tapes, the archive assured intellectual access through a computerized catalog summarizing the content of each witness account in a machine-readable format that can be called up anywhere in the world. Periodically a guide is published to facilitate reader use. Together with her staff, the Yale archivist in charge of the collection assists the many students, faculty, and visiting researchers who come to watch the testimonies in special facilities provided by Sterling Library, as well as many who call to request reference information.

At the center of all this are the men and women who survived and whose individual stories are being preserved, often in remarkable detail. It is our wish to document the tragedy and to show it in its full human detail. But we do not try to make historians of the survivors. We listen to them, accompany them, try to free their memories, and see each person as more than a victim: as someone who faces those traumas again, an eyewitness who testifies in public. What emerges most powerfully in these narratives is the psychological and emotional milieu, the personal thoughts, the everyday texture of living and dying that tends to escape academic historians. Yet in many ways the archive confirms or supplements the historian's important work and reaches out, through vivid portrayals, to both a younger audience in the schools, which is audiovisually oriented, and researchers who know the value of oral history.

Certain basic principles have guided the Yale project. The first is that every survivor or witness should be given the opportunity to speak. The majority of witnesses interviewed had not spoken formally about their experiences, and most were unlikely to record it in written form. We did not seek out an elite but welcomed everyone ready to speak. The second is that the interviewers are there for the survivor: they should never take the initiative away from the person interviewed.

Since questioning may be essential—to get the survivors talking, to release their memories, and to overcome certain resistances—this is not always an easy task. Our training program for the interviewers gives them the necessary historical background and makes a determined effort to screen out any special agenda they may have. Needless to say, this is an ideal not always realized. But at least the ideal is there and very clear: the survivor is to be enabled to talk intimately of harrowing experiences that are often pushed to the margins of consciousness in order for the victim to build a new life. Dori Laub was central in formulating the protocols for this kind of open, or nondirective, interview that encourages a testimonial alliance between interviewer and survivor.

Another principle proved crucial to gaining a less partial, more comprehensive picture of the persecution as a whole. After establishing thirty affiliates throughout the United States, we decided to introduce the taping concept abroad. Most survivors who settled in America after the Holocaust had been persecuted simply for being

Jews, for racial reasons in the light of Nazi doctrine. Filming them alone would not have yielded a satisfactory picture of the political action that took place in Germany in the 1930s, or in France, Belgium, and continental Europe generally in the 1940s.

Even the range over time during which the testimonies are being recorded—starting in 1979 and to be continued at least to the year 2001—is significant. Testimonies differ according to the memory milieu: recall of the same event is influenced by the time and place in which it is recorded. The survivor travail, moreover, did not end with liberation: homecoming, for instance, was a very different experience depending on the country; and many survivors, of course, remained displaced persons in Europe and eventually settled elsewhere as immigrants. Our interviews, therefore, do not focus exclusively on the phase of persecution but bring the story of survival into the present. Perhaps the most important single step taken by Yale, beyond not limiting the duration of the interview, was to initiate this taping in other countries, to respect a diverse memory milieu.

From its beginning the Yale project had also another kind of communitarian purpose. We favor cooperative endeavors: involving universities or research institutes, encouraging interviewers to form study groups, and maintaining a copy of each testimony in the country of origin. We have found secure and curated depositories in many countries. The testimonies recorded in Israel can be consulted at the University of Haifa; in Germany, at Berlin's Wannsee Museum; in France, at the National Archives in Paris; in Belgium, at the Foundation Auschwitz in Brussels; in England, at the National Sound Archives. Publications based on the central archive at Yale, as well as on locally established archives, are increasing. It is our hope that, in the near future, educational or philanthropic institutions will provide funds for scholars to work in these video archives and to research not only specific Holocaust issues but also the best use to which the video testimonies might be put. It is essential that these moving, personal narratives be properly and effectively utilized by public television, museum exhibits, and school programs.

It remains for me to thank those who have given their testimony, as well as the founders of the entire project, and so many others—interviewers, organizers, scholars, donors—who have contributed to make Yale's Fortunoff Archive a reality. Its research and educational potential are enormous. We will continue to do our best to preserve and disseminate the direct words and recollections of those who survived in dark times.

GEOFFREY HARTMAN
Faculty Adviser and Project Director
Fortunoff Video Archive for
Holocaust Testimonies

VIDEO REFERENCES

In this book, profiles of the survivors may be found on the pages in italics below. The testimonies excerpted in this book may be viewed at the Fortunoff Video Archive for Holocaust Testimonies, Yale University, under the following reference numbers:

Abraham P., *p. 22*, HVT-738

Arnold C., *p. 123*, HVT-363

Baruch G., *p. 53*, HVT-295

Bessie K., *p. 110*, HVT-206

Celia K., *p. 86*, HVT-36

Chaim E., *p. 132*, HVT-756

Christa M., *p. 190*, HVT-880

Clara L., *p. 148*, HVT-1850

Edith P., *p. 113*, HVT-107

Edmund M., *p. 205*, HVT-1219

Frank S., *p. 13*, HVT-30

Golly D., *p. 5*, HVT-2475

Hanna F., *p. 143*, HVT-18

Helen K., *p. 164*, HVT-58

Herbert J., *p. 173*, HVT-1386

Jacob K., *p. 235*, HVT-206

Jay M., *p. 93*, HVT-430

John S., *p. 40*, HVT-216

Joseph K., *p. 49*, HVT-61

Joseph W., *p. 43*, HVT-2681

Martin S., *p. 156*, HVT-641

Perla K., *p. 232*, HVT-1369

Renée G., *p. 62*, HVT-5

Renée H., *p. 77*, HVT-50

Robert S., *p. 241*, HVT-1149

Walter S. *p. 168*, HVT-146

Werner R., *p. 181*, HVT-948

FOR FURTHER READING

The following is only a sample from a very rich harvest of works and is not meant to be inclusive. Many important books and articles are not included.

On the Fortunoff Video Archive

Hartman, Geoffrey H. "Learning from Survivors: The Yale Testimony Project." *Holocaust and Genocide Studies*, fall, 1995.

———. "Preserving the Personal Story: The Role of Video Documentation." *The Holocaust Forty Years After*. Edited by Marcia Littell, Richard Libowitz, and Evelyn Bodek Rosen. Lewiston, N.Y.: E. Mellen Press, 1989.

Langer, Lawrence L. *Holocaust Testimonies: The Ruins of Memory*. New Haven, Conn.: Yale University Press, 1991.

Rudof, Joanne Weiner, ed. "The Fortunoff Video Archive for Holocaust Testimonies." *Encyclopedia of Genocide*. Israel W. Charney, editor in chief. Santa Barbara, Calif.: ABC-CLIO, 1999.

———. "The Fortunoff Video Archive for Holocaust Testimonies." *Historical Journal of Film, Radio and Television* 16, no. 1, 1997.

———. "The Things That Sustained Me." *Second to None: A Documentary History of American Women, Vol. 2*. Edited by Ruth Barnes Moynihan, Cynthia Russett, and Laurie Crumpacker. Lincoln: University of Nebraska Press, 1994.

On Holocaust Memory, Testimony, and the Literature of Testimony

Améry, Jean. *At the Mind's Limits: Contemplations by a Survivor on Auschwitz and Its Realities.* Translated by Sidney Rosenfeld and Stella P. Rosenfeld. Bloomington: Indiana University Press, 1980.

Bar-On, Dan. *Legacy of Silence: Encounters with Children of the Third Reich.* Cambridge, Mass.: Harvard University Press, 1989.

Boder, David P. (David Pablo). *I Did Not Interview the Dead.* Urbana: University of Illinois Press, 1949.

Bolkosky, Sidney M. "Interviewing Victims Who Survived: Listening for the Silences That Strike." *Annals of Scholarship* 4, no. 1, winter, 1987.

Bolkosky, Sidney M. and Henry Greenspan, eds. *Holocaust Survivors and Their Listeners: Testimonies, Interviews, Encounters.* Detroit: Wayne State University Press, 2000.

Browning, Christopher R. *Ordinary Men: Reserve Police Battalion 101 and the Final Solution in Poland.* New York: Aaron Asher Books, 1992.

Delbo, Charlotte. *Auschwitz and After.* Translated by Rosette C. Lamont, with introduction by Lawrence L. Langer. New Haven, Conn.: Yale University Press, 1995.

Dwork, Debórah. *Children with a Star: Jewish Youth in Nazi Europe.* New Haven, Conn.: Yale University Press, 1991.

Felman, Shoshana, and Dori Laub. *Testimony: Crises of Witnessing in Literature, Psychoanalysis, and History.* New York: Routledge, 1992.

Friedländer, Saul. *Memory, History, and the Extermination of the Jews of Europe.* Bloomington: Indiana University Press, 1993.

———. *When Memory Comes.* Translated from the French by Helen R. Lane. New York: Farrar, Straus & Giroux, 1979.

Greenspan, Henry. *On Listening to Holocaust Survivors: Recounting and Life History.* Foreword by Robert Coles. Westport, Conn.: Praeger, 1998.

Hartman, Geoffrey, ed. "Intellectual Witness." *Partisan Review*, winter, 1998.

———. *The Longest Shadow: In the Aftermath of the Holocaust.* Bloomington: Indiana University Press, 1996.

———, ed. *Holocaust Remembrance: The Shapes of Memory.* Cambridge, Mass.: Blackwell, 1993.

Johnson, Mary, and Margot Stern Strom. *Elements of Time.* Brookline, Mass.: Facing History and Ourselves National Foundation, 1989.

Koonz, Claudia. *Mothers in the Fatherland: Women, the Family, and Nazi Politics.* New York: St. Martin's Press, 1987.

Langer, Lawrence L. *Preempting the Holocaust.* New Haven, Conn.: Yale University Press, 1998.

————. *Admitting the Holocaust: Collected Essays.* New York: Oxford University Press, 1995.

Lanzmann, Claude. *Shoah: An Oral History of the Holocaust: The Complete Text of the Film.* Preface by Simone de Beauvoir. English subtitles of the film by A. Whitelaw and W. Byron. First U.S. ed. New York: Pantheon, 1985.

Laub, Dori. "History, Memory, and Truth." *The Holocaust and History: The Known, the Unknown, the Disputed, and the Reexamined.* Edited by Michael Berenbaum and Abraham J. Peck. Bloomington: Indiana University Press, 1998.

Levi, Primo. *The Drowned and the Saved.* Translated from the Italian by Raymond Rosenthal. First Vintage International ed. New York: Vintage International, 1989.

————. *Survival in Auschwitz and the Reawakening: Two Memoirs.* Translated by Stuart Woolf. New York: Summit Books, 1986.

Moskovitz, Sarah. *Love Despite Hate: Child Survivors of the Holocaust and Their Adult Lives.* New York: Schocken Books, 1983.

Rudof, Joanne Weiner. "Shaping Public and Private Memory: Holocaust Testimonies, Interviews and Documentaries." *Studies on the Audio-Visual Testimony of Victims of the Nazi Crimes and Genocides,* no. 1, June–July 1998.

Sloan, Jacob, ed. and transl. *Notes from the Warsaw Ghetto: The Journal of Emmanuel Ringelblum.* Reprint of the edition published by McGraw-Hill, New York, 1958.

Vidal-Naquet, Pierre. *The Jews: History, Memory, and the Present.* Translated and edited by David Ames Curtis, with an introduction by Paul Berman and a new preface by the author. New York: Columbia University Press, 1996.

Wiesel, Elie. *Night.* Foreword by François Mauriac, translated from the French by Stella Rodway. New York: Avon Books, 1960, 1969 printing.

Wieviorka, Annette. *L'Ere du témoin.* Paris: Plon, 1998.

INDEX

Abraham P.:
 on aftermath, 220–221, 236–237
 on arrival at Auschwitz, 114–115,
  124–125
 on Auschwitz, 129, 150–151
 biographical information, 22
 on deportation, 105–107
 on evacuations, 178, 192
 on liberation, 206
 on life in Romania in the 1930s,
  19–21
 on outbreak of war, 33, 39
 on Schlieben, 140–141
Aftermath, 219–250
 attitudes toward Germans,
  238–240, 242–243
 attitudes toward Poles, 239
 brutal nature of man, 248
 cynicism response, 237
 Holocaust (television series), 237
 nightmares, 226–228
 relationship with family members,
  223, 225–233, 243–244,
  247–248
 responses to life in U.S., 220–224
 return to Poland, 245–247
Air raids, 186–187, 192, 200
Anschluss, 25

Antisemitism:
 newspapers, 12, 25
 in Poland, post-Holocaust, 216–217
 in Poland in the 1930s, 6–9,
  23–25
 in Romania in the 1930s, 20–21
 in schools, 8–9, 12–17, 23–24
 in Slovakia, 37, 39, 40
Arnold C.:
 on aftermath, 223–224
 on arrival at Auschwitz, 122, 124
 on Auschwitz, 135–136, 144–146,
  159–162
 biographical information, 123
 on death marches, 180, 184,
  186–187
 on *kinder aktsye*, 66–67
 on liberation, 210
 on outbreak of war, 36–37
 on transfers, 73, 111
Arrival at camps, 114–122, 124–125
 belongings confiscated, 115, 120,
  122, 124
 clothing, 115, 121
 hair removal, 119–122
 nakedness, 119–122
 selections for extermination,
  115–116, 118, 124–125, 144

hiding places, 57–60, 72, 84, 93, 101–102
hostage system, 48, 50
hunger, 46, 55
Jewish Councils (*Judenrat*), 45, 52, 68–70
overcrowding, 45–47, 54–55
secret study groups, 47, 54
shootings, 47, 58, 60, 63, 66–68, 70–72
thirst, 46, 47, 72
Glubokoye, Poland, 87–88, 96
Golly D.:
  on arrival at Auschwitz, 115–116, 120
  on Auschwitz, 134, 137
  biographical information, 5
  on death marches, 178, 183, 185, 186, 192–193
  on deportations, 41–42, 78–81
  on *Kristallnacht*, 27–28
  on liberation, 208–211
  on life in Germany in the 1930s, 4, 14
Gorlice, Poland, 48, 50
Grese, Irma, 152
Gross-Rosen camp, 178
Gusen camp, 117

Hair removal, 119–122, 138
Hanna F.:
  on arrival at Auschwitz, 122
  on Auschwitz, 130–131, 135, 137–138, 142, 145–146, 174–175
  biographical information, 143
  on escape and posing as a non-Jew, 84–85
  on liberation, 218
"*Heil Hitler*" salute, 12–13, 12–14
Helen K.:
  on aftermath, 237–238, 247–248, 250
  on Auschwitz, 147, 153, 163, 165, 175
  biographical information, 164
  on deportation, 108

on liberation, 206
on Majdanek, 142, 144, 150, 153
on outbreak of war, 32–33
on Warsaw ghetto, 46
on Warsaw uprising, 101–102
Herbert J.:
  on aftermath, 227–228, 242
  on arrival at camps, 116
  biographical information, 173
  on liberation, 214
  on Mauthausen, 134, 139–140, 157, 172, 174
Hiding, 41, 57–60, 66–67, 70, 72–75, 84–85, 89–91, 94–97, 101, 146, 173, 200, 208–209, 213
Himmler, Heinrich, 238, 239
Hitler, Adolf, 37, 238
  Hitler Youth and, 16–17
  response to election of, 8
Hitler Youth, 9–12, 16–17
Holocaust (television series), 237
Hostages, 48, 50
Hunger:
  in camps, 140–142, 144–145, 170, 199
  on death marches, 178, 180, 182, 186, 189, 192–195
  in ghettos, 46, 54–55

I.G. Farben, 119
Identification papers, 32–33, 84, 87, 96
Illnesses, 50–51, 135, 137–139, 145, 150, 151–152, 167, 170, 199, 203, 204, 206

Jacob K.:
  on aftermath, 234, 235, 236, 238–240
  on antisemitism, postwar, 217
  biographical information, 235
  on ghettos, 58–59
  on liberation, 217–218
  on shootings, 70–71
Janowska camp, 55–56

Jay M.:
on Białystok ghetto, 46, 54, 67, 72
biographical information, 93
on escape from ghetto, 91–92
as partisan resistor, 97–98, 100
Jewish Brigade, 210
Jewish Councils (*Judenrat*), 45, 52,
68–70
Jewish life in the 1930s. *See* European
Jewish life in the 1930s
Jewish star, 37–38, 48
John S., Father:
on aftermath, 240
biographical information, 40
on deportation, 111–112, 114
on life in Czechoslovakia in the
1930s, 25
on role of bystanders, 39
Joseph K.:
on aftermath, 216–217, 248–249
on antisemitism, postwar, 216–217
on arrival at camp, 119
biographical information, 49
on death marches, 182–185, 193
on escape, 193
on ghettos, 48–52, 67
on liberation, 212, 214
on life in Poland in the 1930s,
23–25
on outbreak of war, 34, 42
Joseph W.:
biographical information, 43
on deportations, 42
on escape, 87, 94–96
on ghettos, 55–56, 65–66
on hiding, 94–96
on life in Poland, prewar, 2–4,
23–24

Kapos, 158
Killing Fields, The, 237
Kinder aktsye, 66–67
Kośice, Slovakia, 111–112, 114
Kovno, Poland, 36–37, 66–68
Kristallnacht (Night of Broken Glass), 1,
5, 26–28

Krzywcza, Poland, 2–4

Liberation, 197–218
of Bergen-Belsen, 203
of Buchenwald, 202–203
of Dachau, 203
intolerance to food, 206–207, 210
Jewish Brigade, 210
of Mauthausen, 198–202, 204,
206–208
physical condition of victims, 199,
203, 204, 206
reactions of victims to Allied soldiers, 200, 202–203, 209–210,
213
of Salzwedel, 201, 202
Soviet soldiers, 212, 213
U.S. soldiers, 198, 200–203,
208–210, 212–214. *See also* Herbert J.
Lice infestations, 137, 145
Łódź, 6–7
Łosice, Poland, 57–61, 63–65, 213,
245–246
Lubartów, Poland, 69
Lustig, Walter, 41–42, 78

Majdanek camp, 142, 144, 150, 153
Mannheim, Germany, 26
Martin S.:
on aftermath, 225–226, 237, 248
on antisemitism, postwar, 216–217
on arrival at Buchenwald, 121
biographical information, 156
on Buchenwald, 158, 161
on cattle cars, 108
on liberation, 202–203, 207,
216–217
on outbreak of war, 34
prisoner ID issued in Buchenwald,
158
on Skarżysko-Kamienna, 133–134,
138–139, 141, 151, 152, 155,
171
Mauthausen camp, 134, 139–140,
157, 172, 174, 198–200